D0743064

Municipal Bonds

Municipal Bonds

SECOND EDITION

Robert Lamb
Stephen P. Rappaport

McGraw-Hill Book Company

New York   St. Louis   San Francisco   Auckland   Bogotá
Hamburg   Johannesburg   London   Madrid   Mexico
Milan   Montreal   New Delhi   Panama
Paris   São Paulo   Singapore
Sydney   Tokyo   Toronto

Library of Congress Cataloging-in-Publication Data

Lamb, Robert.
  Municipal bonds.

  Includes index.
  1. Municipal finance—United States. 2. Municipal
bonds—United States. I. Rappaport, Stephen P.
II. Title.
HJ9145.L35   1987   336.3'1   86-27539
ISBN 0-07-036084-7

1234567890   DOC/DOC   893210987

ISBN 0-07-036084-7

*The editors of this book were William A. Sabin and Edward N. Huggins,
the designer was Naomi Auerbach, and the production supervisor
was Thomas G. Kowalczyk. It was set in Baskerville by Byrd.*

Printed and bound by R. R. Donnelley & Sons Company.

To Our Parents,
Robert Keen Lamb and Helen Boyden Lamb,
in memoriam; and
Dr. Bernard Francis Rappaport and Claire Ruth Rappaport

Contents

Part 2   General Obligation Bonds

Part 3   Revenue Bonds

Part 5   The Structural Framework for Public Finance

Part 6   Future Perspectives on Municipal Bond Analysis

Foreword

In the six years since *Municipal Bonds: The Comprehensive Review of Tax-Exempt Securities and Public Finance* first appeared, the market for municipal securities has exploded. The growth in the volume of municipal financings and the vast increase in the number of municipal investors are evidence of the increasing importance of municipal finance, both to the securities industry and to the investing public.

With this growth has come new challenges, both for municipal finance professionals and for investors of all levels of sophistication. Certainly the Tax Reform Act of 1986 will affect the industry profoundly.

This new edition addresses several other challenges facing the municipal finance industry. It is a comprehensive and excellent review of the field and offers a wealth of information for underwriters, counsel, regulators, legislators, issuers, and the investing public.

While the literature on municipal securities has expanded greatly since 1980, reflecting, no doubt, the enormous growth of the industry, this new edition by Robert Lamb and Stephen P. Rappaport maintains the high standards set by its now classic predecessor.

EDWARD I. O'BRIEN
President, Securities Industry Association

November 25, 1986

Acknowledgments

We have retained the following acknowledgments to the first edition of this book, published in 1980, because the individuals contributed as members of their respective firms. The acknowledgments, therefore, are both to the individuals and to the firms with which they were associated.

This book was written with the advice of many individuals whose day-to-day work involves municipal bond finance. While the authors take full responsibility for the contents of this volume, we would like to take this opportunity to thank certain individuals whose advice we sought. Although we cannot list all of those who in one way or another provided such help, there are nevertheless a great number of individuals who must be acknowledged as our principal sources of unfailing support, both moral and substantive.

High on this list were Edward O'Brien and Robert Royer of the Securities Industry Association; Peter Harkins of the Dealer Bank Association; Donald Beaty and Robert Doty of the Municipal Finance Officers Association; Albert Gordon Sr. and Duncan Gray of Kidder, Peabody & Co., Incorporated; Brenton Harries, John Dailey, and Richard Huff of Standard & Poor's Corporation; the late Jackson Phillips of Moody's Investors Service, Inc.; Raymond Lauber of The Chase Manhattan Bank, N.A.; Herman Charbonneau of Chemical Bank; William McCarthy of Blyth Eastman, Paine Webber Inc.; John DeJung of National Securities and Research Corporation; Sylvan Feldstein of Smith Barney, Harris Upham & Co. Incorporated; David Darst of Goldman, Sachs & Co.; and Kevin Collins of The First Boston Corporation.

Other members of the investment banking community who contributed were Richard Ackerman of Merrill Lynch, Pierce, Fenner & Smith Inc.; Lawrence Caffrey and Joan Camens of Paine, Webber, Jackson &

Curtis Incorporated; Alan Weeden of Weeden & Co., Incorporated; John Tamagni of Lazard Frères & Co.; Edward Kresky of Wertheim & Co., Inc.; Richard Jenrette of Donaldson, Lufkin & Jenrette Securities Corporation; John Noonan, Michael Hernandez, Albert Haiback, and Tamara Bund of Kidder, Peabody & Co., Incorporated; Donald Patterson of Blyth Eastman, Paine Webber Inc.; Morgan Murray, William Gibson, and George Friedlander of Smith Barney, Harris Upham & Co., Incorporated; Peter Loeb, Sherman Lewis, and David Troob of Shearson, Loeb Rhoades Inc.; Arthur Petersen of E. F. Hutton; William Deegan of L. F. Rothschild, Unterberg, Towbin; Daniel Lingenfelter of Underwood, Neuhaus & Co., Inc.; Robert Martin and Dick Joseph of Dain Bosworth Inc.; Giles Brophy of First Penco Securities; Robert Stovall of Dean Witter Reynolds Inc.; William Hough of William R. Hough & Co.

Other members of the commercial banking community who were extremely helpful include: John Vella and Michael LaTorre of the Bank of America; James Thompson of the North Carolina National Bank; Larry Clyde and Roy Nahas of Crocker National Bank; John Rowe of the First National Bank of St. Louis; Continental Bank; R. C. Johannesman of Mercantile Trust Company N.A.; George Casey of Wells Fargo Bank N.A.; Amos Beason, Frederic Rosenbauer, and Peter Merrill of Morgan Guaranty Trust Company.

Many other professional associations and individuals provided much support and aid in accumulating material and statistics. In addition to the Municipal Finance Officers Association, the Dealer Bank Association, and the Securities Industry Association cited earlier, those providing the most assistance included: Alex Radin, American Public Power Association; Eric Johnson, American Water Works Association; W. A. Rusch, International Bridge, Tunnel, and Turnpike Association; Raymond Long, National Association of State Budget Officers; Mark Keane, International City Management Association; David Herlinger and William Johnston, Council of State Housing Agencies; Gerald Esser, Municipal Finance Officers Association; Bernard Hillenbrand, National Association of Counties; John Gunther, U.S. Conference of Mayors; and William Cassella, National Municipal League.

Among those who provided much encouragement in the early stages of the manuscript were Philip Fahey, Howard Whitman, John Cooper, E. Eugene Mahon, Jack Kelly, Donald Scalley, Alfred Allen, Neal Sullivan, Bruce Deichle, and Bruce Treitler, all of Thomson McKinnon Securities Inc. In addition, Julian Smerling, Peter Vlachos, and Richard Moynihan of the Dreyfus Corporation provided much interest and enthusiasm for the project throughout all stages.

At Bache Halsey Stuart Shields Incorporated, the following individuals provided much encouragement during the period when the manuscript was in its final stages: William Marlin, the late Edwin Bueltman, Theodore Swick, Samuel Plaia, James Glynn, Ernest Dubin, James Perry, and Ethan Deinard.

Other individuals whose advice we sought include John Winders and Joan Lulkovich, of the *The Daily Bond Buyer* and *The Weekly Bond Buyer*; Christopher Taylor, formerly of the Municipal Securities Rulemaking Board; John Butler of the Municipal Bond Insurance Association; Mathew Malone, Richard Cacchione, and Thomas Cacchione of Fitch Investors Service, Inc.; and former Standard & Poor's staff members: Preston Miller and Robert Margolies; and Robert White Jr. of White's Rating Service. John Brenner and Freda Stern Ackerman of Moody's Investors Service are also acknowledged.

Members of New York University's Graduate School of Business Administration who provided insightful comments were: Wassily Leontief, William Silber, Robert Lindsay, Robert Kavesh, Lawrence Ritter, Arnold Sametz, Ernest Bloch, Edward Altman, Ingo Walter, William Guth, William Berliner, William Dill, Oscar Ornati, David Rogers, Hrach Bedrosian, Jeremy Weisen, George Sorter, Barbara Coe, Lawrence Rosenberg, and Peter Dubno.

Colleagues who responded with enthusiasm for the book include: Demetrios Caraley, Douglas Chalmers, Richard Pious, Charles Hamilton, and Robert Connery, all of Columbia University; Robert Gilmour, University of Connecticut; Douglas Rogers of Kidder, Peabody & Co., Incorporated; Walter Stursberg of Reavis and McGrath, Esqs.; Bernard Axelrod, Esq.; Richard Schmaltz of Morgan Stanley & Co.; and Guenter Weissberg and Sidney Farr of Colby College.

Other writers on finance are also acknowledged here: Lenox Moak, James Van Horne, John Petersen, Alan Rabinowitz, and Wade Smith.

We are grateful to all those individuals cited here and to the many others, especially the municipal bond attorneys and accountants.

Three individuals who contributed enormously to the production of this book were: Melvin Simensky of Gersten, Sherer & Kaplowitz, Esqs.; editor Thomas Rosenbaum; and research assistant Lynn Togut.

Finally, we would like to acknowledge the support of the following organizations, some of whose names have changed as a result of mergers:

American Public Power Association
Bache Halsey Stuart Shields Incorporated
Bank of America N.T. & S.A.
Blyth Eastman Dillon & Co.
The Chase Manhattan Bank, N.A.

Chemical Bank
Continental Illinois National Bank and Trust Company of Chicago
Council of State Housing Agencies
Crocker National Bank
Dain Bosworth Inc.
Dealer Bank Association
Dean Witter Reynolds Inc.
Donaldson, Lufkin & Jenrette Securities Corporation
The First Boston Corporation
First National Bank of St. Louis
First Penco Securities
Fitch Investors Service, Inc.
William R. Hough & Co.
International Bridge, Tunnel, and Turnpike Association
Kidder, Peabody & Co., Incorporated
Lazard Frères & Co.
Loeb Rhoades, Hornblower & Co.
Mercantile Trust Company N.A.
Merrill Lynch, Pierce, Fenner & Smith Inc.
Municipal Bond Insurance Association
North Carolina National Bank
Paine, Webber, Jackson & Curtis Incorporated
L. F. Rothschild, Unterberg, Towbin
Securities Industry Association
Smith Barney, Harris Upham & Co. Incorporated
Standard & Poor's Corporation
Thomson McKinnon Securities Inc.
Underwood, Neuhaus & Co., Inc.
Weeden & Co., Incorporated
Wells Fargo Bank, N.A.
Wertheim & Co., Inc.

Robert Lamb
March 15, 1980   *Stephen P. Rappaport*

For the Second Edition: Encouragement and support are gratefully
acknowleged from George Ball, James Gahan, Leland Paton, Gerald
McBride, Thomas Monti, and Herbert Finn, all of Prudential-Bache
Securities Inc., and Richard West of New York University.

R.L.
November 28, 1986   S.P.R.

A Special Word about
the Case Studies

The case studies that have been selected are classic examples of the kinds
of bond issues they represent. Wherever possible, examples have been
used of issuers which are either large or which enter the market on a
continuing basis. Most of the cases are as recently issued as possible, but
others provide the best examples of the concepts that have been
discussed and evaluated. Case studies have also been selected that are
likely to remain generally viable financings in the wake of the Tax
Reform Act of 1986, and if not, the principles of credit analysis for the
presently outstanding issues of that type should still remain the same.
Finally, the case studies that have been used are located in a variety of
areas around the country.

Nevertheless, cases are not expected to be all things to all people. For
the purposes of this book, the bond issues selected as case studies are
expected simply to highlight certain aspects of the bonds discussed in
each chapter and to underscore important analytical features that go
into evaluating municipal securities. The case studies used here have
also been selected in two other ways. First, space limitations simply do
not allow the cases to be as notable as the discussions about how specific
bonds are evaluated. Second, the material presented here has been
written for a wide variety of audiences, from those who are uninitiated
into the municipal bond field to participants who are considered by most
in the industry to be truly knowledgeable experts. Writing for such a
wide audience presents a challenging task in itself, and it is even more
difficult to provide all readers with examples of bonds that are both
understandable to industry newcomers and interesting to industry
experts. As a result, some of the case studies elucidate specific concepts

in particular bond areas; others explain important bond issues or represent major programs of an ongoing nature; finally, a few apply creative approaches to theoretical issues and then supply a specific example that supports the original hypotheses. What is presented, then, is a vast array of case study materials that should appeal to different audiences.

PART 1
Introduction

1
The Growth of Municipal Debt and Investment

The most dynamic area of the investment industry today, as for the past decade, still remains comparatively neglected in academic or trade literature: the market for municipal securities, which helps finance state and local public services through the issuance of debt. Indeed, the largest number of securities issuers in the world are the federal, state, and local governmental entities. Interestingly, the dollar volume of municipal debt alone issued from 1970 to 1986 was about double the issuance of corporate debt.

A major portion of this increase in municipal debt was issued to supply the critical public needs for both urban and rural services, such as electric power, housing, transportation, education, hospitals, and water and sewer systems. These debt securities were issued not only by cities, states, and counties but also by a rapidly growing number of public revenue authorities. One such authority is the Port Authority of New York and New Jersey, whose annual budget and general indebtedness each exceed those of many states; its budget even exceeds that of many a country.

The magnitude of this development in municipal finance cannot be understated. Yet it took a crisis involving a near-bankrupt New York City in the mid-1970s to make the business, academic, and investor communities aware of the importance of credit analysis of government debt at all levels. Similarly, the technical default in 1975 of the New York

State Urban Development Corporation (UDC)—once purported to be the most innovative state housing, finance, and construction agency—demonstrated the far-reaching impact that these newly created governmental entities could have on the investment community and on the various basic needs of Americans, such as housing. If these financial woes did not impact investors and observers of the American financial scene, the default of the Washington Public Power Supply System (the Supply System, or WPPSS) on $2.25 billion of bonds almost 10 years later in 1984 certainly did.

To a considerable degree since World War II, state and local governments have forgone pay-as-you-go financing for certain basic services, such as highways, hospitals, housing, power projects, water and sewer systems, transportation networks, and port facilities. As a result, the successful financing of these services that people use daily depends on the underwriting and distribution of municipal bonds by investment banking firms and brokerage houses as well as by commercial banks. Moreover, it seems clear that as government and the investment community become more involved in providing financing for more and more public services needed by Americans, the financing will take the form of public debt and bonds.

The explosive growth in state and local debt has resulted in a substantial increase in the number of financial analysts engaged in this work. In a drastic shift of emphasis, investment banking and brokerage firms, commercial banks, corporations, insurance companies, and many other institutions have developed new departments to deal with this expanding debt market. Yet although the credit analysis area has been growing dramatically, there has been little literature on it that is comprehensive and up to date. Before the first edition of this book was published in 1980, the small amount of material written on municipal securities was, for the most part, published before 1939.

The municipal securities industry with its attendant issues, such as credit analysis and disclosure, will continue to play a critically important role in helping state and local governments provide basic public services. Therefore, information about the role of this industry is essential—and this book is the focus of an expanding literature that will bring together the issues and impacts of all public debt with which Americans, particularly the investment community, must wrestle on a daily basis.

The Growth of Municipal Debt

The Tax Exemption

The key feature of municipal securities that may have accounted for their substantial growth in this past decade was their tax-exempt status.

Not only were holders of municipal bonds not required to pay federal income tax on their coupon (interest) income, but their interest was also frequently exempt from most state and local taxes. For example, residents of New York have been exempt from state and local taxes on interest earned on bonds issued in New York State. Regardless of one's residency, interest earned on bonds issued by the Commonwealth of Puerto Rico and certain of its agencies and municipalities has been exempt from federal, state, and local taxes in almost every state, with some notable exceptions. It was generally held that the exemption of interest earned on municipal bonds from federal income taxes was first implicitly granted by the doctrine of "reciprocal immunity" in the important Supreme Court case, *McCulloch v. Maryland* (1819).

This tax exemption of municipal bonds was reaffirmed by the federal government through the Internal Revenue Code, which, in effect, enabled municipalities to come to the capital markets and obtain funds at lower interest rates than those prevailing in the taxable marketplace. The Tax Reform Act of 1986 (establishing the Internal Revenue Code of 1986) has limited the use of the tax-exempt feature for a select number and type of municipal bonds. (This will be discussed in Chap. 21 and the Appendix.) Nevertheless, it is becoming ever more attractive to invest in municipal bonds. Investors in most tax brackets can receive greater returns from municipal securities than may be available on an after-tax basis from most other comparable types of investment; however, this depends on the market relationship of taxable and tax-exempt yields at any given point in time (see Table 1.1). Obviously, the higher an individual's tax bracket, the greater the advantage of this tax-exempt feature.

Current Trends

On New Year's Day, 1978, the lead headline in the "Business and Finance" section of *The New York Times* read: "Municipal Bonds: The Star of 1977." Indeed, 1977 was surely the year of municipal bonds up to that time. New issues of state and local securities increased to what was then a record high of $45 billion in long-term bonds and $66 billion in total new issues, and numerous investment bankers on Wall Street greatly expanded their municipal departments, while other firms founded new ones. This was surely a foreshadowing of events to come. On Monday, January 6, 1986, *The New York Times* again featured municipal bonds in a lead finance article of the new year entitled "Record Borrowings in Tax-Exempts." Later, it was reported that in 1985, state and local governments issued a record $223.4 billion of long-term tax-exempt bonds, two-thirds of the 1986 volume.

However the volume of municipal bond issuance is calculated, the

Table 1.1. Yield Equivalents: Tax-Exempt versus Taxable Income
(Taxable income in thousands)

	1987				1988			
Joint return: taxable income*	$3 to $28	$28 to $45	$45 to $90	Over $90	$0 to $29.75	$29.75 to $71.90	$71.90 to $171.09†	Over $171.09†
Single return: taxable income*	$1.80 to $16.80	$16.80 to $27	$27 to $54	Over $54	$0 to $17.85	$17.85 to $43.15	$43.15 to $100.48‡	Over $100.48‡
% Tax bracket (federal)	15	28	35	38.5	15	28	33§	28
% Tax-exempt yields	% Taxable yields				% Taxable yields			
4.0	4.71	5.6	6.2	6.5	4.7	5.6	6.0	5.6
4.5	5.3	6.3	6.9	7.3	5.3	6.3	6.8	6.3
5.0	5.9	6.9	7.6	8.1	5.9	7.0	7.5	7.0
5.5	6.5	7.6	8.5	8.9	6.5	7.7	8.3	7.7
6.0	7.1	8.3	9.2	9.8	7.1	8.3	9.0	8.3
6.5	7.6	9.0	10.0	10.6	7.6	9.0	9.7	9.0
7.0	8.2	9.7	10.8	11.4	8.2	9.7	10.4	9.7
7.5	8.8	10.4	11.6	12.2	8.8	10.4	11.2	10.4
8.0	9.4	11.1	12.3	13.0	9.4	11.1	11.9	11.1
8.5	10.0	11.8	13.1	13.8	10.0	11.8	12.7	11.8
9.0	10.6	12.5	13.8	14.6	10.6	12.5	13.4	12.5
9.5	11.2	12.2	14.6	15.5	11.8	13.2	14.2	13.2
10.0	11.8	13.9	15.4	16.3	12.4	13.9	14.9	13.9

* Represents adjusted income subject to federal income tax.
† Assumes two personal exemptions.
‡ Assumes one personal exemption.
§ The 33 percent bracket includes a 50 percent surtax and the phasing out of the personal exemptions. This bracket will increase by $10,920 for each additional dependent, and by $11,200 in 1989.
Figures are rounded and subject to verification.

growth in the size of the municipal investment business (as evidenced by the statistics given in Table 1.2) shows dramatic increases in new issue volume from 1976 to 1985. Moreover, while there are 40,000 issuers of municipal securities and approximately 1.3 million issues outstanding, there are 33,000 corporate issuers and only about 63,000 issues of corporate securities. Because of the heavy financial requirements of state and local governments, the total outstanding of state and municipal debt is almost 5 times the amount that was outstanding in 1960. The most significant increases were in revenue bonds for the purposes cited in Table 1.3.

Definition of Municipal Securities

A critical distinction to be made in municipal finance is that between (1) those securities which are general obligations of a state or local government and (2) those which are in a broad category called revenue bonds. *General obligation (GO) bonds* are secured by a pledge of the full faith and credit (i.e., the taxing power) of the issuing governmental entity, while *revenue bonds* are principally secured by user fees or service charges paid by users of a particular government service. Revenue bond obligations almost never constitute debt of the municipality or state in which they are located. It should be noted that there are hybrid forms of these securities.

For decades, GO bonds were considered to be the most secure of all the municipal issues because governments have the power to levy taxes to pay the debt service (principal and interest) on the bonds. For instance, taxes that most Americans pay include those on property, sales, and personal income. These are the revenue sources of states and municipalities that can be increased to pay for debt service on GO bonds. One of the paradoxical problems facing state and local governments is their need to increase tax levies for financing public services, with the resultant possibility that the tax increases would drive out industry and people from the state, thus reducing the number of taxpayers.

Over the last 30 years the issuance of tax-supported GO bonds has declined relative to revenue bonds from over 70 percent to about 30 percent of the total new municipal new issue volume. During the early 1980s there was some discernible movement back to GO bond issuance, but it was not substantial. GO bonds will continue to be an important financing vehicle for such municipal capital improvements as schools, streets, and municipal buildings, but revenue bonds or hybrid-type

Table 1.2. A Decade of Municipal Finance

Bonds	1976	1977	1978	1979	1980
Total	33,844,556,486	45,060,469,916	46,214,763,694	42,260,817,929	47,133,366,006
Negotiated	14,340,689,869	25,034,805,767	24,711,768,991	23,576,075,806	27,644,008,198
Competitive	19,503,866,617	20,025,664,149	21,502,994,703	18,684,742,123	19,489,357,808
Revenue	16,929,341,325	27,172,680,950	28,320,952,734	29,646,045,556	30,786,231,788
General obligation	16,915,215,161	17,887,788,966	17,893,810,960	12,614,772,373	16,347,134,218
Refunding:					
General obligation	938,805,765	2,125,715,300	2,952,297,950	165,135,333	193,679,322
Revenue	2,575,933,300	7,461,152,471	6,331,741,634	1,707,076,000	1,455,853,400
All refunding	3,514,739,065	9,586,867,771	9,284,039,584	1,872,211,333	1,649,532,722
Notes	**1976**	**1977**	**1978**	**1979**	**1980**
Total	21,904,633,078	21,348,918,413	21,642,471,485	20,897,203,230	26,485,274,061
Bonds and notes	**1976**	**1977**	**1978**	**1979**	**1980**
	55,749,189,564	66,409,388,329	67,857,235,179	63,158,021,159	73,618,640,067
Issues	**1976**	**1977**	**1978**	**1979**	**1980**
Bonds	4,768	5,130	5,061	5,116	5,550
Notes	2,613	2,240	2,002	1,815	2,139
All issues	7,381	7,370	7,063	6,931	7,689

Bonds	1981	1982	1983	1984	1985
Total	46,134,227,443	77,179,034,377	83,347,895,020	101,881,559,721	203,954,252,150
Negotiated	29,761,046,118	52,604,116,334	61,614,537,671	78,989,572,823	168,017,569,095
Competitive	16,373,181,325	24,574,918,043	21,733,357,349	22,891,986,898	35,936,683,055
Revenue	32,146,074,621	53,903,344,825	60,764,740,753	74,373,729,638	148,868,547,501
General obligation	13,988,152,822	23,275,689,552	22,583,154,267	27,507,830,083	55,085,704,649
Refunding:					
General obligation	191,995,999	644,859,000	3,100,034,182	2,981,423,813	18,828,257,547
Revenue	999,843,000	3,399,286,000	9,947,442,254	8,408,037,044	39,039,149,057
All refunding	1,191,838,999	4,044,145,000	13,047,476,436	11,389,460,857	57,867,406,604

Notes	1981	1982	1983	1984	1985
Total	34,442,546,349	43,389,650,049	35,848,814,687	31,068,271,916	19,492,434,609

Bonds and notes	1981	1982	1983	1984	1985
Total	80,576,773,792	120,568,684,426	119,196,709,707	132,949,831,637	223,446,686,759

Issues	1981	1982	1983	1984	1985
Bonds	4,242	6,079	6,290	6,392	10,058
Notes	2,410	3,016	2,382	1,791	1,020
All issues	6,652	9,095	8,672	8,183	11,078

SOURCE: *The Bond Buyer 1985 Municipal Statbook*, pp. 8–9. Reprinted by permission.

Table 1.3. State and Municipal Bonds Sold by Purposes 1978–1985 (,000 omitted)

	1985	1984	1983	1982	1981	1980	1979	1978
School	24,200,170	9,754,312	8,734,508	6,563,995	4,362,741	4,754,551	4,924,482	6,239,540
Water and sewer	13,005,545	5,910,052	4,418,780	4,572,682	2,546,000	3,536,900	3,734,590	4,469,944
Highway, bridge, and tunnel[2]	—	—	1,093,101	1,086,488	1,064,686	1,119,088	935,690	1,876,918
Gas & electric	27,900,141	11,239,309	11,337,636	9,479,081	7,441,795	4,839,981	4,714,457	5,991,730
Hospital	30,202,932	10,234,841	9,922,857	9,691,013	5,156,182	3,557,754	3,517,429	3,138,494
State & Mun Housing Finance	37,467,282	20,507,833	18,007,682	15,684,229	6,840,119	14,267,101	12,041,244	—
Industrial	5,911,177	4,527,800	4,482,872	3,510,203	2,178,350	1,485,731	1,339,890	586,076
Pollution control[1]	11,553,598	14,643,962	5,313,819	6,608,345	4,686,635	2,917,055	2,891,735	3,482,361
Transportation[2]	13,283,128	8,761,993	3,533,691	—	—	—	—	—
Other	40,430,275	16,301,452	16,502,944	19,982,995	11,857,716	10,655,201	8,161,297	20,429,698
Total	203,954,252	101,881,559	83,347,895	77,179,034	46,134,227	47,133,366	42,260,817	46,214,763

[1] Includes industrial and nonindustrial financing.
[2] Transportation issues not included in the traditional highway, bridge, and tunnel category were reported separately in 1983. These include airports, mass transit, and road and street repair. All transportation issues are reported in a single category for 1984 and 1985.

The closing date for these figures was March 31. Other *Bond Buyer* reports may employ higher figures because of delayed reporting of some issues.

SOURCE: *The Bond Buyer 1985 Municipal Statbook*, p. 10. Reprinted by permission.

securities will be a major source of funds for providing a whole host of public services in the years ahead.

The tremendous growth in the revenue-backed municipal debt issued since World War II has been the result of the growth of revenue authorities. The Port Authority of New York and New Jersey, created in 1921, was the first major public revenue authority in the United States and is one of the nation's largest public agencies.

The issuance of revenue bonds, however, was originally developed to finance utility projects. Later, under federal sponsorship, such debt was broadened to provide for local public housing projects. As recently as 1957, the bulk of all local revenue bonds outstanding had been incurred for these two purposes. The early 1960s, however, saw the beginning of a rapid extension in the use of revenue bonds to finance types of public services of all bonds. Today, revenue bonds have been issued for such services as housing, electric power, highways, hospitals, water, sewers, airports, mass transit, solid waste disposal, resource recovery, education, pollution control, and port facilities, among others. Providing these wide-ranging services to Americans across the country has made the revenue authority probably the most notable governmental device ever crafted.

State laws govern whether a municipal entity must use GO or revenue bonds. However, when municipalities have a choice of issuing either GO or revenue bonds and desire to have only the users of facilities (not the entire citizenry of a community) pay for their financing, revenue bond financing is employed. Revenue bonds are also sometimes used when voter approval of GO bonds cannot be obtained. Also, revenue bonds may be the most convenient means for financing a capital program that benefits several governmental jurisdictions because they may not be subject to statutory or constitutional debt limitations.

The Issue of Credit Analysis

Unlike the analysis of corporate securities, the creditworthiness of municipal bond securities depends on a whole range of complicated legal, financial, economic, and administrative factors as well as on political considerations that are simply not encountered in the corporate field. This detailed material is harder to come by than is the kind required for corporate securities analysis, and hence a comparatively small group of municipal specialists strongly influences the credit ratings of state and local governments. The rapid expansion in the issuance of municipal bonds that occurred after 1975 led to a vast new interest in municipal bonds and in tools for analyzing their strengths and weaknesses.

Perhaps the most far-reaching effect that the New York City fiscal crisis, the UDC default, and the WPPSS debacle had on the investment community was largely in the field of municipal credit analysis, which was the exclusive domain of the principal rating agencies: Moody's Investors Service, Inc., and Standard & Poor's Corporation. This affected both GO and revenue bonds. With GO bonds, the problem was spearheaded by the New York City fiscal crisis and pointed to the fact that the types of financial data previously used as the indicators of creditworthiness were no longer applicable to the budget-balancing dilemmas and revenue-raising capacities of municipalities. Similarly, the UDC and WPPSS problems pointed to difficulties in analyzing revenue bonds—particularly to the inherent uncertainties involved in predicting demand for a given service and to the more general problem of constructing a major project on time and on budget.

The public's demand for more and better government services should keep analysts and investors busy for many years ahead. Indeed, by the mid-1980s many states and municipalities either began planning or embarking on major "infrastructure" programs for rebuilding and adding to such vital services as mass transportation systems, water and sewer treatment plants, highway networks, bridge and tunnel facilities, and public buildings programs. Many of these programs are estimated to cost well into the billions of dollars, and most will involve the development of municipal bonds with new forms of security. This may have at least some impact on the ability of states, local governments, and ultimately the public to pay for them. In the final analysis, investors and analysts of municipal securities will make the ultimate credit determinations on these debt obligations. Therefore, it is to the complexities in the analysis of municipal bonds that this book is directed.

Risks and Returns of Municipal Bonds

Risks

While it is certainly true that municipal bonds have, on the whole, been relatively safe investments over the years and that their default record, even during the great depression, was far less than that for corporate bonds, municipal bonds are not risk-free. Like virtually all other types of securities, municipal bonds have certain risks associated with them, and of necessity some municipal bonds have more risks than others. Therefore, it may be important for investors and bond analysts to consider the comparative risks of certain types of municipal bonds versus certain other municipal bonds, as we will do in the following chapters. All municipal bonds have certain common types of risks; nevertheless, different categories of municipal bonds have different specific risks associated with them in particular. Eight kinds of risks that can be associated with municipal bonds are listed. Several are interrelated, possibly because, in part, they involve the loss or change in value of the bond's principal or the loss or change in value of its interest payments.

1. *Default.*   If a municipality goes bankrupt, it might not pay back the principal and interest on its bonds.

2. *Delayed payments or delinquency.*   Although technically this is a kind of default, if payment quickly resumes, it is not a full-scale default.

3. *Loss resulting from a rating change.*   This is the risk of changing credit quality.

4. *Liquidity.*   This risk would be due to an investor's inability to obtain cash immediately or quickly in exchange for the bonds.

5. *Marketability.*   There may not be any buyers.

6. *Call.*   Loss may result when bonds are *called*, or paid back, long before their maturity or expiration date.

7. *Loss of asset value.*   This occurs when the inherent value of the bonds' principal falls. (A bond's price goes down when the yields on current prevailing bonds go up.)

8. *Loss of interest.*   If investors have to sell during periods of lower interest rates and if they cannot reinvest principal at as high an interest rate as before, they lose interest. (It is the same as risk of call except that the investor—not the issuer—initiates the sale.)

For certain individual or institutional investors, certain risks (for example, credit quality or default) will be of greater concern than others (for example, liquidity). It should also be noted that some buyers are prohibited from investing in certain securities that carry certain types and degrees of risks. Lawyers, accountants, bankers, brokers, dealers, and investors in the bond market have quite different perceptions of what is and is not a risk.

While, obviously, different individuals have different risk profiles (some try to avoid risk entirely, some try to avoid certain risks only, and others seek or welcome risk), we cannot catalog every individual's perception of risks. Nevertheless, we can bracket several types of risk profiles and identify the types of bonds each would perhaps choose or avoid.

Bond dealers' perceptions of risk, for example, are strongly colored by the fact that they are 80 to 90 percent leveraged at all times. They would therefore tend to worry about making any serious mistake and tend to turn over their portfolios very rapidly. Long-term risks would thus be less important to such dealers, whereas avoiding the liquidity risk would be vital.

Institutional investors might well view risk from the standpoint of their fiduciary relationship to clients' investments and would almost certainly avoid investing in municipal bonds that lacked sufficient rating or credit quality (as, for example, those below investment grade, unrated securities, defaulted securities, or discount bonds). Marketability risk would be important for institutional buyers who buy in large blocks and who must therefore be concerned about buying unfamiliar credits or small issues of local bonds.

Yield Measurements

Strange as it may seem, there is no general agreement on what *yield* really means. Therefore, the meaning of any given calculation of yield, or rate of return, is related to specific situations and the specific techniques employed for its measurement. *Yield to maturity, yield to call, net interest cost, Canadian interest cost, running yield,* and other terms denote some of the different measurements of overall return that are employed by different buyers, dealers, brokers, underwriters, etc.

Each different class of participants in the municipal bond market may use a different set of yield calculations and measurements of return because of the participants' quite different needs. For an ordinary investor, the simplest method of calculating yield, or return, is probably best; but for institutions or funds, more complex measures are needed. Certain market participants are forced by law to use a specific measure of yield. For example, underwriters of bonds are usually required by state laws to use net interest cost. This is because the municipal issuer of the bonds is in many states required by law to select, from among the competing underwriters, bids that have the lowest net interest cost.

Net interest cost (NIC) is a technique for reducing bids from all different underwriters to a common standard of measurement. NIC is relatively simple and can be computed with a pencil and paper. (Today's more complicated measurements of yield and return must be figured on computers.) Although the total NIC of a new bond issue is a fixed measure, it can result from many different individual yields on the various bonds in a new offering. For example, a long-term bond has more impact on the NIC calculation than a short-term bond because it generates more cash than a short-term bond. High coupons on the short-term bonds and lower coupons on the longer maturities result in a lower NIC. By manipulating which yields they will offer on which maturities, underwriters seek to select a low enough total NIC to win the bidding. The NIC measurement has come under criticism because it fails to take explicit account of the time value of money, and thus other techniques that do acknowledge this factor have begun to gain a following, e.g., the Canadian interest cost.

Whereas underwriters are forced to think in terms of NIC, in contrast, bond traders and investors tend to think in terms of *yield to maturity*. The calculation of yield to maturity was long thought to be simple and accurate; however, it is in fact very deceptive. This is because the actual yield to maturity always depends upon the interest rate at which one can reinvest the coupons when they are received. If one cannot get as high a rate of interest for the coupons as the original yield rate on the bonds, then the actual yield to maturity will be lower than the stated yield to maturity. If one can get a higher interest rate at which to reinvest the coupons, then the actual yield to maturity will be far higher. The range of yields to maturity on exactly the same bond is quite considerable. These two most popular measures of yield, the net interest cost and yield to maturity, have no necessary relationship.

Running yield, or *current yield*, is another popular measure of return and is simply the coupon rate divided by the price of the bond. It is a useful measure of a bond's current value if the investor wants current income. However, for a long-term investor, yield to maturity might provide a better guide to long-term return.

Yield to call is yet another measure of a bond's return. Many municipal bonds, especially newer ones, are callable, and some may have more than one call provision. A *call* is a payment of the principal back to the bondholder at a time well in advance of the maturity date printed on the bond. As already noted, if the bond is called, the investor has the problem of reinvesting the principal at a rate of return equivalent to or better than the rate of return received under the old bond. The current rate of interest may be lower than the rate the investor was getting on the bond, which is one primary reason why bonds are called and why refunding of bonds has become so popular.

Discussions of yield measurements could take pages of material, but this summarization should suffice for the purposes of this book.

2

The Municipal Bond Market: Buyers, Sellers, and Underwriters

This chapter will briefly summarize all the operations and major facts about the buying and selling of municipal bonds in the United States today. The first half will concentrate on the buyers of municipal bonds in both the primary and the secondary market. The role of individual investors and intermediaries for individual investors will be contrasted with the role of major institutional investors, such as commercial banks and insurance companies. The functions of brokers, dealers, and various types of bond funds will also be discussed. The second half of the chapter will cover the selling of municipal bonds. We will examine syndication of bond offerings and the different forms of underwriting arrangements by competitive sale and negotiation.

We can split each of the many bond markets into its participants: its buyers and sellers. Whether we analyze the market for general obligation bonds or revenue bonds or those of states, cities, school districts, or public authorities, the roles of the different participants in those markets will bear certain similarities but also reveal many crucial differences. This is partly because the nearly infinite variety of municipal bonds, which are unquestionably more diverse than corporate securities, creates a quite distinct market within each narrow type of bond and within each range of price, yield, quality, and maturity.

Within each group of buyers and sellers of each of these securities, one can look at the *primary market*, meaning the creation and placing of new securities, in contrast to the trading of existing securities in what is known as the *secondary market*. Indeed, among these groups as well we must reduce each to investors, dealers, and brokers and break these still further into bank or nonbank. Finally, among the dealers we must look at the role of individual underwriters and syndicates.

The Small Localized Bond Market

Numerically, a large proportion of all new municipal issues in the United States consists of small- to moderate-size loans to municipalities for such things as a fire engine, school bus, or bridge. These bonds might not ever truly enter the national public bond market at all. In a small community, especially when buying some specific piece of capital equipment with a definite estimable life, the town managers will simply ask a local commercial bank to provide a loan in order to purchase the equipment. Working together, they will structure the loan as a collection of tax-exempt municipal bonds by negotiating directly the terms and rate of interest. These bonds will probably never be resold or leave the community, the state, or indeed the bank's vault at all, for they were tailor-made for that particular bank customer in order to secure the loan to that municipality. (Occasionally, local banks will sell these bonds in order to be able to keep buying new local bond issues.) Other local investors will also buy small bond issues to hold until maturity. The very special nature of local bonds, with their very limited liquidity and marketability by the standard of other nationally sold bonds, makes it clear that this small-issue municipal bond market is of a totally different nature from the large-scale national and regional municipal bond markets with which this book is primarily concerned. It should never be forgotten, however, that this local market has always existed and to some degree or other will certainly continue.

The Buyers

In 1986 the U.S. state and local debt outstanding totaled approximately $635 billion. Each year approximately 8000 issues come to market from the 40,000 governmental units that are permitted to issue federally tax-exempt debt. These issues stretch in maturity from only a few months to 30 years or more.

Because of the extraordinary variety of municipal bonds, which are infinitely more diverse than corporate bonds, the individual or institutional investor can pinpoint exactly the type, yield, price, risk, quality, and length of maturity of the bond desired.

As Table 2.1 demonstrates, the buying side of the municipal bond market has been dominated by three groups that together have over 90 percent of all outstanding municipal bonds: individuals, commercial banks, non-life (or fire and casualty) insurance companies, and mutual funds. In the United States recently, by far the largest institutional holders of municipal bonds were still the commerical banks, who owned nearly half of all state and local debt outstanding. Municipal bonds were bought by commercial banks not only because of their track record of safety but also because of their federal tax exemption and their yield and because they ensured that the institutions are seen to be supporting local communities.

Individuals owned approximately one-third of all municipal bonds, and they have been strong participants in this market over the past decade. During this period, commercial bank investments in municipal bonds have grown but have remained far more stable as a percentage of the total purchase of new bonds.

Among the other buyers of municipal bonds, the fire and casualty insurance companies were followed by corporations, life insurance companies, and foreigners. Mutual funds have become very large buyers.

To be sure, the purchasing habits of all investors in municipal bonds will change in the wake of the Tax Reform Act of 1986, which will be discussed in Chap. 21. The following sections on buyers will analyze buying decisions made before this legislation.

Institutional Investors and the Municipal Bond Market

Most organizations owning portfolios of municipal bonds are not run exclusively for the purpose of buying municipal bonds. Instead, they are run as part of a large profit-making enterprise that is only incidentally or partly an investor in tax-exempt bonds. Obviously, major exceptions to this generalization would be the closed-end and open-end municipal bond funds. However, to take two examples from among the major buyers of municipal bonds, neither insurance companies nor banks regard buying municipal bonds as their central reason for existence. Therefore, inevitably, their decisions to buy and sell municipal bonds are governed by many considerations based on factors that frequently have little or nothing to do with supply, demand, price, or other changes in the municipal bond market itself.

What, then, are the major reasons for and patterns of such institutional purchases of bonds? First, the different ways in which banks and

Table 2.1. Holders of State and Local Government Debt 1975–1984

(Billions of dollars)

Holder	1984	1983	1982	1981	1980	1979	1978	1977	1976	1975
Households	201.4	169.9	129.0	99.9	89.9	83.2	72.7	70.1	70.1	68.1
Nonfinancial corporate business	4.0	4.2	3.5	3.5	3.5	3.7	3.7	3.5	3.4	4.5
State & local government, general fund	9.5	9.0	8.2	7.2	7.0	6.8	7.2	7.9	7.3	5.0
Commercial banks	172.1	162.6	158.7	154.2	149.2	135.6	126.2	115.2	106.0	102.9
Saving and loan associations	0.9	0.9	0.8	1.3	1.2	1.1	1.3	1.2	1.2	1.5
Mutual savings banks	2.1	2.1	2.5	2.3	2.4	2.9	3.3	2.8	2.4	1.5
Life insurance companies	9.5	10.0	9.0	7.2	6.7	6.4	6.4	6.1	5.6	4.5
Other insurance companies	87.2	86.7	87.0	83.9	80.5	72.8	62.9	49.4	38.7	33.3
State and local gov't, retirement funds	1.7	2.2	3.4	3.9	4.1	3.9	4.0	3.5	3.4	1.9
Brokers and dealers	2.0	1.4	1.0	1.2	1.1	1.0	0.9	1.1	0.9	0.6
Mutual funds	44.9	31.4	21.1	9.3	6.4	4.0	2.7	2.2	0.5	—

Because of rounding, components may not add to totals.
NOTE: Directly comparable figures are unavailable for 1985 and 1986 at the time of this writing.
SOURCE: Flow of Funds Accounts, Federal Reserve Board of Governors.

insurance companies are taxed determine to a considerable extent their purchases and sales of tax-exempt municipal bonds. These types of institutions receive tax shelters for their total profit-making activities from their municipal bonds, but they need such tax protection at different times, often for different reasons, and in response to different cyclical trends.

Large commercial banks whose primary purpose is to make loans are only residual users of funds for the most part. In other words, if they *cannot* make loans and they *can* anticipate taxable profits, then they will tend to buy municipal bonds. Their buying is therefore residual, or leftover, and occurs after they have either met their loan demand or reached a level of loan demand that they find acceptable. They are more likely to sell municipal bonds to make loans than vice versa. Only over the long run are banks net municipal bond buyers, but in the short term their rate of municipal bond sales changes, and can change more rapidly and more frequently than does that of insurance companies.

The pattern of insurance company buying is partly governed by what their actuaries believe is the acceptable level of insurable risks. They need only keep enough funds readily available to cover that level of insurance claims. The rest of their funds will tend to be constantly invested. For this reason, insurance companies are virtually always net investors in the municipal bond market, except in cases of catastrophic losses or during a severe economic downturn. Their municipal bond sales therefore tend to be primarily for the purpose of reinvesting in higher-yielding securities, among municipal bonds or elsewhere. The pattern of insurance company securities purchases is partly governed by the underwriting cycle, so that when their insurance underwriting is going well, they tend to buy municipal bonds, but when their insurance income is small or their losses are large, they tend to buy taxable bonds instead.

What is important to note about the large institutional players in these markets is that they provide a kind of price leadership both because of the size of their transactions and because of their high visibility. The hefty volume of their buying and selling gives them a strong bargaining leverage in any given negotiation, especially so because in municipal bond deals, for many types of bonds, the most common issuance is only for $10 million to $20 million or less. Therefore, a major institution in certain instances can effectively influence the price by taking a large fraction of the issue.

Individuals

In total, the number of individual investors in municipal bonds is so large that some analysts place the figure as high as 8 or 10 million. It is significant that some individuals' municipal bond holdings and tradings are larger than those of many of the smaller institutions. Even more important is the collective impact of these individuals, whose municipal bond transactions during a year can outstrip the movement of institutions, particularly in their ability to create sharp up or down trends in markets. In the years before 1986, it was estimated that fully 70 percent of all municipal bonds were held by those individuals with marginal tax rates of 50 percent; the remaining 30 percent of municipal bond buyers included perhaps 2 million investors below the 30 percent tax bracket.

Obviously, as inflation has pushed salaries higher with the cost of living, more and more Americans have been escalated into higher tax brackets. Thus with each year a whole new layer of wage earners has been confronted with a higher tax charge for the same effective purchasing power. It is these groups to whom the benefits of municipal bonds held an ever more appealing allure as the governmental tax bite worsened.

Institutional Bond Funds for Individuals

Since individuals' accounts in various types of funds are frequently handled and actively managed by banks and financial institutions, it is important to see how these players as buyers and sellers affect the market. While some funds turn over constantly, several times each year, most do not. On the other hand, unit trust funds of municipal bonds created in 1961 do not and cannot by law change their portfolio of bonds once the bonds are bought. Hence, they have occasionally become victims of souring interest rates, which cause them to lose asset principal. These unit trust fund investment companies are registered with the Securities and Exchange Commission (SEC), but their individual investors are not taxed as a corporation. Individuals can buy units of small amounts and get the advantages of diversification of risk as if they held many. While individuals may sell all or a portion of their units, they cannot substitute new bonds. When all the units are retired at expiration or when all are sold ahead of expiration, the trust simply disappears as a legal entity.

The major disadvantage of these unit trust funds for investors is that because they cannot exchange, sell, or trade bonds declining in market value, they tend to be hit very hard during periods of soaring interest rates, as we have experienced during certain periods. Also, since they are locked into a portfolio from a previous time, the individuals who must sell before the redemption date can lose a portion of their asset principal because of a depressed market.

The unit trust funds were created by many of the major bond dealers over the past 25 years (whose buying departments accumulate the portfolios for a trustee). The unit trust funds were split into two groups: those retailed for a sales charge by registered sales representatives and those issued as *no-load funds*, which were sold via direct mail and carried no sales charge to individuals. Because a typical fund is only $50 million, it is when many funds are clustered under one firm that the magnitude of this municipal buying and selling can be appreciated.

The goal of all such unit trust funds is to provide a reasonably stable stream of bond interest income over a long period of time. Two other specialized types of unit trust funds exist that concentrate on bonds of only one state or one intermediate maturity to benefit particular types of investors, who, for example, can frequently avoid state and local taxes. Also, a resident may know his or her state's municipal credits better than those elsewhere and feel more comfortable investing there.

In addition to the several billion dollars of bonds in these unit trust funds, there developed in late 1976, as a result of an alteration in the federal law, the creation of new open-end municipal bond funds that, unlike unit trust funds, could allow active management or trading of the bonds in the portfolio. Like unit trust funds, these are also split into two groups: those which charge a commission and those which do not. They are also split into those which are extremely actively managed, turned over, or traded versus those which anticipate holding most bonds until maturity. Once again, the major advantage to investors is argued to be that they can enter this market with a fractional share of $100 or $250, far smaller than the $5000 cost of the typical municipal bond. Investors also gain the advantages of diversification of a portfolio of bonds instead of the risk of putting all their eggs in one basket.

Dealers

Dealers both underwrite new issues and make over-the-counter markets for holders of tax-exempt municipal bonds. In the United States today, there is an ongoing dealer market for every type of municipal bond (including markets for defaulted issues). An insight into this dealer market comes from *The Blue List*, which shows most new issues and secondary markets of the best-known credits. It is commonly held that *The Blue List* at any given time shows between 50 and 75 percent or more of the total dealer inventory in both new and old bonds. In the past two decades the number of dealers has risen markedly, largely made up of new bank dealers, whose number has quadrupled from 50 to nearly

200. Since many firms, including perhaps 30 percent of *The Blue List* firms, have gone out of business and others have merged or been acquired, this dealer market should not be seen as unchanging but as participating in the larger financial shifts taking place on Wall Street and elsewhere.

While the failure rate of financial brokerage firms has been spectacular, the truly significant occurrence has been (1) the sudden start of municipal departments and divisions by practically every financial firm and (2) the dramatic increase in staff of those firms which already had a municipal department or division. Thus, in total, the sales growth of municipal bonds has been responsible for keeping large segments of the securities business alive and for employing a large portion of the stockbrokers, underwriters, and traders who were forced out of business by the failures, mergers, and acquisitions of firms in the past.

Dealers can be divided between bank and nonbank or between those which are exclusively municipal dealers and those which are wings of larger firms or banks. It has been noted that the smaller dealers have the following key characteristics: Most are corporations that hold no long-term debt but usually have huge short-term debt to finance an extraordinarily highly leveraged position. Because of their heavy potential expenses if they hold any bonds for long, most dealers hold particular bonds to maintain a position only for the minimum time it takes to sell the bonds to an institution or an individual (who will frequently hold the investment for the life of the security).

The larger, more diversified dealers at banks or large brokerage firms trade, swap, and otherwise exchange municipal bonds and even corporate securities with the federal government and federal agencies so that they can maintain an active market in each. They are constantly looking for the slight edge or fractionally undervalued security into which they will move. This movement into and out of the municipal market is frequently influenced not so much by what is happening in it as by what is happening in other quite separate securities markets.

Dealers in municipal bonds may also be ordered by the higher management of their firm to act in their trading in such a way as to maximize the firm's total position regardless of the current position of the municipal market, or to act for the current tax benefit of those receiving the firm's profits rather than for the long term. What is crucial but rarely understood is that despite the very heavy leverage or bank borrowings required by dealers in the municipal market, the interest on those borrowings used to finance municipal purchases was not usually a tax-deductible item (or if it was so used, the income from the coupon accrual was not tax-exempt).

Sales Trading and Back Office

The three separate operations engaged in by all municipal dealers and brokerage firms are sales, trading, and back-office technical work. These are all quite separate from the work of underwriters, which will be discussed later in this chapter. The larger the dealer firm, the more people in each operation and the greater the likelihood that they will be spread apart or regionalized. In the largest firms, interconnected microphones in front of every trader and salesperson in different parts of the country enable constant communication.

Brokers

In contrast to dealers, bond brokers do not trade on their own behalf but exclusively for customers among bond dealers, from whom they get commissions. Not only are there far fewer brokers than dealers, but the very largest brokerage firm only employs a staff of 100.

J. J. Kenny, which is fully specialized and automated, handles 500 or more separate bonds on any given day and must be aware of all the credit information that is up to the minute and pertinent to all these different securities. J. J. Kenny's brokers must be able to make virtually instant decisions about the best times to buy and sell during a day's trading.

Risk

Over the years, municipal bonds have come to be generally regarded as extremely safe investments. High-grade bonds are frequently considered safe, and medium-grade bonds have a large margin of safety to satisfy even conservative buyers. What many point to is the strong track record displayed by even the lowest-rated 10 to 15 percent of the market during depressions and recessions. The fact is that even during the great depression the vast majority of municipalities kept afloat financially, a remarkable feat considering the corporate and bank experience of the same period. Thus, relative to other securities, tax-free municipal bonds have performed well, and the number of defaults has been (except during the great depression) quite minimal. This is not to say that there is no risk in buying municipal bonds or that one's asset principal could not drastically change in value during the life of a bond before it is redeemed. Current markets fluctuate considerably in response to a whole range of factors.

In examining the day-to-day risks and performance of bonds in the trading market, it is clear that the daily participants are constantly looking at the whole municipal bond universe of prices, yields and credits, long and short terms, and searches for the undervalued securities. Just as with any other bond, the key factors are liquidity, or closeness to cash; the marketability, or ready range of buyers; the credit name, or familiarity to buyers; and above all, the official ratings by the two major rating services. The prices and yields of all other securities at that moment in the broader municipal and other securities markets are closely examined by all municipal analysts because they supply the range of immediate alternative investments. Just as with corporate bonds, the credit name and rating are the most critical factors; indeed, these factors are far more critical than for corporations because of the vast number of municipal bonds. In fact, because there are 1 million municipal bonds issued, compared to only 10,000 corporate bonds, and the unusual and unfamiliar credits among municipal bonds are many, both the individual and institutional investor are far more dependent on the rating services for guidance in obtaining municipal bonds than for obtaining corporate bonds. Also, since neither Moody's nor Standard & Poor's (S&P) rates even 40 percent of all municipal bonds, most of the large institutional investors are unable or unwilling to invest in the unrated bonds at all.

Moreover, only those issues which trade in giant volume can accommodate the large institutional investors. Thus there is something akin to follow-the-leader kinds of pressures that develops among those funds which actively manage or frequently swap, trade, or turn over their portfolio of municipal bonds. Because there is an abiding question about whether interest rates can be forecast, there is an ongoing dispute between those who argue that managing a municipal portfolio to get the best interest rate is totally impossible and those who argue that it is essential. This dispute gained added fire in the last two decades because of soaring interest rates, dramatically changing bond yields and prices, and the entrance into this municipal bond market in force of the new funds and institutions. Also important were masses of individuals ricocheting from their painful experience of getting burned in the stock market to municipal bonds for the first time, expecting these to provide a safer haven. With so many newcomers to this municipal market, among both investors and fund managers there were bound to be certain tendencies that were mistakenly carried over from stock market investing or corporate bond investing into the municipal market before participants learned how very different, indeed unique, this market is.

Price Characteristics of Municipal Bonds

General market bonds that cross state lines in search of buyers on the national or regional scale must obviously be priced in relation to one another. However, countless small municipal bond issues are bought and held locally and never leave the municipality. Their characteristics are often less uniform than those of general market bonds. In general, however, local bonds of the large populous states, such as New York and California, do move in price and yield quite closely to price levels in the general market because the same individual and institutional investors look at them as they look at other alternative securities and, consequently, force considerable uniformity. It is thus in the less populous states, cities, and regions that deviations start to occur from the general levels of bond prices and yields. There, the difference between the unknown name and the better-known credit becomes critical. As a result, higher prices become required in order to justify these variations in relative marketability of these unknown bonds.

The effect on bond prices and trading behavior caused by a new issue's size is difficult to gauge for the buyer and seller. In evaluating the pricing level, most sellers of a $50 million issue know it is frequently the fate of the last $10 million that determines the price. For the buyer, it is the size of this issue that can affect the presence or absence of an aftermarket. Whereas standard borrowings by large states that are regularly in the market for a set amount are considered easy to price and evaluate, it is the extra-large issues that can pose a problem. Especially small issues can also result in bond prices that are out of line with the average. This "size leverage," as it is sometimes called, is noted by many participants, but in general it is significant that there are not wider variations in bond prices, given the variety of differences involved within this multiplicity of bonds.

Like the various stock markets and the corporate bond market, the municipal bond market tends to move together. While some bonds of different grades also tend to move together, there are strong tendencies for the highest-grade bonds to act as market leaders and let others follow. Leads and lags of different particular securities are watched daily, even hourly, but for the most part the participants' expectations that different groups of bonds will be bid and traded in line with the general trend tend to be fulfilled.

What is significant is not the minor variations, which must of necessity always occur in such sectional lags and leads, but rather the basic underlying trend, which is for the high-grade credits to maintain their price stability better than the lower-grade credits. A result of this could be that when the whole market slides down in level 30 basis points, the high-grade bonds might hardly change, while the lower-rated bonds will slide away far deeper on the downside. Likewise—in the opposite direction—when the market is rising, the reverse happens as the low-grade bonds make up for their decline by rising faster.

The Municipal Market

The market for municipal securities has two parts: (1) the primary market and (2) the secondary market. The primary market, or new issue market, exists for securities when they are first issued. As greater demands are made upon state and local governments to raise the money needed for building and replacing, investors will have a continuing choice of new bonds that will finance educational facilities, mass transit, pollution control, housing, and urban redevelopment, to cite only a few examples.

The secondary market, or trading market, in municipal securities—although it begins even before the securities are issued in the "when issued" trades—really refers to the market in which older, seasoned issues are bought and sold before their final maturity. This nationwide market is made up of dealers and brokers who are in contact via telephone and wire networks. This system offers a trading market for municipal securities and enables one to buy or sell municipal securities comparatively easily. The existence of the secondary market allows investors to change their portfolios in terms of the types of bonds they own, their maturities, and their ratings. In addition, the secondary market allows them to take tax losses or gains when appropriate because of changes in the investors' tax bracket.

The Sellers and Underwriters

Underwriting and Syndication

The simplest form of selling municipal bonds is when a municipality asks its local bank to structure a loan for a specific piece of equipment in the form of a set of tax-exempt bonds. While such sales remain the most numerous, the overwhelming dollar volume comes from bond sales transacted between bond issuers and dealers in the primary, or new issue, market via a system known as underwriting and syndication.

Underwriting is a common practice throughout the municipal markets whereby investment bankers and commercial banks join in a syndicate contract with a bond issuer to buy the entire new bond issue at a set price (whether reached competitively or through negotiation) and then resell that issue in smaller wholesale or retail pieces to the public.

The underwriting of massive blocks of bonds sold by municipalities, in amounts of over $25 million and up to $500 million and more in one issue, cannot be handled exclusively by one dealer or bank. This is not only because of capital limitations but also because each bulk buyer of bonds wishes to carefully spread, or diversify, its risk should this issue, for whatever reasons, not be readily salable at the intended reoffering scale.

These bulk transactions between municipalities and bond dealers in this new issue market are of two types: competitive or negotiated. Since the financial managers of cities, towns, and states are often required by law to do so, they request competitive bids for their municipalities' bonds rather than relying on negotiation with only one underwriter or one group and one price. However, when money is tight in the nation's debt markets and large bond issues are hard to sell, a negotiated sale may well be the best solution for the issuer. In other cases—where the bond issue is very large or of an entirely new type, where an entirely new market must be developed, or where a new issuer is coming to market for the first time—a negotiated sale can make great sense.

If a municipality decides to do a negotiated underwriting, it contacts a number of leading managing underwriters and asks them to submit a presentation of their credentials. It then selects the firm or management team that it believes, for a combination of reasons (capital, distributing ability, management record, municipal finance expertise), will be the most competent and will achieve the lowest net interest cost in marketing the issue. The selected managers assist in structuring the issue, performing due diligence in the preparation of the official statement, conducting a premarketing sales campaign, and, finally, negotiating in good faith the terms of the sale.

In most states the law explicitly requires that issuers sell GO bonds by competitive bidding, usually by submission of a sealed bid. It is for this reason that most bond issues still come to market via competitive bids. GO bonds tend to be easier to sell on the whole than revenue bonds and to need less explanation in order to be sold. They do not require the extra care and services that many revenue bonds require. GO bonds have no holding restrictions as to ownership, while revenue bonds do. Nor are there any limitations as to the type of investment dealer who can bid to underwrite them.

In contrast, revenue bonds tend to come to market via negotiated transactions with an underwriter or a single syndicate for the following reasons: The infrequency of coming to market was in the past a primary reason why most revenue issues were negotiated. Only a limited number of dealers were willing to assume liability for such new untested issues, and a vast amount of legal and financial groundwork was needed before financing was possible. Underwriters were understandably reluctant to give their guarantee of purchase to such bond issues regardless of the state of the bond market. Today these conditions are changing somewhat with the far more substantial size of the revenue bond issues, but a large number still tend to come the negotiated route because of these factors and others, such as tradition or the ability to find a market "window" or to have a presale effort.

Revenue bonds often come to market in a single-term issue, while GO bonds come to market in serial form over a span of years. Since it may be more difficult to find a large number of buyers for an issue of bonds all maturing in one year, say 2013, the sale of these bonds may take more time. Each buyer of a brand-new and unknown revenue issue (such as a joint action power agency combining several municipalities together for the first time under a power supply contract) will require time to evaluate the sources of future earnings, sinking fund provisions, the cash flow of the authority, the cost of the power to the users, the quality of the management, and the level of debt coverage. All these factors account for some of the newest issuers coming to market via negotiation. However, even many of the best-known names come to market via negotiation. Uncertainty in different bond markets at different times is pointed to as the reason why they choose negotiated sales, but other key factors include the unusually large size of an issue and perhaps the difficulty of selling it in total to retail customers, especially when many issues are coming to market at one particular time.

The dollar volume of negotiated issues has risen over recent years compared with that of negotiated sales. Both competitive bidding and negotiated sales are usually quite constrained by local legal requirements in state constitutions and statutes as well as in local town or city statutes. For these legal reasons peculiar to the locality, the generalized description of competitive bidding and underwriting procedures, which follows, will vary somewhat from one municipality to another.

The exact method of advertising a forthcoming bond sale by a municipality is usually set down in local laws, and it involves not only a public notice in *The Bond Buyer* or some other financial publication but also a list of details concerning the bond issue:

- Date, time, and place of sale
- Amount of issue, maturity schedule, and call feature (if any)
- Manner in which bid is to be made (sealed or oral)
- Authority for sale
- Type of bond (revenue, GO, etc.)
- Limitation as to interest rates plus the payment dates of the interest
- Denominations and registration privileges
- Amount of bid (at par or better or discount allowed)
- Amount of good-faith check

- Names of approving attorneys and a statement to the effect that these attorneys will furnish an unqualified legal opinion approving the legality of the bonds and also a certificate that no litigation is pending which will affect the issuance of the bonds
- Bid form
- Method and place of settlement for the bonds
- The right to reject any or all bids
- Manner of obtaining a copy of the official statement or prospectus

The Syndicate

Whereas a negotiated bid is sought by an issuer's proposal to an underwriter or single group of underwriters to enter a bid, in contrast, competitive deals will be advertised by the issuing municipality in *The Bond Buyer* a week or more before the day set for the award of the bonds to the winning underwriting syndicate. Competitive deals and negotiated ones begin with investment bankers and/or commercial banks joining together into groups called municipal securities "dealing accounts," or "syndicates," to make bids on these new bonds being offered for sale. These syndicates have formed over time in an informal manner. Because of traditional associations, they usually bid in substantially the same groups as they did for some previous issue of bonds for this same issuer. This is not to say that there are not shifts among those belonging to these groups over time. Some dealers leave the proposed syndicate on a new issue because they feel that (1) the bond price the other syndicate partners have agreed upon is too high or too low or (2) the underwriting spread is inadequate. Other syndicate members are dropped from the syndicate when they have not in the past shown themselves able to sell their whole allocation of bonds.

For large states or cities that come into the debt markets 1, 2, or 3 times every year, it would be relatively impractical for underwriting syndicates to regroup into different partnerships each time. Firms that have bid together as a syndicate in one state are therefore expected to join together for the next syndicate offering of municipal bonds by that state. It definitely conflicts with standard underwriting practice for firms to shift back and forth repeatedly between syndicates, and most syndicates stay relatively intact for some time.

Within syndicates the largest dealers have a better capacity to handle the mechanical operations of the syndicate as a whole, and they become known as the managing underwriters. Although some deals are "comanaged," others of the very largest dealers will usually be designated "joint managers." Then, there follows a clear bracketing of the different members in the syndicate into tiers, depending on what share of the loan issue they are able to underwrite. This clear-cut status is very important in maintaining the pecking order within the syndicate and is watched very closely. The order of the names of the syndicate members printed in financial publications' advertisements, known as "tombstones," is first by bracket, then by the size of each member's share of participation in the issue, and finally alphabetically within each bracket. Underwriters have been known to resign from syndicates rather than to appear listed below what they deem lesser firms, and so the manager must be quite careful to be aware of the objections of different members.

The syndicates sometimes merge when an especially large issue is being brought to market. They also can split up for smaller issues, but there tends to be a good deal of continuity of syndicate membership because of the crucial need for absolute trust, cooperation, and honesty. Dependability and, especially, familiarity on a personal basis with the individuals with whom you work in the syndicate are the basic reasons that syndicates endure. Even when a firm drops from the syndicate on one deal, because of overpricing or some other reason, it will remain a member of the next syndicate unless it "is asked to find another home." Because there are so many municipal issues offered for sale during any particular year or month, it is not uncommon for syndicate members who are working together on one deal to be competitors at the same time on another deal in which, for whatever reasons, they are part of separate syndicates.

The syndicate manager, upon seeing a municipal bond advertisement in *The Bond Buyer* for a new issue, contacts former members of the syndicate and arranges a meeting to discuss a bid. The manager also circulates to all the account members actual written contracts requiring that they be bound by the rules of the account. This does not mean that they cannot drop out of the account after signing. They can drop out right up until the very last minute before the syndicate makes its final offer, but once the syndicate has won the bid, all members are bound to the terms of participation that they have contracted for in advance.

The legal syndicate letter sent by the managing underwriter directly to each member of the syndicate spells out the duties and obligations of each to the other for the time that the syndicate lasts (usually 30 days—however, 45- and 60-day agreements are sometimes found). While this may appear to be a kind of partnership, the letter spells out specifically that it is not. Instead, it is a form of joint venture in which the liability of each member is detailed in a special fashion. The manager can borrow funds, advertise, pledge securities, submit the bid, and otherwise act as the official agent for the whole syndicate. The manager's mistakes, except for ones that result from "want of good faith," will usually not result in any legal action by other syndicate members.

The price ideas of the different members of the syndicate, which are shared in their first meeting, reflect each participant's assessment of the bond markets, interest rate levels, and general economic outlook of the municipal and national economy at that moment. From this general pricing discussion emerges a scale of proposed prices for each broad 5-year period in the new bond issue. With these 5-year "spots" running until the final maturity of the bonds, the manager is easily able to scale all the intervening years' prices and hence develop a full schedule of prices, yields, and profit spreads for the entire issue. The manager always tries to remove risk from the syndicate's membership with a bid that is high enough to be profitable but low enough to be competitive against the bids being submitted by other syndicates.

The next meeting of the syndicate occurs the following day, approximately an hour before the time the bonds are to be sold. This is usually a meeting of all members in person, although sometimes it is held in a conference call. The lead manager at this final meeting announces the interest rates at which the members generally feel that investors will be attracted to the issue. Those who disagree with the interest rates generally agreed on for the whole issue have the right to drop out of the syndicate. Each member firm's name is read out, and each firm's opinions are sought with regard to the rate and whether it wishes a larger or smaller "participation," or share, of the total underwriting—or whether it will "drop." The critical problem for the manager is then to determine whether there are enough dealers left at the agreed-upon price to fully underwrite the loan to the municipality.

The manager can decide that not enough members remain at this price and hence that the rate of interest must be increased to attempt to win back into the account some of the members who have dropped. Alternatively, the manager can decide that too many members wish to increase their participation. The rate of interest must be too high and must therefore be lowered in order to ensure that it is truly competitive and retains a chance of being the winning bid in the competition.

In these hectic minutes just before submission of the final bid, the manager's computer is used during the meeting to determine the very best coupon rates to use for the bid, given a whole variety of factors. The computer projections of prices, coupon rates, yields to maturity, and profit spread are all added together in various combinations to find a net interest cost figure that will be relayed to the issuer at the last possible moment. Usually, the bid is phoned to a contact near the issuer to make sure that these last-minute negotiations of the members at the manager's office can proceed with all the very latest market information before the bid is transmitted to the issuer. Since sometimes hundreds of millions of dollars are at stake in one offering, it is understandable that these last minutes are somewhat tense as each partner assesses its degree of risk or exposure in pricing too high or too low and thereby suffering a loss. Sizable losses on underwriting are certainly frequent enough, today as in the past, to give each of the underwriters pause. For this reason, the pressure is quite strong for members of the syndicate to come up with realistic rates of interest when bidding. No underwriter wants an unsalable issue on its hands.

Finally, at the designated time and place the municipal issuer opens the bids from the different competing syndicates, and they are compared. Usually the award is made to the account that promised to pay the lowest net interest cost. This method of awarding the sale of bonds has been attacked on the ground that it fails to explicitly take into account the actual time value of money. Nevertheless, this remains the predominant method of awarding underwriting contracts.

The winning syndicate, as part of its original computation of its bid, has agreed upon a reoffering price for these bonds—for every bond in every maturity. Therefore, the instant the winning bid has been accepted by the municipality, the selling departments of the syndicate members start making telephone calls or sending teletype messages around the country to all their normal or special customers to announce the details of the new offering.

In advance of the final actual bid, these same customers have usually been contacted at least once for their interest in buying. However, no customer is definitely committed until the syndicate has won the bid. The result is that often certain eager buyers who expressed interest accept right away and agree to buy a certain number of bonds, while others say that the final agreed-upon rate is too expensive and they will pass this issue by. During these first hours, known as the *order period*, if the underwriting is very successful, all orders are gathered together, the whole issue is sold, and the syndicate closes. If the syndicate manages to sell the underwriting in a period of but a few days, its members will usually be able to profit from their risk taking in this venture, and this is another reason that widespread canvassing of customers in advance is so thorough and why timing is of the essence.

Yet if the U.S. Federal Reserve Bank intervenes in the bond market, if the bond markets as a whole encounter a bad time, or if many other issues come to market at this very same time with better rates of interest, then by the end of the first week all the bonds in this particular issue may well not be resold by the syndicate. It will be forced to "break" and sell the bonds for whatever lower price the general prevailing bond market will now require to "unload" these bonds. At the point at which the syndicate breaks, the manager sends out bills to the members reminding them of their original share participation and asking them to pay for the loss on the account. They must then buy their share of bonds at their agreed-upon price regardless of the price at which they can now resell the bonds. The bonds that are left will be prorated among all the members of the syndicate. These remaining bonds will be advertised in *The Blue List* and either sold at the lower market rates or held by the former syndicate's members in their own account until a later time when they find an acceptable buyer. The two final alternatives can each be quite expensive and are the two situations in which underwriters incur substantial losses.

While most competitive offerings attract several bids—which may result in *close covers,* or bids very near the winning one—it is very unusual ever to hear of a tie bid. Underwriters of the winning syndicate as well as customers they contact are especially pleased if there was a close cover or very near alternative bid by another syndicate because it is a clear indication that the price of these bonds is very competitive, indeed. Usually, the farther away the next bid is, the harder it will be to sell the issue. These bids and their range are published in *The Bond Buyer.* The dispersion of the many bids can usually be greater than 10 basis points, or 0.1 percent; nevertheless, the closest cover bid is usually less distant than 0.05 percent, suggesting that the underwriting market is quite competitive.

The member firms of the underwriting syndicate are subject to two separate types of assessment: (1) the western, or divided, account versus (2) the eastern, or undivided, account. Today, most accounts or syndicates are undivided as to liability because most dealers do not wish to take on the risks inherent in divided accounts. Many will not even bid on the underwriting of divided accounts. In brief, the distinction between these two types of accounts in terms of member firms' liability is as follows: In an undivided account each syndicate member's sale of its underwriting participation reduces its liability. In a divided account it does not because each member's liability is broken down by brackets of particular types of bonds; for example, the first 10-year bonds, which are generally easier to sell, are shared by all members of the syndicate, and one firm's sale of all of them does not reduce its liability for the sale of the more difficult last 30-year maturities. In this scheme, a single firm's sales reduce somewhat the total liability of others in the syndicate but may not discharge that firm's total liability.

Regional Investment Firms

Among the less well publicized aspects of the municipal bond market is the role of the regional investment firms. They serve as local underwriters and brokerage institutions and in some regions still dominate the municipal market.

The range of local investors is frequently better known by regional firms than by firms in New York or even a national organization. For this reason it has been common for major national underwriters to ask important regional firms to join an underwriter syndicate as comanagers or major-bracket partners in a new underwriting for a municipality in their state or region. Major regional banks may also be asked to join particular national syndicates for the same reason. Municipal bond selling (unlike the selling or underwriting of corporate securities) tends to require so much more on-the-spot local knowledge of a particular town, school system, public facility, or public authority that the regional firm has an advantage over the New York investment firms in knowing a specific municipality, its economic and debt trends, its financial position, the caliber of its management, and the market for the bonds.

In the 1970s many national brokerage firms joined in especially powerful syndicates to go after new regional underwritings, and they became known as "barracuda accounts." Because they were then thought to threaten the existence of the regional investment firms, there developed a tense rivalry between New York and the regional firms. While the outright tension has decreased somewhat, the pressure from the New York firms, which have been expanding their branch offices across the country and out into the regions, has continued as they have bought up weaker (and some stronger) regional firms in order to gain hefty regional distribution for their new issues. Because such national brokerage firms have a whole network of regional and national offices and such a wide range of financial services, they have increasingly put new pressure on the smaller regional firms.

This regional versus national competition should be seen as part of the larger battle between many investment institutions today. The failures, mergers, and acquisitions that have occurred during the last decade are widely expected to continue in the next decade as the various investment organizations attempt to enlarge their capital base, computerize their back-office operations, offer a full range of financial services, and put down ever stronger regional roots to ensure their sales distribution systems.

3
The Rating Agencies: Their Role in the Municipal Marketplace

Over the last four decades, the rating of municipal bonds by independent analysts has grown from next to negligible importance into a central and, in many cases, controlling factor as to whether an investor or institution will buy a municipal bond. Yet the degree of faith attached by the individual and institutional investors to a rating on a municipal bond issue has been matched only by their lack of knowledge about how a rating is reached. This occurred partly because little or nothing had been written or publicized about the rating process.

To fill the vacuum, this chapter grew out of lengthy discussions with analysts at Standard & Poor's Corporation, Moody's Investors Service, Inc., Fitch Investors Service, Inc., and White's Rating Service—four advisory services in the United States whose systems of ratings for municipal bonds are used throughout the country. Policy discussions were also held about the role of ratings with representatives, senators, regulators, and the rating agency directors.

The Meaning of a Rating on a Municipal Bond

The concept of a rating is simple: What is the probability of the timely repayment of principal and interest? While the following pages cannot give all the details of how ratings are reached—primarily because of the number, diversity, and complexity of the variables involved—they will spell out the fundamental credit analyses conducted by the major rating agencies.

The sheer size of today's public market for corporate and municipal debt (involving huge reservoirs of money through insurance companies, savings banks, trusts, mutual funds, profit-sharing plans, pension plans, and so on) has made the traditional word-of-mouth assessments of credit values totally insufficient. Therefore, independent rating agencies have been developed to help investors by providing an easily recognizable set of symbols (i.e., A, B, C) that grade, on the same scale, a range of issuers of debt stretching from Exxon to foreign governments (such as Japan) and to municipal issuers as varied as New York State and the Pinellas County, Florida, Water and Sewer District. The simplicity of the rating symbol is especially important because many issuers sell bonds with varying security pledges ranging from first mortgage bonds and sinking fund debentures to bonds that are convertible or double- or triple-barreled in their backing; in short, the range is extremely complex.

As the number of municipal bond issues has multiplied each year, the ratings of bonds by these agencies have increased in importance and complexity. Also, since ratings affect the eligibility of bonds for purchase by institutional investors, they can influence the interest rate a community must pay on its bonds. Owing to federal and state regulations, many institutional investors, particularly banks and pension funds, can only buy bonds of a specified quality. Most trusts and estates today are guided by what is called the "prudent person" rule in buying their investment bonds. A high rating for a given bond issue will broaden the market for that bond and should reduce the net interest cost to the issuer.

Basic Similarities and Differences between the Rating Agencies

Moody's Investors Service and Standard & Poor's Corporation are the two major municipal rating agencies. They rate bonds on request by the issuer for a set fee based upon time and effort; they continue to maintain and renew the rating until the bond has been redeemed. Prior to 1968 (S&P), 1970 (Moody's), and 1974 (Fitch), the agencies derived all their income from the sale of publications that provided information on municipal bond issues for the benefit of the financial community and investors. The research for ratings was done at no charge to the municipality whose bonds were being rated. However, the crippling financial expense of doing free analysis and the growing complexity and volume in the municipal financing field caused them to change to a fee policy.

The rating agencies rate virtually all types of GO and revenue bonds, encompassing bonds of states, counties, cities, school districts, and special-purpose taxing districts. Both limited- and unlimited-tax GO bonds of these issuers are rated. In addition, all three rate the following revenue bonds:

- Enterprise systems, such as electric, water, sewer, gas, airports, parking, ports, toll facilities, solid waste disposal, transit, hospitals, housing, racetracks (under certain conditions), stadiums (if additionally secured), telephone, marinas, and auditoriums

- Special tax revenue bonds, such as sales, franchise, hotel, utility, cigarette, business license, and fuel

- Special revenue bonds, such as higher education (tuition, etc.), student loan, tax increment, special assessment (if additionally secured), lease-rental obligations, debt service makeups, and insured bonds

Some believe, however, that there are differences of philosophy and policy between Moody's and Standard & Poor's that dictate differences in their approaches to rating municipal bonds. Nevertheless, rating agencies are thought to be remarkably similar with regard to bonds in four vital aspects: independence, symbols, general criteria, and warning.

Independence. Each believes that its ratings are of value only so long as it is considered totally objective, independent, and disinterested, i.e., credible. That credibility is very fragile, and so each is cautious to have no corporate or governmental influence.

Symbols. While their symbols have slight differences, they are virtually identical. Moody's ratings for municipal bonds are, in descending order of quality: Aaa, Aa, A, Baa, Ba, B, Caa, Ca, and C. Standard & Poor's ratings are: AAA, AA, A, BBB, BB, B, CCC, CC, C, and D. Ratings under Baa and BBB are considered by most to be under what is commonly known as investment grade. (Short-term ratings of municipal notes will be discussed in Chap. 16.) In addition to these rating categories, the symbols Aa1, A1, Baa1, Ba1, and B1 are used by Moody's to identify the bonds in those groups which possess the strongest investment attributes. Standard & Poor's uses + and − (for all categories from BB to AA) to indicate, respectively, extra strengths and weaknesses.

General Criteria. Each bases its ratings in varying degrees on the following considerations: (1) Likelihood of default—capacity and willingness of the obligator as to the timely payment of interest and repayment of principal in accordance with the terms of the obligation;

(2) nature and provisions of the obligation; and (3) protection afforded by, and relative position of, the obligation in the event of bankruptcy, reorganization, or some other arrangement under the laws of bankruptcy and other laws affecting creditors' rights.

Warning.   Rating agencies warn that a rating is not a recommendation to purchase, sell, or hold a security. This is because the rating agency does not comment as to the market price or suitability for a particular investor of a particular bond. Also, the rating does not mean that the rating agency has performed an audit. Nor does it attest to the authenticity of the information given to the agency by the issuer and on which the agency bases its ratings. Ratings of all three agencies can be changed, suspended, or withdrawn as a result of changes in information or a municipality's refusal to provide information. The agencies also attempt to make it clear that they are not saying that one bond issue is better than another; their rating is simply an assessment at a single point in time of the nature of the security underlying the specific bond issue. Once a decision has been made that an issue will be sold, whether competitively or by negotiation, a rating request to one of the rating agencies is initiated by the issuer or its authorized representatives.

Prior to the assignment of many ratings, the agencies usually meet with representatives of the issuing entity at their offices or on the site and give the issuer an opportunity to make a presentation. The purpose of the meeting is to resolve questions and uncertainties concerning the proposed bond issue; it also allows the rating agencies the opportunity to assess the quality of the management of the issuing body.

Each of the rating agencies aims to determine whether the issue is investment grade or speculative grade. The term *investment grade* was originally used by various regulatory bodies to connote obligations that are eligible for investment by various institutions, such as banks, insurance companies, and savings and loan associations. Over time this term has gained widespread use throughout the investment community. Issues rated in the four highest categories are generally recognized as investment grade. Securities rated below Baa or BBB are generally referred to as "speculative securities."

Once established, municipal bond ratings remain in effect for as long as financial information is furnished regularly or until the next bond sale. For most issues, the rating agencies need annual audits and budget documents on an ongoing basis. For revenue bond ratings involving construction financing, they also need at least quarterly progress reports covering the project involved. In a lease-rental situation in which the lease-rental payment depends upon the completion and/or acceptance of the project by the lessee, they request a copy of a certificate of completion. For Standard & Poor's, Moody's, and Fitch, the failure by municipalities to supply all the above information on a timely basis necessitates a suspension or withdrawal of the rating, inasmuch as their first rule is that a rating must be based upon all the adequate facts.

Rating of General Obligation Bonds: Moody's

While Standard & Poor's and Moody's share four basic criteria in analyzing municipal bonds (examining the entity's debt, economic base, finances, and management of the municipality), a fundamental difference exists in their approach, although this is not a hard-and-fast difference as a rule. According to Moody's, debt and the debt ratios that follow from it are among the first factors to analyze. The first questions asked in the analysis leading to the rating are "(1) what has the debtor pledged to pay and (2) what is the probability that he can fulfill this pledge."[1] On the other hand, for Standard & Poor's *the economic base* is the first factor.

For example, Moody's states:

> The analyst is concerned with the total impact of all debt obligations on the reasonable ability of the taxpayers of the issuing unit to meet them. To this end, his central and first task is to derive a measure of the debt burden. In simplest terms, this is the relationship between the total debt of all governmental units and the taxable wealth located within the borrower's boundaries.
>
> The overall net debt is related to the broadest and most generally available measure of the wealth of the community—assessed valuation of all taxable property adjusted to reflect market value as nearly as possible. The adjustment is made through application of an equalization ratio, which generally reflects a state government's appraisal of local assessment practices. Empirical evidence indicates that there is good reason to expect difficulty in meeting debt obligations when the debt burden exceeds the 12% range and when an exogenous factor, such as an economic recession, comes into play.[2]

In contrast, Standard & Poor's states:

> The economic base is the most critical element in determining an issuer's rating. A community's fiscal health derives from its economy, affecting such major revenue sources as sales, income, and property taxes. Economic conditions also dictate the quantity and quality of services deliverd in such categories of expenditures as welfare, community development, health care, and the like.[3]

The Standard & Poor's approach will be discussed in the following section.

Moody's analysis, concentrating on debt and debt ratios, is the more established and more traditional approach. Moody's spells out its own debt analysis in the following list:

Debt Analysis[4]

1. Debt policy: the uses, purposes, and planning of debt issuance • the type of instruments used • debt limits.
2. Debt structure: adequacy of plans for debt retirement • the relation between rate of retirement and purpose of debt, resources of the community, and existing and future debt needs.
3. Debt burden: gross and net debt related to resources and a comparison with other communities • overlapping debt and pyramiding.
4. Debt history and trend: the record as to defaults, refunding of maturing bonds and funding of operating deficits • rapidity of debt growth relative to purposes for which it has been incurred.
5. Prospective borrowing: authorized and uninsured bonds • adequacy of capital programming • obsolescence or inadequacy of capital plant • existing debt structure.

The Moody's analyst also examines the structure of the debt and how the issuer plans to reduce it. Unnecessary deferral of debt payment raises questions, and as a general rule the analyst prefers payment to be reasonably related to the life of the improvement that the debt is used to finance. The payment of one-half of the debt of a community over the ensuing 10 years is generally recognized as being prudent; it accounts theoretically for some depreciation, besides maintaining the capacity to borrow in the future. Another aspect of debt structure the analyst seeks to determine is irregularities and any special problems that might be incurred in meeting them.

Other aspects of the analyst's appraisal of the debt of a community include examining the community's debt history, the reasons as to how and why the community issues debt to meet both its needs and resources, and the probabilities of future borrowing by the community. The latter factor is of utmost importance. It involves an assessment of a city's capital planning relative to its own position in history. For a deteriorating older city or for a rapidly growing newer city, future borrowing policy dictates particular and careful planning. While turning to other factors in the analysis, the analyst must bear in mind the possible future debt policies of the borrowing unit.

Economic Base of Municipal Bonds According to Standard & Poor's

Among the factors Standard & Poor's considers in evaluating the economic base are income levels and the rate of income growth. Both per capita and per household income levels and growth rate are measured against those for the region in which the community is located, its standard metropolitan statistical area (SMSA), the state, and the nation.

Next, Standard & Poor's analyzes the employment mix to isolate areas of potential vulnerability compared with state, regional, and national trends, considering both short- and long-term aspects. While unemployment figures can be useful in some cases, the stress at Standard & Poor's is usually on the growth of the labor force. These figures give a real indication of the expansion or contraction of the local economy and are a measure of its economic viability.

Then Standard & Poor's analyzes population growth using a four-decade trend as well as recent estimates, the age of the population (under 18 and over 65 are considered "dependent" population requiring more costly services), and educational attainment levels as they relate to wage-earning capacity.

The leading employers and taxpayers are weighed carefully in relation to the types of industry involved, their commitment to the area, expansion plans, etc. Any significant shifts in taxpayers or employers are analyzed for their impact on the economic base. Building activity is another good indicator of economic vitality and of course translates into assessments and revenues from higher property taxes. Standard & Poor's looks carefully at the mix of building activity (residential versus commercial and industrial) and the effects of various economic conditions on building activity. Other economic indicators include the age and composition of the housing stock, retail sales activity (which indicates whether a community is a locally, regionally, or nationally important center), and bank deposits.

In summary, communities with higher income levels and diverse economic bases, which provide protection against economic fluctuations, clearly demonstrate a stronger capacity to pay the long-term bondholder. As previously stated, assessments of the economic viability of a community must take a long-term perspective because the issuer's ability to meet debt service is a long-term consideration. Economic change is generally slow but persistent, and a high capacity to pay at present may not translate into a long-term trend.

Financial Analysis of Municipal Credits

Both Moody's and Standard & Poor's use much the same techniques for their financial analysis of a municipality's credit. Historical budget and audit report analyses are conducted with an emphasis on the issuer's revenue structure and how well it responds to various economic conditions. The translation of resources into revenues to pay expenses, including debt service, requires periodic and constant examination of the issuer's accounts.

Their examination of the financial operations of the community for the latest period available serves to confirm its performance under existing conditions. Current account analysis includes examination of the absolute size of the current budget, the trend in budget growth related to growth in population tax base, and the revenue/expenditure balance or imbalance over a period of years.

For analyzing the municipality's current account, the rating agencies concentrate on the main operating funds that are basically tax-supported, such as the general fund, debt service fund, and road or welfare fund. The special revenue fund would be included if federal revenue-sharing monies were used primarily for operating rather than for capital purposes. The municipality's reliance on outside federal and state aids or on short-term borrowing or any other sign that the community's tax calendar is not geared to its rate of expenditures is taken as a signal that cash flow problems are likely because the community is counting on outsiders to constantly bail it out of temporary or permanent imbalance.

Next, the rating agencies analyze all the major revenue sources, their changing importance as part of the entire revenue picture, and the suitability of these revenue sources in terms of their economic bases. Expenditure trends and categories are analyzed, as is the balance sheet, to determine the accumulative effect of each year's revenue and expenditure scorecard. Comparing this year's budget with actual operations is a key test of both financial and managerial strengths.

Critical to all rating agencies is the analysis of the revenue system to determine the municipality's reliance on the community's property tax, the trend of assessed valuation, and tax delinquencies. All the agencies concur that a balanced composition of revenues, sufficiently diversified so that the community is not unduly reliant on one or two big taxpayers or outside financing sources, is necessary to give the issuer of municipal bonds the necessary flexibility to meet all its obligations.

The rating agencies give some weight to an assessment of the management of the municipality. They meet with the managers personally to size up their knowledge and professionalism and are especially concerned with the availability of adequate financial documents, annual budgets, reports, and planning for land use, capital expenditure, and future income and future expenditure projections. Cost controls and management systems zoning are each signs of professional management. They indicate that management is thinking about how services are to be provided in the future to perpetuate the municipality's growth and strength.

Obviously, managers are restricted somewhat in their ability to plan by charter, statutory, or constitutional limitations on tax rates, levies, and bases of assessment, and so a knowledge of the governmental structure and traditions of the municipality is essential for the rating analyst. Intergovernmental relations are today an increasingly significant key in assessing the cooperation and competition between this municipality and others.

In general, the range and level of services in relation to the communities' ability to provide such services (and the sharing of responsibility with other overlapping governmental bodies) are the central focus in the assessment of managers by the rating agencies. Their ability to deal with possible litigation, labor relations, and tax collection in a future recession or depression are all evaluated by the rating agents.

For each of the rating agencies, the crucial problem is how the separate analyses of the economic base, debt, finance, and management are blended together and weighed in order to arrive at a single rating. Each agency warns against a rigid mathematical formula or blanket rule for making this final rating determination.

Analyzing GO and Revenue Bonds

The approach of a rating agency to the different types of municipal bonds obviously varies according to the category and credit involved. While the major differences in rating approaches are between GO and revenue bonds, even within GO bonds there are different methods of analysis that depend upon whether a district is a state, county, city, or school district or a special district. This is because although the conceptual analysis is the same, state governments have sovereign powers or unique fiscal options that must be reflected in the creditworthiness of state GO bonds. Since states can unilaterally establish funding levels for certain local programs, they have an increased control over expenditure levels. Funding levels are usually statutorily, not constitutionally, determined, with the result that the statute sets the limits. Political practicality, however, dictates that once a given level of funding is reached, the bureaucratic law of incrementalism usually makes it difficult to cut the level—and nearly impossible to decrease it. Because of their unique powers, states have great discretion in setting, establishing, or changing due dates for taxes and major-disbursement dates for state aid. This discretionary power can immediately and favorably impact the cash flow calendar of a state.

While the same broad areas of analysis (including debt, economic base, management, and finance) are important for almost all municipal bonds, the difference between the rating analyses of GO and revenue bonds centers on the former's general taxing power of the community, as opposed to the latter's specific credit backing of the revenues. When an issuer sells a GO bond secured by its full faith, credit, and taxing power, it is attaching to that issue its broadest pledge, encompassing such things as its ability to levy an unlimited ad valorem property tax or other revenue taxes, such as sales or income taxes.

In contrast, in its simplest terms a revenue bond security almost always involves an enterprise whose debt is related to its earnings. Therefore, revenue bond analysis encompasses a closed system with a fixed and limited number of variables, which are more amenable to simple quantification and comparison. The enterprise provides a community benefit (such as a water system, sewer service, toll bridge, or road), but it is a benefit that depends upon consumer usage. Therefore, the crucial points for the analysis of a revenue bond are the bond's demand and its legal protections for the bondholder in case the user demand declines.

There are specific types of analysis that must be performed on revenue-producing enterprises, such as engineers' appraisals of the soundness of the physical plant and system; special consideration of the secular, cyclical, and operating characteristics of the industry in which the enterprise is operating; and an examination of the particular system being built. The legal protections are far more important for revenue bonds than for GO bonds because in most cases revenue bonds do not have the backing of the taxing power.

Each rating agency also focuses on the specialized aspects of each type of revenue bond that force their rating analysis to break down by category. This has led to specialization among the rating experts, who usually handle only a given type of bond—e.g., housing, public power, hospital—or, for GO bonds, a given area. The analysis of specific kinds of revenue bonds will be detailed in Part 3.

Fitch and White's Ratings

Fitch Investors Service, while employing methods similar to those of Moody's and Standard & Poor's, tends to specialize in hospital ratings and may do more of these than does any other service. Fitch maintains an office in Denver from which most of the hospital ratings originate and another in the Wall Street area from which all other ratings are done.

The other quite unique rating service is White's Ratings. White's, in contrast to the traditional credit research method of Fitch, Moody's, and Standard & Poor's, uses a system of analysis based on the study of the trading market, e.g., how bonds actually are priced and find their level in the market. White's uses a relative market value index that lets the bond market be the rater of each bond. It does this by translating each yield into a scaled number from 1 to 100 and listing them. Each bond is scaled to a 0.05 in basis points of its yield and given a White's rating that changes with its performance periodically in the actual bond market.

Just as Standard & Poor's and Moody's have increased their municipal staffs, so has each of these two smaller rating services, thus demonstrating an across-the-board growth in this field. While the number of bonds issued has soared in the past 10 years, the proportional growth of the rating analysts far exceeds the increasing number of bond issues and thus reflects the rating services' need to take on more specialists to supply more in-depth coverage of municipal bonds. This is an assessment with which they each concur.

The Power of the Rating Agencies

While the rating services insist that ratings are no more than approximate guides of relative bond values, and *not* absolutes, ratings are definitely viewed by many as *being* absolutes. This is a crucial point, because not only do many individual investors see ratings from this perspective, but the federal government insists upon making the ratings of Moody's and Standard & Poor's a cornerstone for bank portfolio audits. The critical distinction between investment grade securities (unlike speculative grade securities), therefore, is not simply linguistic, but is in fact a category as to what banks, other financial institutions, and fiduciaries may invest in for trusts and other portfolios.

A substantial number of studies during the past 20 years have concluded that interest cost, or the cost of capital, definitely varies directly with the rating: (1) the higher the rating, the lower the interest cost, and (2) the lower the rating, the higher the interest cost to the municipality. Yet despite the unanimity of these studies, it remains uncertain just how much influence this rating effect will have on any particular bond during any particular period or on any particular type of market.

Risk is an important concept in municipal bond analysis, yet what is not generally realized is that credit risk is not just the chance of outright default or the delay of timely interest payments. Instead, risk for the investor involves the consequences of financial changes in value during the whole life of the bond. In other words, if the market value of the bond drops substantially at some point in the future just when the investor has to sell the bond in a hurry, long before the bond's expiration date, the investor is faced with a loss, an unforeseen cost, a risk.

It is clear that there are many other factors besides a bond's rating that can affect the bond's price. Among these factors, the most important are the bond's name, its issuer's familiarity in the market, and the geographic region. Of any single factor, however, ratings have been shown in all studies to have the most consistent effect on bond prices.

Are these general changes in rating standards important, and are changes in particular ratings significant in the overall bond market? These questions have been analyzed by many studies in response to the prevailing view today that market participants fully anticipate these changes in advance and discount or revalue bonds ahead of time. Nevertheless, the moment that a rating change is announced, the market price of the bond experiences a jolt. After a change, the yields on upgraded bonds decrease and those on downgraded bonds rise. Changes in yields come faster and in a more pronounced fashion than could be accounted for by changes in the perceived credit of the municipality itself.

In conclusion, the crucial point is that ratings have a very important effect on a bond's price in the market, and this is widely recognized and realized.

Notes to Chapter 3

1. Moody's Investors Service, *Pitfalls in Issuing Municipal Bonds*, 1982, p. 16.

2. Ibid., p. 19.

3. Standard & Poor's Corporation, *Debt Ratings Criteria: Minicipal Overview*, 1986, p. 29.

4. Moody's, op. cit., p. 17.

PART 2
General Obligation Bonds

4

Revenues,
Expenditures,
and Regional
Finance

So intricately entwined are state, local, and federal financial systems today that an interrelated analysis of all three systems is essential for an accurate picture of their fiscal operations. It was not always so. Traditionally, for the first 150 years of our nation, the American system of government functioned so that there existed three separate tiers of governmental financial systems, namely, the federal, the state, and the local. The financial operations of each tier were seen to be separate and distinct. And in reality, during the early years of the American Republic, there was little movement of funds from one tier to the other, as governments of each tier found it neither financially necessary nor morally incumbent upon them to provide monies as well as financial services for the other governments. This early picture was aptly dubbed the "layer cake" model of federal-state-local fiscal relations.

As the character or, perhaps more accurately, the mission of the U.S. government changed in the years following the great depression, so did the fiscal relations among the three governmental tiers. The federal government virtually reversed its position of noninvolvement in the economic affairs of the nation and also to a degree reversed its noninvolvement with state and city finances. With increases in income taxes as well as other revenue sources and with the establishment of major social programs, such as welfare, aid to education, and social security, the government of the United States began to discharge its constitutional obligation to promote the general welfare.

To be sure, the federal government was not alone in funding such general welfare programs: Funding was, in fact, undertaken on a cooperative basis between the federal and state governments. More often than not, the federal government provided grants-in-aid and matching grants, so that the state governments were required to pay their proportionate share for the government programs and services that their own populace would receive. The federal government, under the U.S. Constitution, could not legally "mandate" such programs for states and municipalities because the Constitution confers certain powers on the federal government, and it reserves many powers for the states. Nevertheless, federal involvement resulted from the federal power to "tax and spend for the general welfare." With the United States providing matching grants and "seed monies" to the states, and with the states, in turn, providing funds in those ways to their localities, which were in essence "creatures of the states," the carrot-and-stick approach actually brought forth a new era in fiscal relations in American government. As a result, the layer-cake model of American finance neatly gave way to what was termed the "marble cake" theory.

It cannot be overstressed that here was the first major change in the pattern and the philosophy of American government finance. It came suddenly and with great force. The laissez-faire policy of the eighteenth and nineteenth centuries that pervaded American economic affairs gave way to the image of a veritable federal octopus. Yet this virtual about-face in economic philosophy came to fruition without violence.

The marble-cake picture of fiscal relations among the tiers of government laid the basis for the next and final metamorphosis in government financial affairs. This change was accomplished through the issuance of tremendous amounts of debt via new fiscal entities, created at all three levels of government, that were known as revenue authorities, or public authorities. Many states developed, for example, public housing authorities following the U.S. Housing Act of 1937. Public power authorities, turnpike authorities, port authorities, and many other varieties sprang up and multiplied in number and in complexity. In the 1960s a state form of public authority with a "moral obligation" pledge by the state was introduced, and it added further complexity to the already confusing array of revenue authorities.

What is important is that since World War II, a large part of the dramatic growth in the issuance of state and local debt can be attributed to these various sorts of revenue authorities. The increase in revenue bond underwritings since 1945, for example, has been almost 80-fold.

Public authorities had been operating in the United States since the nineteeth century, when, after a series of cyclical depressions, states adopted constitutional restrictions on the borrowing powers of their legislatures and the use of state credit. Beginning with the early canal companies, these revenue enterprises were designed to circumvent the prohibitions by borrowing outside the purview of state responsibility, that is, by borrowing without the backing of state funds to deliver the government services to which most Americans were becoming accustomed.

However, the proliferation of these revenue enterprises on a large scale was spawned by the New Deal in the 1930s. The national government, as noted earlier, virtually mandated, in fine federalistic fashion, the establishment of local public authorities for such services as housing and transportation.

The establishment of revenue authorities, endowed with almost limitless debt-creating ability, brought forth a quasi-corporate financial mechanism for issuing public debt that changed the nature of federal-state-local fiscal relations. In some cases, federal and state funds were funneled to these debt-creating mechanisms for such services as housing, transportation, public power, and even education. In this way, the marble-cake analogy of interlocking levels of government finance gave way to a "mixed marble cake" of overlapping, frequently changing, and often conflicting government service financing. As a result, finding the security behind many municipal bonds today has been said to resemble tracing a New York subway line to its origin.

How, then, does the ordinary investor or bond analyst go about the task of evaluating municipal bonds if these new fiscal interrelationships of states and municipalities with the federal government *and* with revenue authorities are so complex?

One approach to this problem is to analyze each revenue category and each expense category (in order to spot the largest or the most important trends). A second approach is to see if they balance. In other words, is the state or municipality accruing a surplus or is it incurring a deficit?

State and Local Revenues: The Property Tax

Wealth emanates from the land, wrote many early political economists. Yet any cursory evaluation of the American political scene today shows that not only has the property tax become less significant as a revenue source for both state and local governments over the past 60 years, but it also is under attack throughout the nation. Property assessments have been increasing dramatically and straining the taxpayers' budgets well beyond what many of them consider reasonable. Put differently, although the property tax has declined in significance as the source of staple governmental revenue, present tax rates are so high that a nationwide backlash has developed with a potential for reducing the property tax to an even less significant portion of total governmental revenue. If other revenue sources do not make up for the gap created by the future limiting of property assessment rates, then fewer government services will be provided.

It is interesting to note that it appears that taxpayers' views, in the last 50 years, have finally come full circle—moving slightly back toward a laissez-faire philosophy. This may not take the form of radical limitations on the property tax rate that the nation has seen in California through the enactment of Proposition 13, which amended the California constitution. The heart of the measure was the limitation of ad valorem real property taxes to 1 percent of the market value of property based on the property owner's 1975–1976 tax bill, with the possibility of increases that would not exceed 2 percent annually. At the time of passage, property tax rates in California averaged approximately 2 percent of full market value. As a result, although outstanding GO debt, which was approved by local voters, was exempt from the 1 percent limit, additional GO bonds secured by ad valorem property taxes were effectively limited.

How significant is this property tax revolt for the municipal bond market as a whole?

There are a number of ways to chart the development of the property tax as a revenue source for state and local governments over the past half century. In 1932 the property tax, the mainstay of local revenue, accounted for over 97 percent of all local revenue from any source at the local level of government. By 1978 only 80 percent of total local governmental revenues accrued from property taxes, a proportion that has remained relatively constant to the present. The property tax, however, varies in importance as a revenue source in terms of both government and area. Town governments and school districts rely most heavily on the property tax. The tax makes up over 60 percent of the revenues of townships nationwide and over 45 percent of the revenues of school districts. For counties and other municipalities, the property tax is only one-third of the available revenues. As a percentage of all taxes, however, the property tax is still overwhelmingly important. On the average for school districts and townships, the property tax as a percentage of all taxes totals 98 and 96 percent, respectively. Counties use the property tax to the extent of approximately 85 percent of all taxes, and other municipalities derive 65 percent of their revenue from the property tax.

Over the last few years the property tax has become the subject of widespread and extensive public policy debates and initiatives aimed at questioning its inherent economic inequities and limiting it as a revenue source. Previously, there had been much attention devoted to the property tax in academic literature by economists, political scientists, and jurists. Taking their lead from differing court rulings, these academic investigators tended to concentrate their analyses on whether the use of the property tax as a basis for public school financing was just or unjust. During the 1970s, as a result of debate over the financing of public education with property taxes, a variety of other larger issues emerged concerning the status of the property tax as the major source of local governmental revenue. Proponents argue that the tax is one that is inherently stable, providing consistent revenues during times of economic difficulty. In contrast, sales, income, and other nonproperty taxes are much more subject to cyclic economic conditions. In addition, they argue that the wealthier individuals who hold more property must bear a substantially greater share of the tax than must less fortunate individuals.

However, detractors of the property tax suggest that it discourages improvements on property, lest the property be taxed at a higher rate. Second, during periods of inflation, assessments (which are usually made at the local level) are not raised commensurately with the theoretical changes in the value of property. Thus the property tax is more inflexible than other sources of revenue. It is likely that the debates and sophisticated academic studies on the property tax will continue.

There are distinct state and regional patterns in the contribution that each revenue source makes to the entire state or local revenue system. For example, the states of the northeast and midwest relied more heavily on the property tax than did the other regions of the nation. Such revenue-raising statistics are important in determining which states are able to capture additional revenues as a result of inflation or in discerning which states must cap expenditures and exercise fiscal restraint when inflation-induced revenues are comparatively low.

In general, although the personal income tax and the local property tax are both capable of adding unanticipated revenues to budgets during inflationary periods, the personal income tax is the most reliable revenue source. As a result, those state or local tax structures which rely more heavily on the progressive income tax, as opposed to sales or property taxes, have more resilience during times of inflation. States that do not rely on it must resort to fiscal austerity measures to keep pace with inflation and to stockpile budget surpluses.

Newer State and
Local Revenues

For decades the property tax in this country was thought to be insensitive to the business cycle and to be an ironclad support for municipal securities. Many credit analysts of that period were still reacting to fears from the great depression of the 1930s; these fears colored their interpretation of each factor in GO bond evaluation. This perspective tended to warn them against any municipal tax, revenue, or support mechanism that was overly dependent upon the business cycle. This bias tended to lead to higher credit ratings for municipalities that were exclusively dependent upon property taxes and to lower credit ratings for municipalities that were overly dependent upon other sources of income that would, in turn, be overly dependent upon the business cycle.

Today, in contrast, confidence has waned in the property tax as an unquestioned support of GO bonds, whereas income tax and sales tax revenues of states and municipalities, which are pegged to the rate of inflation and the growth of the gross national product, are considered stronger revenue supports than they once were.

Nonproperty taxes may be divided into four *major* categories: (1) individual income tax, (2) corporate income tax, (3) sales and gross receipts taxes, and (4) motor vehicle tax. The individual and corporate income taxes need no further explanation here, but it is sufficient to state that the individual income tax constitutes almost 30 percent of all revenues from local nonproperty taxes. The sales and gross receipts taxes, however, account for over 50 percent of all the nonproperty tax revenues of local governments. This tax category may be divided into two broad subcategories: the general sales tax and the selective sales tax. The general sales tax supplies the larger portion of the revenues from sales and gross receipts, accounting for approximately 35 percent of the nonproperty tax revenues of local governments. The selective sales tax accounts for almost 20 percent of all nonproperty tax revenues of local governments and is composed of taxes on such items as motor fuel, public utilities, and tobacco products. Motor vehicle and license taxes include almost 3 percent of all nonproperty tax revenues of local governments. In addition, nontax revenues account for about 15 percent of the nonproperty tax revenues. Nontax revenues cover a wide variety of service charge items, including parking fees, educational expenses, hospital charges, park and recreational fees, water and transportation charges, and certain other special assessments. Taken separately, each accounts for only a small portion of the total nontax revenues, but taken together, they are an ever-growing source of revenues for both state and local governments.

Intergovernmental revenues were touched on earlier in this chapter when federal aid to states and localities was discussed. There is also a variety of kinds of state aid provided to localities, and there are a myriad of methods through which such aid is administered. What is most important to realize about all such programs and such aid is that in one form or another they have become an integral part of the American federal, state, and local systems of government finance. For the investor or bond analyst, the extent to which such aid constitutes a significant part of a single state's or municipality's total revenue, however, is a critical dimension in analyzing its credit. A discussion of this aspect of intergovernmental aid will be covered in some of the following chapters.

Most federal and state grants and transfer payments to a municipality are looked upon as fiscal leverage that gives great financial support to the municipality. However, this may be very deceptive. Virtually no federal or state grants cover 100 percent of the costs of the projects or programs they support. Most grants are partial, frequently matching what a municipality puts up, and thus cover only the start-up costs, marginal costs, basic costs, or capital costs, but almost never the *full* costs. Since some of these federal programs (e.g., environmental and pollution control standards for water and sewage treatment plants) are in effect mandated or forced upon municipalities, it is possible for a municipality to find itself strained by the financial costs of accepting federal and state grants. While subsidies and grants definitely help a municipality to adjust its cash flow (and certainly they supply vitally important revenues for municipalities today), these external funds do not come free, as many observers assume, but instead can carry considerable hidden costs.

General Expenditures by State and Local Governments

Expenditures by state and local governments have soared in dollar volume and by function over a period of 35 years. Expenditures for education since 1950 have been and still are by far the largest single budget item. Today, although spending for education still remains the largest expenditure, the percentage increases registered by the functions of health and hospitals and by miscellaneous functions (including police, fire, general administration, sanitation and sewage, housing and urban renewal, public welfare, and interest on a general debt) have outstripped the percentage increase of expenditures for education.

Nevertheless, as a percentage of total general expenditures, education expenditures have constituted approximately 40 percent of all expenditures since 1960. This fact is important for two reasons: (1) Education remains the most important expenditure item, with expenditures far exceeding the monies spent for every other government service, and (2) this stability stands in contrast to the decreasing growth rate for highway expenditures on the one hand and to the increasing rate of growth for public welfare expenditures on the other.

Indeed, as a percentage of total expenditures by state and local governments, monies spent for highways have been cut in half since 1960. At that time, expenditures for highways constituted over 18 percent of the total general expenditures for all government services. By 1990 this percentage should hover at approximately 9.0 percent. Expenditures for public welfare, however, have shown the opposite trend. In 1960 monies spent on public welfare constituted only about 8.5 percent of the total state and local general expenditures. By 1990 public welfare expenditures should consitute about 12.0 percent of total expenditures. For the past 30 years the rate of growth in public welfare expenditures has outstripped the rate of growth in monies spent on education, sanitation, highways, police, or administration in the United States.

The Regional Perspective

One way to view the economic and financial variables discussed previously, a way that has received wide coverage in the nation's press, is from the "regional" perspective. To be sure, viewing state and local finance from a regional perspective does not really reveal much about the creditworthiness of a particular state, municipality, or revenue authority. Creditworthiness may be more easily shown through an analysis of fund balances and detailed economic and financial data. Yet discussion of regional trends points up the fact that a state's economy does not begin and end inside its precise geographic boundaries; indeed, more often than not, economic zones cross state boundaries and may actually cover large areas in two or three states. A regional perspective also introduces the reader to the basic terminology of state and local financial measurements, which form the basis of more precise analyses of general obligation debt. Most important is that regional analysis provides a picture of America—its economic and financial trends, and its taxing and spending preferences—and also serves up a comparative perspective on the economic and financial structures of America's states. It is this comparative perspective that is at the heart of municipal credit analysis.

In the 1970s there was much publicity given to broad-based statistics that seem to show that the southern regions of the country were growing at faster economic rates than the nation's more mature regions. Such statements implied that municipal credits in the south were stronger than those of other areas, and this fact has had a psychological spillover effect that has impaired the marketability of many municipal issues in the northeastern region. Nevertheless, there was still some evidence that ran counter to the argument made against northeastern credits during that period. A study (noted at the end of this section) was completed at that time; it focused on the four regions of the country and then divided the regions into two subregions for each. The northeastern region included New England and the mid-Atlantic subregions, the midwest included the Great Lakes and Great Plains, the south included the south-Atlantic and the south-central states, and the west included the mountain and Pacific subregions. The general findings of the study included two salient facts. First, it was found that there were great disparities within the regions of the country over a broad series of financial and economic characteristics; in other words, in some cases the subregions of any region differed substantially from one another across the gamut of important economic and financial variables. As a corollary, many subregions of different regions had financial and economic characteristics that resembled those of other subregions more than they did those of the subregions within their given region. Second, when compared against the other regions of the country, particularly the midwest, it also appeared that the northeast did not have as many problems as it was generally perceived to have.

For instance, per capita income in the northeastern region was still the highest and did not register a more substantial decline than any other region of the country did in the 1970s. Also, New England's income growth had not been less than the average across all the regions of the United States. During the early 1970s the northeast showed the lowest percentage of population increase of any of the other three regions of the country, but the population increase of New England was much higher than the population increase of the midwest. In addition, the northeast showed the highest unemployment during this period, but it was not much higher than that of the west or of the Great Lakes subregion.

It had long been held that the northeast levied the highest state and local per capita taxes. It was found, however, that states in the northeast levied some of the highest but also some of the lowest per capita taxes on a state and local basis. When the regions of the country were compared on a state-tax-effort basis (state and local taxes as a percentage of personal income), it was found that the northeast was not measurably different in state tax effort from the west and that many states within

New England registered lower state and local taxes as a percentage of personal income than did many other states around the country.

If the 1970s marked a time of general decline for the northeastern economy and of controversy about the continuation or retardation of that decline, then the 1980s are surely a decade of renewed confidence and prosperity in the northeast, relative to other regions of the country. Indeed, one of the clearest recent trends is a pronounced convergence among all regions in terms of per capita income. The importance of this finding is that the era of financial and economic dominance of certain regions and of the apparent weaknesses of others is giving way to an evening out of these distinctions. Unemployment has also been relatively low in the northeast as industry has renewed its commitments to the suburban communities of New York, New Jersey, and Connecticut and is establishing strongholds in Massachusetts, New Hampshire, and the southern portions of Maine and Vermont. Without detailing further the long laundry list of positive economic developments in the northeast, it is simply sufficient to note the continuing trend of relative economic prosperity.

NOTE: This chapter was written by Stephen P. Rappaport in reports entitled "Revenue and Expenditure Patterns in State and Local Finance" and "Why Not the Northeast?: An Economic Analysis of Regional Trends" at Thomson McKinnon Securities Inc., 1979. Reprinted by permission.

5

General Obligation Bonds: A Framework for Analysis

If there has been one single event that has changed the nature of municipal credit analysis, it was the fiscal crisis of New York City in 1975. Prior to this event, aside from the rating agencies, there was far less analysis done either on Wall Street or by the large institutional bond purchasers than there is today. GO bonds secured by the full faith and credit and taxing powers of the issuers were rarely really questioned beyond their credit ratings by either Moody's or Standard & Poor's. If Wall Street firms, bank trust departments, and insurance company portfolio managers did have in-house analysts of municipal bonds, these analysts tended to focus only on municipal revenue bonds and oftentimes carried out the corporate bond evaluations as well. The continuing saga of the WPPSS crisis has reinforced the trend toward more comprehensive analysis.

The New Interest in General Obligation Bond Analysis

The notion that states and cities could default on their GO debt was, of course, known because of the defaults during the great depression.

NOTE: This chapter was adapted almost entirely from the first edition's chapter by Sylvan G. Feldstein, Robert Lamb, and Stephen P. Rappaport. Sylvan G. Feldstein is manager of the municipal research department of Merrill Lynch Capital Markets.

However, modern bond defaults by cities and states were generally thought to be so remote a possibility that they were usually considered only in reference to a deeply depressed national economy, such as that of the early 1930s. And, as many bond salespeople were quick to point out, even during the great depression the repayment records of municipal bond defaults were far better than those of corporations. There seemed little reason for Wall Street underwriters and institutional purchasers to invest sizable staff resources to evaluate GO bonds. In fact, because of the legal right of communities to levy a property tax and other taxes without limitation as to rate or amount, GO bonds were long considered to be one of America's safer and less volatile investments.

However, the near bankruptcy in 1975 of New York, the nation's largest city, and the resulting liberalization in federal procedures for municipal bankruptcy catapulted GO bond analysis to the forefront of importance in the fixed-income investment community. In 1975 the New York City bondholders and noteholders were, from a legal standpoint, first in line to get paid, but they unhappily realized that a GO bond issuer would not, in order to pay noteholders and bondholders, forgo providing the municipal services demanded by strong political constituencies. The credit analysis of GO bonds today springs largely from this realization.

Methods of Credit Analysis of General Obligation Bonds

There are several different approaches to the credit analysis of GO bonds. There are those who follow Standard & Poor's concentration on the socioeconomic base of a community, and, in contrast, there are those who follow Moody's concentration on the debt burdens and ratios. Since GO credit analysis involves the same four main factors of (1) debt burden, (2) economic base, (3) administration, and (4) local governmental revenues, the differences between the credit analyses of any particular GO bond tend to stem from the relative emphases placed on each of these four categories.

Subtle Differences between the Standard & Poor's and Moody's Approaches

Many believe that the credit analysis of GO bonds centers on two issues: (1) the municipality's ability to pay and (2) its willingness to pay its bonded indebtedness in a timely fashion. This approach to municipal bonds therefore centers on the debt ratios of each municipality, which are used to determine a municipality's past, present, and future debt payment. It focuses on debt trends over a 10-year period, whether rising, falling, or holding constant, and undertakes an elaborate analysis of debt ratios that compares the rate of borrowings with trends in other factors, such as property assessments, property tax collections, personal incomes, and budget operations. From these an assessment is made of how well a community has been paying its debt and its potential ability and willingness to pay off new debt issues.

The Moody's analysis of a state bond might, for example, concentrate on the state's debt issuance, debt burden, debt history, and debt payout schedule over the life of each past, present, and presently known future bond. The ratio of debt to wealth would be an important ratio to be compared with the ratios of other states. Strong emphasis would be placed on the state's statutory debt limits and the strength of its budget operations. Finally, an effort would be made to make sure that the term of the bonded debt matched the useful life of the facility being funded by the new bond.

In contrast, the credit analysis of Standard & Poor's for the same state bond might tend to emphasize socioeconomic factors of the state's population and income. In looking at exactly the same bond that Moody's is analyzing, Standard & Poor's might concentrate on the per capita growth trends and total personal income and would use these measures to compare one state with another or with the national averages. Also of critical importance for a credit judgment might be the employment rate and employment mix of the state, trends of employment and population influx or exit, and the actual age and makeup of the population. For municipalities, school districts, and counties, local building activity, the age of the housing stock, and its composition would be explored in detail along with (1) trends in property assessments and (2) trends in the mix of industrial, commercial, and residential properties. To undertake such an analysis, great reliance would be placed on documents from the Bureau of the Census, the Department of Labor, and the Department of Commerce, and their statistics would be vital sources quite distinct from those supplied by the issuer.

From Standard & Poor's perspective, it might be the bond issuer's economic base that usually helps pay off its debt. From Moody's perspective, a bond is a debt, and therefore the debt and budget characteristics of the issuer might be emphasized. However, the agencies have no set rules on this. Although each rating agency obtains many of the same pieces of background information about the municipal bond issuer, they tend to weigh them differently in terms of the credit risks.

Recent Developments in Credit Analysis

One method of credit analysis of GO bonds overlaps Moody's and Standard & Poor's approaches, but it also raises additional potential questions favored by a number of municipal bond analysts on Wall Street and by major investment firms, banks, and insurance companies. We, too, look at a bond issuer's debt structure and economic base, but along with these factors we emphasize the management capability, the political and legal settings, and the revenue and budget characteristics of the local government. These latter considerations are especially important today because they reveal (1) the degree to which a bond issue is independent of or overdependent on outside revenue sources and (2) the degree to which the issuer is willing and able politically to maintain genuinely balanced budgets.

Reviewing the value of intergovernmental aid programs is quite complex. The investment community has the traditional viewpoint that any local government overly dependent upon outside sources of income is in a less desirable position than one that pays its own way. Yet the budget operations of a municipality may be significantly strengthened by that outside support. For example, the school districts in certain cities received a large percentage of their revenues from the state. In these instances it is a state constitutional provision and a resulting state law which ensure that if those cities lose their property tax revenues, the state will make up the difference. As the property assessments decline, under state law the amount of state aid increases. Therefore, does this clear dependence on state aid make such GO bonds stronger credit risks or poorer ones?

Another area of new concern is whether or not the community presents clear, complete, and timely accounting records. Full disclosure in footnotes and explanations of any and all changes in accounting procedures are simple tests of financial and managerial competence. Noting whether the municipality uses or does not use a certified public accounting firm and whether its reports are stated to be in conformance with generally accepted accounting principles (GAAP) and local laws are other easy and quick checks on the financial competence of the municipality's managers.

Another relatively simple test of a municipality's health is to compare the projected budget with the actual performance of operations for the previous year. Such a comparison shows how reliable the municipality's managers are in managing their finances. A final, quite useful check can be made of the tax-supported operating funds, such as the general fund and debt service fund, which can easily be compared with the capital fund and special revenue fund to determine whether there is a clear segregation of these monies and whether the local government is indeed living within its means.

Two critical factors which both Standard & Poor's and Moody's include and which we stress in particular are (1) the actual political structure of the municipality and (2) its management's ability and willingness to maintain balanced budgets. Although full-scale systems of management administered by professionals were absent in most American cities, counties, and school districts until recently, such professional management is becoming a necessity now. The presence or absence of professional managers will directly influence such credit analysis questions as the updating of property valuations and assessment trends. Likewise, it will have an effect upon the direction of tax collections, delinquencies, and levies. The presence or absence of long-range land use, industrial planning, clear management control systems, and zoning standards will also give a quick indication of the professional caliber of a municipality's management. The political strength of the governing body's members, their length of tenure, and the rate of turnover are usually readily obtained facts that indicate governmental continuity. Also important is management's ability to resolve labor disputes: How forceful has the political leadership been in dealing with collective-bargaining issues?

Basic Questions to Ask When Analyzing a General Obligation Bond

We must point out that there is no universally accepted method or theory of credit analysis. To a considerable extent it remains more an art than a science. It requires individual judgment and personal interpretation of a range of important factors. We hope the following material will provide some simple, clear guidelines for the investor or bond analyst to consider when reviewing a GO bond.

Information relating to the analysis of GO bonds may be grouped into four categories: (1) debt, (2) budget, (3) revenues, and (4) the economics of the community.

These four categories, with slight modifications, may be applied to the GO bonds issued by states, counties, school districts, towns, or cities.

Information Related to the Debt

First, ask what is the total amount of GO debt outstanding. This figure would include all bonds and notes secured by the general taxing powers, limited and unlimited, of the issuer.

Several issuers have *limited-tax* GO bonds outstanding. These bonds are secured by the limited power of the issuer to raise taxes. Some limited-tax bonds, although they are general obligations, are secured only by the revenues generated by a property tax. Nevertheless, when calculating the issuer's true total GO debt, the limited-tax bonds and the *unlimited* ones, which are secured by the full taxing powers of the issuer, are initially combined.

Next, information is also required on the GO debt trend for the previous 5 years. These figures show whether or not the issuer has been using debt to an increasing degree, possibly during periods of local economic adversity and decline when capital improvements are not required. An increase in debt is not automatically negative, however, if one takes into consideration the impact of inflation and the genuine needs of the community. On the one hand, many growing suburban communities have shown rapid increases in debt as they financed the construction of water and sewer systems, new roads, and schools. On the other hand, some declining areas have turned to GO debt as a way of financing budget deficits and priming the local economy. While determining the GO debt trend for 5 years, one also must be consistent in reporting the GO notes issued. If the record of debt outstanding at the end of the issuer's fiscal year is used, one could overlook the notes that were issued and redeemed during the course of the year. To avoid this omission, one must determine the bonds outstanding at the year-end and must also indicate the notes sold during the course of the year.

The Security for General Obligation Debt. The security behind the GO bonds sold by states, counties, school districts, and municipalities usually includes a pledge that the issuer will use its full taxing powers to see that the bondholder receives bond principal and interest when due. Under various state and local government constitutions and charters, providing such security usually involves the levy of unlimited taxes on property, a first claim by the bondholder to monies in the issuer's general fund, and the legal duty of the governing body to pass any legislation needed to increase revenues. In order to enhance further the security for their bond issues, some states have formally waived their rights to immunity from suits by bondholders, thereby making it easier for the bondholder to seek a mandamus against the state.

The Double-Barreled Bonds. While most GO bonds are secured by only the general taxing powers of the issuer, and perhaps by whatever monies are available in the issuer's general fund, some bonds are also secured by earmarked revenues that flow outside the general fund. For example, some bonds are general obligations of the state and are secured by the gasoline taxes in the state's transportation fund. Because, as a matter of actual practice, debt service is paid from monies in the transportation fund, the bonds are considered to have a "double-barreled" security. We believe that if all other factors are equal, bonds having a double-barreled security should be considered a stronger credit than the issuer's straight GO bonds.

Net General Obligation Debt. In order to determine the debt ratios, it is necessary to determine the amount of the issuer's GO bonds that is not double-barreled, or supported by earmarked revenues. To obtain this figure, one has to review the accounting reports of the issuer. While certain funds outside the issuer's general fund may be used to pay debt service, the source of monies in the specific fund will determine whether the bonds are operationally double-barreled or just straight GOs. Some states have issued GO bonds for housing that are secured by monies in the respective state's housing fund. Although the annual debt service on these bonds is indeed paid out of the housing fund, the bonds are not genuinely self-supporting or double-barreled. This peculiarity arises because most of the monies in the fund are appropriated by the state for grants to local governments; these monies are credited to the fund by the state comptroller for payments owed the fund by the local governments.

The net GO figure should include all those bonds which require monies from the general fund to pay debt service, for the purpose of the figure is to show the amount of GO debt that the general taxing powers of the issuer (as characterized by the general fund) support. Since it is not always certain what these reserves are invested in, we would tend not to deduct these amounts from the debt figures.

Overlapping Debt and Underlying Debt. Still another debt figure necessary for the analyst to determine is the total amount of GO debt for which the issuer's taxpayers are responsible. If the issuer is a municipality, the overlapping debt would include the GO debt of its county, school district(s), and special districts (such as water and sewage authorities) that have issued GO bonds secured by unlimited property taxes. In determining how much of a county's outstanding GO debt must be included in the municipality's overlapping debt, one must determine the percentage of the real estate property values of the municipality vis-á-vis that of the county. That percentage represents the county's overlapping debt that pertains to the municipality's real property taxpayers. Similar approaches are used to determine the overlapping debt of school districts and special districts applicable to the municipality's taxpayers.

When the issuer is a county government, the same procedure is used to determine the applicable GO debt of other jurisdictions. Here, however, the debt is known as underlying debt, not overlapping debt, although the concept is the same. One must be careful in determining what overlapping or underlying debt the taxpayer is indeed responsible for paying.

State Debt. Normally, when determining the overlapping debt or underlying debt of school districts, counties, or municipalities, the GO debt of their state is not considered. This is because, unlike local governments, states have broader revenue sources and potential powers under their constitutions to pay debt service on their GO bonds without reverting to property taxes, which are the major revenue sources of most local governments.

Special Debt. Besides the net GO debt and the overlapping or underlying GO debt, there are also three other debt obligations which many states, counties, and municipalities incur and which should be considered part of the issuer's debt load. They are outstanding leases, moral obligation commitments, and unfunded pension liabilities.

Lease Debt. Many states and local governments have entered into leases or lease-purchase agreements for the construction of new buildings, highway repairs, and rentals for office space and data processing computers. The rental payments come from various sources, including general fund revenues, earmarked tax revenues, student tuition, patient fees, and amusement park fees. In some instances, such as the lease or rental of computer equipment, the leases are also secured by the equipment itself. This area of borrowing has become increasingly important in the last 25 years. While New York state was a leader in the issuance of such debt, most GO debt issuers have lease-rental debt outstanding. Since this debt usually has a legal claim to the general revenues of the issuer, analysts should include it in their overall debt figures as well.

Moral Obligation Debt. During the last 20 years many states have been issuing moral obligation municipal bonds. These bonds, structured as revenue bonds with 1-year debt reserves, carry a potential state liability for making up deficiencies in their debt reserves, should any occur. Under most state laws, if a drawdown of the reserve occurs, the bond trustee must report the amount used to the governor and state budget director. The state legislature, in turn, may appropriate the requested amount, although there is no legally enforceable obligation to do so. Bonds with this makeup provision are the so-called moral obligation bonds.

Since 1960, over 20 states have issued bonds with this unique security feature. The first state was New York State with its Housing Finance Agency (HFA) moral obligation bonds. This feature was developed by a well-known bond attorney, John Mitchell, who had extensive experience and knowledge of state constitutions and laws. In the history of moral obligation financing, most of this debt has been self-supporting—no state financial assistance has been required. However, in all the instances in which the moral pledge was called upon, the respective state legislatures responded by appropriating the necessary amounts of monies.

Unfunded Pension Liabilities.   Still another special debt figure that the analyst must develop is the current unfunded pension liability of the issuer. That is, what is the difference between the expected assets of the public employee pension system at current annual contribution rates and the future benefits to be paid out to the issuer's employees? In assessing this figure the analyst must determine when the pension system was last audited, who performed the audit, and what the auditor's assumptions were concerning, among other factors, the average age of public employee entry and retirement. The credit analyst should also determine whether the issuer has a plan in operation to reduce the unfunded liability and, if so, how long it will take (10, 20, or 50 years, for example) to eliminate the liability. Still another question to raise concerning pensions is their legal basis. That is, can pension benefits unilaterally be reduced by the local governments? Such reduction is allowed in some jurisdictions but not in others. An example of the latter would be New York State, where the state constitution prevents the reduction of pension benefits once they are granted to the public employees; therefore, the unfunded pension liabilities of local governments in New York must be taken much more seriously than in states where such guarantees do not exist.

For purposes of determining the special debt figure, which represents the potential debt liability in a worst-case environment, the lease obligations, the moral obligations, and the unfunded pension liabilities are combined, and one figure is used.

Straight Revenue Debt.   Besides the general obligation, special lease, moral obligation, and pension liability, many governing bodies have also issued revenue bonds that are secured solely by the monies generated by the revenue-producing enterprises. Municipalities have issued water and sewer revenue bonds, and many states have issued toll road revenue bonds, most of which do not have a legal claim to the general taxing powers of the respective municipality or state. Nevertheless, the credit analyst should tabulate the issuer's outstanding revenue debt. Although this debt is not factored into the debt ratios, it is important to know the total borrowing activities of the issuer.

Future Bond Financings. While some GO issuers have small amounts of debt outstanding, they may be required to borrow significant amounts of money in the future. In order to factor this possibility into the credit assessment, the analyst must learn what the future financing plans are. As an example, a municipality that will have to issue large amounts of GO bonds to finance the construction of mandatory federal improvements for pollution control is of weaker quality than one that has already met the standards.

However, not all large-scale programs of capital construction are in themselves undesirable. Issuers who are borrowing heavily today to construct their physical infrastructures, such as new roads, schools, and water systems, may be better long-term investments than those issuers who have postponed making improvements and, as a result, have much less GO debt outstanding. The latter may very well face the prospect of extensive capital expenditures somewhere down the road in order to remain attractive for continued economic development and just to meet the service demands of the taxpayers.

Debt Limits. For many years, credit analysts viewed debt limits as major safeguards for the bondholder. Those GO debt limits which are restricted by the need for electoral approvals before bonds can be sold are still meaningful checks on excessive borrowing. However, debt limits that are tied to percentages of the issuer's real estate wealth have become less significant. This has resulted from the experience of New York City in 1974–1975. In spite of state constitutional debt limits, the city had sold, over many years, amounts of GO bonds that were beyond its financial means and yet several billion dollars below its debt limits. The experience of New York City reveals the weakness of debt limits as real safeguards for the bondholder.

Information Related to the Budget

The second general category of information required by the analyst is related to the budget. Here, we are concerned about questions of executive powers, budgetary control, public services, accounting history, and the potential impacts of taxpayer revolts.

Powers of the Chief Executives. Learning the form of government of the GO bond issuer is very important to the analyst. Governments that have strong executive systems (i.e., strong governors, strong county executives, or strong mayors) are, in general, preferred to those which do not. This preference results because strong centralized executive systems have the potential to deal quickly and efficiently with unforeseen budgetary and economic problems. Perhaps the importance of this is best seen in the city of Cleveland, which has a weak executive form of government, having very little power beyond access to the press. Its limitations include the need for electoral approval for increasing property and personal income taxes that are above the state-allowed levels; no control over many of the city's essential services; limited appointment and removal powers; and a term of office that is only 2 years, so that it must consistently focus on reelection strategies rather than on policy directives. As a result of this fact and of the city's overall economic and political problems, the city defaulted in 1978 on its GO notes.

In the 1970s the cities of Detroit, Baltimore, Newark, and Boston all had similar economic problems—in the cases of Newark and Detroit, economic problems far more serious than those of Cleveland—but they all managed to avoid defaults. One possible reason why these cities have been able to manage their problems is that they have strong executive forms of government, whereas Cleveland does not.

There are three basic components of a strong executive, regardless of whether the chief executive is a governor, county executive, or mayor. First, the chief executive must have at least a 4-year term of office with the right to seek reelection without limit. Second, the chief executive must control three aspects of the annual budgetary process: (1) the preparation of the budget, which is presented to the legislative body for approval; (2) line-item veto powers over the approved budget; and (3) control over the implementation of the budget, including the power to determine allotment periods, to fill personnel lines, and to award contracts. The third component is the ability to control the bureaucracy through extensive personnel appointment and removal authority.

Services Directly Provided. In order to project future budgetary demands, it is necessary to determine the services provided by the issuer. In general, issuers that provide a full range of services have a weaker credit quality than those which provide only basic minimum services. For a municipality, basic services include utilities (such as water and sewage treatment), garbage pickups, street maintenance, police and fire protection, and recreational programs. Large municipalities that provide additional services, including extensive welfare programs, hospital care, housing, mass transportation, and higher education, usually have bureaus and departments that are captives of pressure groups which demand these services without regard to budgetary consequences.

General Budget Appropriations by Function. While many issuers provide the same services, quantitative distinctions should be made in order to determine what the budgetary priorities of the issuer really are. This is best done by determining the general budget appropriations in the current fiscal year by function, amount, and percentage of the total budget appropriation.

Accounting Procedures and Funds. The most desirable accounting system is known as a *modified accrual system.* In general, in this system revenues are only considered received when they are physically in the issuer's general fund. At the same time, expenditures are deemed to have occurred when contracts and other legal liabilities are entered into by the issuer, even though warrants for payment of these obligations may not have been made yet. The modified accrual system is the most honest and fiscally conservative accounting system. Many issuers, however, prefer other accounting systems that allow their governing bodies to have greater flexibility in the budgetary process. For example, for issuers who define *revenues* to include monies that are due but not necessarily received, a budget can quickly be balanced. The governing body levies a new tax or increases projected revenues from existing taxes and then adds the new amount to the revenue side of the budget. On the expenditure side, those issuers who use *cash expenditure accounting* can easily close their fiscal year with a budget surplus by just delaying actual payments until after the new fiscal year has begun.

Audit Procedures. Auditing is yet another important area of concern for the investor and bond analyst. The best auditing procedure is for the issuer to be audited annually by an outside certified public accountant (CPA) who applies generally accepted accounting principles, using the modified accrual system of accounting. For sound cost-related reasons, however, many issuers (states, in particular) do not have such audits performed.

If no audit by an outside CPA is commissioned, the next best safeguard for the bondholder is to have the issuer's accounts annually audited by a public official who is politically independent of the chief executive. Many states and municipalities have treasurers and comptrollers who are also elected public officials or appointees of the legislative branch. The institutional rivalry and competition between these elected public officials can provide checks and balances in the accounting areas.

Budget Trends. In order to determine the overall budgetary soundness of the issuer, it is necessary for the analyst to determine the revenues and expenditures of the issuer's general fund and all operating funds for at least a 3-year period. In this way one can see whether the issuer has balanced budgets, budget surpluses, or budget deficits. Clearly, those communities which have yearly budget deficits are serious investment risks, regardless of how positive the other analytical variables may appear to be.

Still another related question to ask is: What was the cash fund balance in the issuer's general fund at the end of the most recent fiscal year? While some issuers may show budget deficits during the previous 3-year period, the deficits may be planned in order to reduce a fund balance surplus. Surpluses sometimes accumulate in state governments that have elastic revenue structures made up of income and sales taxes. During expansions in the local economies or during inflationary periods, these revenues will greatly increase. Many states build substantial budget surpluses during such periods. They can then draw upon these surpluses either to meet revenue shortfalls caused by recessions or to meet increased wage and salary demands caused by inflation.

Short-Term Debt as a Percentage of the General Fund Receipts of the Prior Year. In order to determine how well the issuer matches revenue flows to expenditure flows, it is necessary to determine the percentage of short-term debt in relation to the issuer's general fund revenues of the prior year. The short-term debt does not include the issuer's bond anticipation notes (BANs) but does include both tax anticipation notes (TANs) and revenue anticipation notes (RANs). Issuers who are committed to policies that require them to borrow large amounts of money to meet expenditure schedules are clearly less attractive than issuers who have coordinated their expenditure flow with their revenue flow so as to minimize the need for issuing annual short-term debt.

Budgets and Taxpayer Revolts. In looking at budget trends, one must also assess the potential impacts of newly enacted or anticipated budget and tax limitation measures. An example is Proposition 13 in California, which significantly restricted local property tax revenue growth, the issuance of new GO bonds, and other functions. While each measure must be carefully reviewed, in general it can be said that taxpayer attempts to reduce taxes and government expenditures on the local levels by these measures have positive benefits for GO bonds. At the same time, these measures may have negative consequences for the overlapping GO bonds of the state governments. On the local level such restrictions on budget expenditures and tax collections can result in reductions in some municipal services; these restrictions can also provide governing bodies and budget directors with the legal weapons and supportive political climates for resisting constituent demands for increased services and for bargaining with their local organized public employees—i.e., with the unions representing fire fighters, police, schoolteachers, etc. In recent years the militancy of these unions has been very costly. Since approximately two-thirds of the annual expenditures by local governments are for salaries, pensions, and related purposes, curbs in these areas can be very beneficial in slowing down the escalating costs of local governments.

While the political activities and effectiveness of public employee unions and other pressure groups are lessened at the local government level, they may be correspondingly increased at the state government level. This pressure results from their attempts to have the states provide increased state aid to local governments or to have the state governments begin to finance and operate public programs that were originally the responsibility of the local governments.

When looking at both the GO bonds of the local governments and those of the states, credit analysts must determine both the direct and the indirect implications of specific tax and budget restrictions. This is important in order to determine in a budgetary sense who benefits from the specific restrictions, who is not affected, and who is hurt. Obviously, to answer these questions, analysts must study and make conclusions about the relationships and interdependencies between pressure groups, such as public employee unions, political parties, and political leaders. Credit analysts invite criticism by speculating on the political implications of proposed tax restrictions, particularly if they are later proved to be incorrect. They must nevertheless offer investors their opinion of the direct and indirect political effects of the proposals.

Information Related to Revenues

The third general category of information covers data relating to the nature of the issuer's specific types and amounts of revenue.

Primary Revenues. The initial question is: What are the issuer's primary revenues? In general, states have the most diversified revenue sources, which can include personal income taxes, a variety of corporate and business taxes, real and personal property taxes, death and gift taxes, sales taxes, motor vehicle taxes, severance taxes, user fees, and federal grants-in-aid. The attractiveness of state credits over the credits of counties, municipalities, and school districts is largely a result of the diversity of a state's revenue sources and a state's ability, under its own laws, to make its revenue base even broader.

The local governments, in contrast, rely primarily on property taxes for their revenues. Some counties and municipalities have broadened their revenue bases through sales and income taxes. Such diversification is usually very difficult for a local governmental unit to initiate, since state legislative approvals are normally required. Nevertheless, many cities in recent years have convinced their respective state legislatures to grant them taxing powers beyond the property tax.

General Fund Revenue Trends. Besides learning what the overall primary revenue sources are, the credit analyst should determine what the specific revenues have been in the issuer's general fund over a 4-year period. This is the governmental fund account in which all unrestricted revenues that can be used for debt service are placed. The reason for going back 4 years is to identify trends that may be developing in the issuer's revenue flows.

In the case of issuers who pay debt service on their GO bonds from a debt service fund (which, for example, may receive property taxes that do not pass through the general fund), this fund should also be included. The reason for separating general fund revenues from the restricted ones is that many revenues received by issuers, such as certain federal grants, are restricted as to purpose and cannot be used for debt service on GO bonds. Since many local governments, such as school districts and municipalities, include restricted monies in their general fund reporting, the credit analyst will have to separate the unrestricted portion from the restricted portion.

For urban counties, school districts, and municipalities, real property taxes, state grants, and federal aid monies are the major sources of revenue. In many cities, state and federal monies have displaced the property tax as the major revenue source. In most suburban and rural areas the property tax is the dominant source of revenue.

Economic Factors

The fourth major category of information required by the analyst concerns the overall economic health of the issuer. Indicators of economic activity and well-being include the trends of real estate valuation, population, unemployment, and total personal income.

While separately these economic indicators provide incomplete assessments of the economic vitality of the issuer, taken as a whole they provide clues as to the strengths and weaknesses of each community. Obtaining the data for the informational categories is easy, since data is available from either the local governments themselves or publications of the U.S. Bureau of the Census and the U.S. Department of Labor.

Real Estate Valuation Trend. A major index of the growth of a community is the yearly change in its real estate value. Here, analysts are not as interested in the assessed real values, which are used for tax purposes, as they are in the full, or market, values of the real estate. This would only include the taxable real property. Tracking these values over a 4-year period provides a good indication of the health of the community and provides clear indications of a declining or stagnant community. It is also important to keep in mind that in an inflationary environment, growth in real estate values is not enough to indicate that a community is becoming wealthier; the annual growth must be higher than the annual inflation rate.

Ten Largest Taxable Properties. In looking at counties, municipalities, and school districts, it is useful to identify the 10 largest taxable properties in terms of their full real values and business purposes. In so doing, the analyst can determine how much of the real estate base may be dependent on railroads, utilities, and private corporations. Additionally, certain communities may be dependent on one major shopping center or manufacturing plant for most of their property taxes; therefore, the viability of that single property will determine the community's overall economic viability.

Properties: Taxable or Tax-Exempt? When reviewing counties, municipalities, and school districts, it is necessary to learn what percentages of the total real estate wealth are exempt from local property taxes. Although a municipality can add new office buildings, hospitals, and governmental structures to its inner core, their contributions to the general real estate wealth of the community will be limited if they are tax-abated or -exempted. A corollary is to determine the distribution of the community's taxable property by purpose: What percentage is residential, commercial, industrial, held by a utility or railroad? From these figures the analyst can determine accurately which segment of the community's real estate is carrying the burden of the property taxes.

Building Permit Trend. In looking at counties, municipalities, and school districts, another component of economic vitality is the building permit trend. Here the analyst is looking for at least a 3-year record of the annual total dollar value of all permits granted by the local governmental bodies for building and construction improvement. These figures are checked to make sure that building permits for tax-exempt properties are not included. One major value of this indicator is its ability to show the degree of business confidence in the future of the local economy.

Five Largest Employers. It is important to learn who the five largest employers are in each county, municipality, or school district to be analyzed. The analyst should determine the number of workers as well as the nature of the business. In this way the analyst can determine how stable the community is and how dependent the local economy may be on one industry.

Population Trend. Another useful index for investigating states and local governments is the population trend. An increasing population usually means a growing economy, while a declining or stagnant population usually indicates economic weakness. Besides having the raw population figures, it is worthwhile to break down the population by age group and by income level. A community that has a high percentage of senior citizens may have greater political demands for municipal services and reduced property taxes than one that does not. Also, communities with large numbers of unemployed or low-income residents usually require costly social services, and these services increase the budgets of the local schools, courts, welfare systems, and police departments.

Job Trend. Employment data are very necessary to the credit analyst. A 10-year comparison of the absolute number of employed people and their percentage of the population provides another clue as to the economic direction of the area. It is also helpful to determine the distribution of the nonfarm employment for at least the most recent year. The employment categories include manufacturing; retail-whole-sale trade; services; contract construction; and federal, state, and local government employment. This breakdown of employment according to type of job helps indicate, among other things, whether or not the economy is being supported by increased governmental jobs or by a vibrant private sector.

Unemployment Trend. It is helpful to compare local unemployment trends covering at least 3 years. It is useful to examine both the annual unemployment rate and the average number of workers unemployed during the year. For counties, municipalities, and school districts, the comparisons should focus on the unemployment rates within the boundaries of the local area, the state, and the nation. If the unit of local government is within a metropolitan area, it is also useful to include the unemployment rates of the metropolitan area.

Economic Activity Indicators for States. When reviewing the economies of states, there are five categories of information that are particularly useful:

1. Statewide personal income trend for the past 3 years
2. Statewide retail sales trend for the past 3 years

3. Statewide motor vehicle registration trend for the past 3 years

4. Total number of people within a state who have received federal welfare for the past 3 years

5. Per capita personal income today, compared with the figure 5 years ago and with the national per capita income figures

The information gathered for these categories will quickly show whether a state is becoming wealthier both in absolute terms and when compared with other regions of the country.

Economic Activity Indicators for Counties. When reviewing counties, municipalities, and school districts, the analyst will find that the following seven categories of information are useful:

1. Percentage of the population in the low-income bracket

2. Number of residents receiving federal welfare

3. Per capita income, compared with the national average

4. Median family income

5. Median home value

6. Percentage of owner-occupied housing

7. Age distribution of the population

Important Debt Ratios

The analyst should also develop debt-related ratios. The value of the ratios is twofold: (1) The ratios are among the analytical tools for evaluating the creditworthiness of the issuer's GO bonds, and (2) the per capita data allow the analyst to compare bonds of different communities.

Net GO Debt per Capita. This figure represents the non-self-supporting GO bonds divided by the population. In theory, it represents the amount of debt per person that is supported by the general taxing powers of the issuer in the issuer's general fund. In general, the lower the number, the more attractive the issuer.

Net GO and Overlapping Debt or Underlying Debt per Capita. This ratio applies not to states but to the local units of government. It is a per capita debt figure that includes the issuer's own net GO debt as well as the GO debt of overlapping debt or underlying debt jurisdictions.

Net GO Debt as a Percentage of Full Real Estate Valuation. This percentage indicates the debt as compared with the real estate wealth as represented in the most recent real estate evaluation. This statistic is perhaps one of the most important figures for the credit analyst, since it indicates the issuer's ability to pay.

Net GO and Overlapping Debt or Underlying Debt as a Percentage of Full Real Estate Valuation. For counties, municipalities, and school districts, this figure is also used. It represents the relationship of the issuer's full real estate value to the sum of the issuer's own GO and overlapping GO debt.

Net GO Debt as a Percentage of Personal Income. For a state, this figure is another major indicator of the ability of the taxpayer to support its debt. While this figure is desirable when reviewing all GO bond issuers, often such data are only available concerning states.

GO Debt Payout in 10 Years. This figure shows whether the issuer has a relatively rapid debt retirement schedule, which is desirable, or a debt service stretched out to, say, 30 or 40 years. In some cases payment of debt service on bonds may continue beyond the useful life of the capital projects financed by the original bond proceeds. While the debt payout schedule is not a debt ratio, it is necessary for evaluating the actual ratio figures. For example, high debt ratios may be less significant if most of the issuer's debt will be retired within 10 years. But above-average debt ratios combined with a slow debt retirement schedule certainly weaken a security substantially.

Conclusion

After having determined whether the GO bonds are double-barreled or not (and if so, what the quality of the specific revenue stream is); after having gathered the information about the issuer's debt structure, budget, revenue operations, and economic forces; after having checked for trends; and after having studied the issuer's ratios of various debt burdens, the credit analyst can make a generalization about the investment quality of the bond under review. While all these elements together are important indicators of bond quality, each provides (if taken separately) only a single isolated element not in itself sufficient for full-scale anlaysis. Therefore, the analyst must carefully review all these indicators so as to arrive at a judicious credit conclusion concerning the degree of risk involved in purchasing an issuer's GO bonds.

Case Studies

State of New Hampshire: General Obligation Bonds*

The state's population increased from 805,000 in 1974 to 977,000 in 1984, registering a growth of 21.4 percent. The influx of high-technology firms and service industries provided much employment during the same years. The state's personal income per capita increased 159 percent during these 10 years, with manufacturing (as the state's primary economic activity) accounting for about 31 percent of the gross state product. Additionally, the state's nonagricultural employment increased over the same time period by 37 percent, compared to only 16.6 percent for New England and 17.4 percent for the United States. Also, the unemployment rate of the state was the lowest in the country for 1983 and 1984.

State revenues are derived from business and specialized taxes, user charges, and certain income from state enterprises. The state does not levy any personal earned income tax or general sales tax; as a result, state and local taxes per $1000 of personal income are the lowest in the nation. For the fiscal year 1984, the state reported a general fund surplus of $1,332,709 on a budgetary basis and estimated that the cumulative surplus for 1985 would be $37.8 million. The 1986–1987 biennium budget forecasted an accumulated surplus, on the basis of generally accepted accounting principles, for the fiscal years 1986 and 1987. Direct debt of the state was calculated to be $367,200,000, and contingent debt was $107,344,000. Total debt was therefore $474,544,000 and, less self-supporting debt of $245,586,000, resulted in total net tax-supported debt for the state of $228,958,000. Other debt statistics were as follows: Direct debt per capita was $376, and net tax-supported debt per capita was $234. The ratio of direct debt to personal income was 2.9 percent, and the ratio of net tax-supported debt to personal income was 1.8 percent. The ratio of direct debt to estimated full value of property was 1.1 percent, and the ratio of net tax-supported debt to estimated full value was 0.7 percent. Debt service as a percentage of general fund revenues was 7.4 percent.

City of Dallas, Texas: Dallas County General Obligation Bonds†

The bonds were direct general obligations of the City of Dallas payable from ad valorem taxes levied within the limits prescribed by law on taxable property within the city. The bonds were being issued to provide funds for the city's capital improvements. Taxable assessed valuation at 100 percent was $42,792,236,827, and total general obligation debt was $581,890,710. Self-supporting debt totaled $85,424,617, leaving total funded debt payable from ad valorem taxes at $496,466,093 and funded debt at $429,797,881.

---

* Data from Official Statement of $154,525,000 State of New Hampshire, General Obligation Refunding Bonds, $81,875,000 Series A Bonds, $72,650,000 Series B Bonds, dated July 15, 1985.
† Data from Official Statement of $43,335,000 City of Dallas, Texas (Dallas County), General Obligation Bonds, Series 1985, dated June 1, 1985.

The ratio of total general obligation debt to taxable assessed value was 1.36 percent, and the ratio of net funded debt outstanding to taxable valuation was 1.0 percent.

The population of Dallas was 947,950. The per capita assessed valuation was $45,141.87, the per capita total general obligation debt was $613.84, and the per capita net funded debt was $453.40. (It should be noted that the civil statutes of Texas provide that total funded debt payable from ad valorem taxes may not exceed 10 percent of the city's taxable assessed valuation.) Fund balances stood at approximately $31.1 million and $34.4 million in 1983 and 1984, respectively. Over the last 3 years, total current tax collections averaged approximately 96 percent. Southwestern Bell Telephone and Texas Utilities Electric Company were the largest two taxpayers, with taxable assessed valuations of approximately $796.5 million and $591.6 million, respectively. In the Dallas–Fort Worth standard metropolitan statistical area (SMSA), the distribution of nonagricultural employment by industry showed that wholesale and retail trade was 27.14 percent, services 20.14 percent, manufacturing 19.15 percent, and government 11.51 percent. The unemployment rate of Dallas was approximately 3.8 percent.

PART 3

Revenue Bonds

6
The Public Revenue Authority

One of the most interesting, if not most remarkable, aspects of the evolutionary process of American state and local government finance and the financing of public services has been the advent and widespread growth of the public revenue authority device. The use of revenue authorities in the United States is generally considered to have taken hold in the early part of the twentieth century with an effort to provide government services without exceeding constitutional debt limits on public borrowing. Another benefit that proponents suggested would result from the public authority device was that its operations would be "taken out of politics" and given to an entity that was generally considered to be of a more corporate character. The lineage of the word *authority* can be traced back to the Port of London Authority in England. As the legend goes, the creators of the Port of London sought to give this new entity a name, and when they were unable to find something with broad enough appeal, they reread its enabling legislation, wherein many of the powers given to the Port of London were granted with the phrase "Authority is hereby given . . . ." Not surprisingly, those vested with the powers to name London's port decided on the name "Port of London Authority." One of the earliest uses of the public authority device in America was the creation of the Port Authority of New York and New Jersey in 1921.

In general, the financing of authority operations was to be by user fees and any of its borrowing would be secured by revenues from individuals and commercial enterprises that would use this governmental device. Originally, the authority device was used for toll roads, but it gradually evolved to provide a wide variety of services. Nevertheless, through most of the early and mid-twentieth century until about 1960, the vast majority of government services were still provided by state and local governments through the issuance of general obligation bonds. After this period, the growth of public authorities and the issuance of revenue authority debt climbed steadily; today, most of the large issuers are similar in nature to the early public authorities and also issue the largest percentage of debt. Revenue authority debt is now issued for many different types of services, including public power, water and wastewater, housing, hospitals, resource recovery projects, education, transportation, pollution control, airports, bridges, tunnels, recreational facilities, and many other projects.

The nature of the revenue authority serves up to the investor or analyst a corporate-type enterprise for which a different analytical perspective must be marshaled. Most individuals who evaluate the security of bonds issued by revenue authorities have lumped the structure of their analysis under four basic headings—financial, administrative, economic, and legal—and assign each area the same approximate weight to the evaluation. It might be somewhat more useful, however, for the investor and analyst to evaluate what really can be analyzed, in the first instance, and then try to understand the driving financial force behind an authority's operations. As a result, it may be more useful to evaluate authorities generally according to three basic categories in the following order of importance: (1) the demand for service and the future economics of providing such service, (2) a cash flow and financial analysis of the authority itself, and (3) the legal protections and safeguards afforded the investor. The quality of the management or administration of a revenue authority is very difficult for an analyst to appraise. (Without strong demand for the revenue enterprise, solid cash flow, and sound legal protections, the caliber of management may be relatively unimportant to bond security.) Noting whether financial and other reports from the authority are available, up to date, consistent, and complete is a start, and obviously there are other characteristics of management that should weigh heavily in the evaluation of a revenue authority. Yet in today's world, demand, cash flow, financial analysis, and the legal protections afforded the investors are certainly the most critical analytical features and represent those which can be evaluated to a significant degree.

The Demand for Service and Its Economics

Regardless of what service the revenue enterprise issues debt for, individuals and/or institutions must need the service, and it must be financially worth their while to use the particular service provided by that revenue authority. As a result, the feasibility study for the issuance of debt by a revenue authority has become of almost historic importance in the evaluation of the security of revenue authority bonds. Most feasibility studies provide comparisons of the cost of this service versus the other alternatives within the given service area. The studies trace historical demand trends and projected demand for that particular service years into the future. The competitive nature of the revenue authority within its service area is of the utmost importance.

Of primary importance to this kind of projected use study is an analysis of the future economic viability of the service area and the surrounding community. This evaluation would entail an analysis of the community's historical and projected trends of population and industrial growth, level of employment and unemployment, and income levels of its population. All of these characteristics are highly important indicators of the economic well-being of a community both past and present. Therefore, very often revenue bond official statements include detailed economic information about the service area in question. It is also useful to evaluate the service area's debt ratios, both past and projected. In short, the approach used is not unlike that employed when evaluating a government's general obligation debt.

Cash Flow Analysis and Financial Analysis

From the demand for service and the projected economic growth of the community, the feasibility consultant provides a cash flow analysis of the project. This includes both historical and projected revenue and expenditure patterns under different economic scenarios. This is often similar to a sensitivity analysis. The extent to which detailed data is provided depends upon the kind of revenue bond in question and whether or not it is a start-up-type project. Furthermore, information is provided about the diversity of revenues and the components of expenditures for the revenue enterprise, including the important item of operating and maintenance costs and their projected growth. An analysis of the balance sheet and income statement should be completed, and the authority's future financial plans should be factored into the evaluation.

From this financial analysis, the investor or analyst should derive a variety of financial ratios. Some are important for certain revenue-type debts and others are less so. In general, however, there are some medians and means that should be observed; in most cases, the most important is the debt service coverage, ratio, which usually hovers between 1.10× (times) and 1.75×. Listed below are some of the major ratios used to evaluate the financial operations of revenue authorities.

$$\text{Debt service coverage } (x) = \frac{\text{net revenues}}{\text{debt service required}}$$

$$\text{Debt service safety margin } (\%) = \frac{\text{gross revenues } \textit{minus} \text{ operating and maintenance expenses } \textit{minus} \text{ current debt service}}{\text{gross revenues}}$$

$$\text{Debt ratio } (\%) = \frac{\text{net debt}}{\text{the sum of working capital plus plant}}$$

$$\text{Net takedown } (\%) = \frac{\text{net revenues}}{\text{gross revenues}}$$

$$\text{Operating ratio } (\%) = \frac{\text{operating and maintenance expenses}}{\text{operating revenues}}$$

$$\text{Interest coverage } (x) = \frac{\text{net revenues}}{\text{interest payments required}}$$

Legal Protections for Bondholders

Perhaps the most unusual and interesting aspects of analyzing the security behind certain municipal bonds comes in the evaluation of the legal protections afforded bondholders by issuers of revenue authority debt. The mechanisms, contracts, and security provisions involved in this area are unique to security analysis and bring the revenue bond device and its evaluation closer to that of its counterpart in corporate finance. Most revenue bonds have a series of funds, whose revenues ultimately provide for the security of the bonds through the payment of debt service, for the operating costs, and for a variety of other items. These funds are provided for in the trust indenture of the bond and, although not totally alike for all revenue bonds, generally follow the form of a debt service fund, an operating and maintenance fund, a renewal and replacement fund, a construction fund, and a surplus fund, among others. Revenues coming into the authority fill each of these funds to a prescribed level and then flow to the next fund, and each fund is required to be maintained at a certain level for the life of the bonds.

Other legal protections involve the authority's ability to raise revenue to pay its bills. The rate covenant is the requirement that the issuing entity or guaranteeing entity set rates for its services at a level so that net revenues will be sufficient to cover the debt service on the bonds, plus operating and maintenance expenses and perhaps other costs for any given year. Coverage generally above 1.1× (times) is required and is usually calculated using the required maximum yearly principal and interest payment. If coverage falls below this level, rates must be raised to meet the coverage test and refill the debt service reserve fund and other funds, if necessary.

There has always been a question as to whether a revenue authority should be able to pay debt service (principal and interest payments) on its bonds on a net or gross lien basis. What this really means is paying debt service from revenues either after paying operating and mainte-nance expenses or before such costs. It generally used to be considered that gross lien bonds provide more security because they are backed by a larger amount of revenues. Today, however, analysts and investors realize that in almost all cases, in order for an operation to continue providing sufficient service, operating and maintenance expenses must be paid. Therefore, net revenues are usually used in the calculation of revenue debt service coverage.

Another significant legal protection is the requirement for the issu-ance of additional bonds or more debt. There is usually a provision that requires three tests: one for projected revenues divided by historical debt service, another for projected revenues divided by future debt service, and a third for past revenues divided by maximum future debt service. The use of these tests may vary, but generally the revenues derived from the future improvements to the service, as a result of additional bond issuance, must be covered by the projected revenues from the project or at a certain level of coverage in any given year.

NOTE: This chapter was written by Stephen P. Rappaport in a paper entitled "The Public Revenue Authority in American State and Local Finance" at Prudential-Bache Securities Inc., 1986. Reprinted by permission.

7

Public Power Bonds

What the New York City financial debacle of the 1970s was to general obligation bond analysis, the Washington Public Power Supply System's (WPPSS's) default in the 1980s was to revenue bond analysis. The thought that WPPSS would ultimately default on about $2.25 billion of bonds was certainly not a consideration during the project's early years. Yet huge cost problems, construction delays (and the lessening of demand), and public outcries against the project were among the major contributors to the WPPSS financial morass. It is difficult to say what is at fault in the Supply System's problems, and most people have different opinions with different emphases, yet if there is one important statement that could be made about the problems, it is that they have had a tremendous impact on the analysis of municipal bonds and that this effect will certainly continue into the foreseeable future. Public power bonds will never again be evaluated the way they had been for years. Indeed, the economics of a project, its projected demand, its financial feasibility, its construction schedule, the political milieu in which it is being constructed, and the validity of its contracts are certainly items that will be more closely examined in the future. Nevertheless, WPPSS is still one single case; although it is a major case, to say that it is representative of power issues nationwide or revenue bonds generally is simply not so. The WPPSS problem is also discussed in Chapter 19, but presented here is a general analysis of public power bonds.

The issuance of municipal bonds for the creation of public power facilities had its roots in the 1930s during the eras of the great depression and the New Deal. It began in a quite-concentrated form in California, Nebraska, and the northwest, especially Washington and Oregon. The public power legislation, which was the forerunner of all public power authorities, grew out of a congressional desire to harness the gigantic power of the Columbia River and its tributaries in order to provide rural electrification for the entire northwest. Since that time of hydroelectric power, public power issuers nationwide have built projects for oil, coal, and nuclear fuels and have been the largest issuers of all revenue bond debt during the 1970s and early 1980s.

It is generally considered that there are four different basic types of utility systems in the municipal finance arena. The first type is a municipal distribution system that purchases its electricity at wholesale. The second generates, purchases, and also distributes electricity. The third generates and distributes electricity. The fourth is the bulk power supplier, which includes most state agencies, joint action agencies, and combinations of them as well as generation and transmission coopera- tives; bulk power suppliers build electric power–generating units and supply power to their participants or members.

Bulk Power Supply and Joint Action

In the past, large municipal utilities had characteristics that distin- guished them from small utilities. While a few of the large traditional utilities generated power, all the small ones acted exclusively as distrib- utors. Small utilities sold small bond issues, and the proceeds could be used only within the particular localities. Both of these traditional conditions are now changing. Many municipal power systems continue the recently instituted programs for bulk power that guarantee long- term power contracts to their purchasers. However, the fact that some federal contracts to supply cheap power have ended means that certain power systems must immediately seek new supplies for bulk power. This requirement subjects them to the same demands with which small municipalities must contend.

The new utilities that must now secure bulk power include three types of wholesale power purchasers: (1) those which own exclusive generat- ing capacity and which finance projects for their own area, (2) those which purchase power from large municipal electric systems and which are not involved in the planning and acquisition of public power, and (3) those which had purchased power originally from low-cost federal hydroelectric facilities that no longer have excess capacity. Local utilities may also buy bulk power, but on an individual basis they are far smaller users.

Today is a particularly critical time for the entire municipal utilities industry because they are forced by obsolescent plants to invest vast sums in new facilities. They are also beset with higher fuel costs, shortages of supply, environmental complaints, and higher rates of interest that affect any new municipal bonds they sell. The result of increased capital costs and operating expenses is obviously that the cost of power has risen sharply. Most small public municipal utilities have been coping with these soaring costs by binding together for direct or indirect participation in giant generating units in order to maintain an adequate supply of bulk power.

Because of the vast new uncertainties of the public power environment, most smaller systems have started considering joint action, joint operation, or direct and indirect cooperation of some kind with a group of other public utilities. Traditionally, they had financed their power needs almost exclusively through rate increases. Many had neither experience with seeking external financing nor any power-generating capacity. The new pressures of inadequate supply and rising costs have forced small facilities to find an entirely new way of doing business. The same economic, financial, and supply pressures have also forced large systems to reassess future bulk supplies.

Moreover, any large municipal power system or agency that purchases from a private or public power project is dependent on the owner-operator. While there may be no problems with this arrangement, occasionally (and increasingly during the 1970s) there have been problems of power scarcities and allocation disputes. Thus, because municipalities fully recognize the hazards of overdependency, many have started joining together to construct their own power-generating systems. To do so, they must go through a lengthy approval and construction process, with all its attendant problems and risks. Many municipalities consider these difficulties to be preferable to their past dependence on external power supplies, because once new systems are built, the generation of power is generally under their own control.

There was another major reason for the surge in joint action financings. Because of the antiquated bond resolutions under which most large systems operate, they have been forbidden to issue additional bonds, to finance improvements or buy new supplies, or to enter into new contractual agreements with purchasers. The *additional bonds test*, which each municipal bond resolution included, was based on a decades-old conception of the technology and cost structure for building and maintaining a public power system. This so-called legal straitjacket has forced many public power agencies to explore alternatives in order to continue to supply their requirements for bulk power supply. These have included (1) direct ownership of a generating facility by issuing new bonds, (2) issuing new or refunding old bonds, and (3) long-term contracts for financing power supply from another source.

Because of the long heritage of legal constraints, direct ownership plans have been somewhat hampered in efforts to finance vast new power expansions via the existing bond resolution. It was believed that this would place an excessive burden on the existing ratepayers. Furthermore, because the lead time necessary to build a new power plant is frequently a number of years, the current burden on ratepayers for financing a new facility could be crippling. Although some smaller capital additions in the past could be financed by rate increases, such financing is no longer possible because of the vast amounts of capital expenditures that would be required.

Some municipalities attempt to pay off the old bonds and issue new ones under a new bond resolution that has far more flexibility than the existing resolution. This may be accomplished by refunding the old issue. The new bonds will sometimes then have a second lien on the revenues of the same utility system. These bonds will therefore carry a lower rating and a higher relative interest cost than the previous bond issue. Nevertheless, to remove their legal straitjacket and to achieve flexibility, many municipalities have issued such second lien bonds.

Another key alternative, one that municipal utilities have employed to avoid restrictive legal covenants, has involved the creation of power supply systems under a separate legal resolution and the issuance of new bonds secured by a power supply contract with the original system. These new bonds usually burden the facility with another operating expense or additional debt service payment, either of which usually has a lien on available revenues. This lien may take precedence over all currently outstanding debt if it is payable with operating and mainte-nance expenses. It weakens the debt service coverage, and some suggest that it constitutes an attempt to avoid the additional bonds test. Some bond resolutions therefore explicitly prohibit their use. Relying solely on another municipal utility, or the long-term contract for power supply, leaves the municipality lacking control. It has no right to review the costs, expenses, or availability of supply of the seller. In any case, for all the above reasons, joint action programs for bulk power supply have spread rapidly.

New Issues

With bonds that are being issued for public power by a new agency or a municipal entity that has not issued such bonds before, the credit analysis must be far more extensive than for most ongoing issuers. New issuers have no track record, and they frequently have yet to construct a power-generating or power-distributing system. In these situations, construction risks are paramount and involve failure to complete construction, delays that sometimes last years, and problems in engineering that can result in an improperly or inadequately functioning power system. In the case of a new issuer, the engineer's *feasibility study* is crucial, and institutional investors, the rating agencies, and the issuer all rely on the engineer far more heavily than usual. In addition, the caliber and past experience of the management itself must be weighed. New start-up municipal power authorities issuing bonds for the first time raise additional analytical questions about the relative autonomy of the issuer in setting rates, its right to issue such bonds, and its right to have a monopoly on offering power to residents within its geographic area.

Because of new federal and state laws and regulations, not only the broad design but also the detailed specifications of start-up public power situations have to be carefully analyzed by any major investor. Frequently at each stage of financing and construction, the permits and approvals must be obtained from each level of government for siting, environmental compatibility, construction strength and safety, and operational adequacy. The project has to be started on time, each stage must be fully completed by set deadlines and according to specific standards, and all fuels have to be purchased under long-term contracts. When completed, the whole facility must undergo rigorous testing and operational checks. Throughout this process, there are many sources of cost overruns and chances of delay as well as legal risks. Among the concerns of investors and analysts are the possibilities of a failure to complete a new project, an operating failure of the utility before construction is completed or before the utility is fully functioning, or a failure once the plant is operational.

Governmental standards for safety, health, conservation, and environmental safety, as well as those for disclosure and liability, have all been upgraded recently. As a result, they have raised the costs of each new electric utility project and increased the lead time required to plan and construct a power plant or distribution system. Until an entire system is finally complete and its operations certified as acceptable, it does not earn money. Thus the longer the delays continue, which could last for years, the higher the fuel costs; and the higher the fuel costs are, the higher the rates that must be charged in order to recover the additional expenses.

Methods of Credit Evaluation

The Demand of the Service Area: Economics

Absolutely key to the analysis of a public power revenue bond is a detailed evaluation of the economics of the service area as well as the projections of demand as a result of that analysis. A service area should at least be stabilized and hopefully be a growing area that is not dependent on a single company or a single industry. The customer mix should be balanced among residential, industrial, and commercial users, with not more than 10 percent of the energy purchased by any one single customer. An analysis should be made of the projected influx and outflow of residential, industrial, and commercial users as well as the strength of the various customer bases. In the case of joint action agencies, it is especially important, as has been shown in the past, to analyze the economic base and the demand characteristics of all the participants. To be sure, this is an involved task, but the record shows that the strength of these agencies lies in the strength of their participants. Without an analysis of the economic base of these participants, an evaluation of the quality of a public power bond, especially a joint action agency one, could be improved. As part of the economic analysis of the public power project, it is important to take note of the financial strength of the municipalities or participants that will use the project. This is quite apart from analyzing the financial strength of the project itself, which (as discussed later in this section) is a whole other area in the analysis of public power projects and most other revenue bonds. However, the point must be made that the economics of the project, as seen from the perspective of demand, has inherent within it the economic as well as financial characteristics of those who will use the output from the public power project.

Engineering and Financial Projections

In the past, bond analysts seriously considered only actual figures for historical growth trends in load supply, customer demand, revenues, costs, and overall experience. Indeed, many start-up situations were unratable because they had no track record. There had been an increasing willingness among bond analysts to accept engineers' projections and financial consultants' expectations for a new facility or an expansion of an old one. Market participants together simply dictated that if there were going to be more start-up utilities, including new joint ownership and joint action municipal power projects, then expert projections simply had to be used to evaluate the creditworthiness of the new bonds; otherwise, the bonds would not be sold successfully.

Today, both historical and projected figures are carefully compared with the on-line resources of the enterprise under development in order to assess the adequacy of both sets of figures as standards of measurement. Obviously, any utilities that overbuild capacity which they cannot market must absorb heavy, added fixed costs. Utilities with too small a power capacity are forced to purchase power during emergencies at prices that may necessitate a rate increase or throw financial operations out of balance. For these reasons, the reviews of past forecasts are compared with actual operating experience. The engineering consultants should be pressed hard on all assumptions and forecasts, especially those regarding the escalation of costs.

Perhaps the most common reasons for financial difficulties in the public utility area are projected cost and revenue miscalculations. Because of this fact, investors and analysts are particularly anxious that only nationally recognized engineers and financial consultants be chosen by the utilities issuing bonds. They are believed to have the experience, skill, and track record necessary for making the most realistic assumptions.

Unrealistic projections of revenue frequently emerge when bond issuers attempt to force projections of sales figures to satisfy artificial constraints instead of objectively estimating the natural level of demand, and there are numerous other reasons for miscalculation that engineers and financial analysts would not be expected to foresee. Nevertheless, if a utility's management has been accurate in its past forecasts, kept its rate increases in line with budget requirements, appeared to cope over time with peak load requirements, and maintained a long-range plan, then its track record is considered a reliable measure of its future forecasts. New projects do not have the benefits of previous records; in these cases, projections should be of the most conservative sort.

The Financial Feasibility Study

Critical to the analysis of public power bonds, as with most revenue enterprises, are the feasibility study and the financial and engineering projections made by it. The feasibility study should present revenue and expenditures on a historical and projected basis, with an analysis of the construction costs figured into the projections.

The analysis should evaluate the project's historical and projected capital improvement program and how it will be financed. What is critical to assess is the degree to which any new capital improvement or enlargement actually adds to the facility's earning potential without greatly increasing its cost, because most power projects are of a scale that requires additional construction almost throughout the greater portion of the project's life. This has been the case in the past, even though it may not continue to be so in the future. The principle of analysis, however, remains the same for any capital construction program. Operating projections should go as far into the future as possible, hopefully 5 to 15 years. Leeway should be left for construction delays, with the added potential burden of increases in construction costs. Projections of peak demand should be made, and average revenue per kilowatthour, average number of customers, and monthly average revenue per customer should be presented by the study and evaluated by the analyst. Generating capacity should be ascertained through peak load, existing capacity, reserve capacity, and reserve margin. An analysis of sales revenue for residential, commercial, and industrial users should be provided and evaluated. Projections of net income should be made as a result, and financial ratios of the kind employed for most revenue bonds should be ascertained and evaluated. These ratios and operational data would give the analyst some idea of the quality of management. A similar type of analysis, although somewhat less detailed, should be made of the participants' electric systems if the bonds are issued for a joint action agency.

If there is one significant point to be made about the analysis of public power revenue bonds in the wake of a few problems, it is that the analyst and investor must make some determination about the validity of the assumptions in the feasibility study, most especially concerning construction cost estimates, construction schedules, and projections of demand. This, however, is much easier said than done. There are many individuals who argue that they are able to discern inaccurate cost assumptions and demand projections, but there are equally as many people who have great foresight when viewing matters in hindsight. To be sure, it is most difficult for investors and even analysts to make evaluations of demand projections and cost estimates when these are presented to them in feasibility studies authored by consulting firms of national recognition with access to highly sophisticated computer models. Gross exaggerations in a feasibility study can be detected by comparing it with studies of similar enterprises. For the most part, however, analysts and investors alike must rely on themselves to ask the kinds of questions that would elicit answers leading them to some kind of conclusion about the legitimacy of feasibility assumptions. A corollary to this, in the area of construction cost estimates, is that analysts must make evaluations of management's ability to adequately control and supervise the construction of a public power project, especially if management does not have any track record in this area.

Fuel Mix

Traditionally, hydroelectric plants provided the lowest-cost power, especially in the Pacific northwest and along the Tennessee River. They were therefore considered vastly superior to plants powered by oil, coal, gas, or nuclear fuel. Having continual river power, hydroelectric plants had no fuel expense and no pollution or other environmental hazard. Today, however, there are almost no readily available river sites for constructing massive new plants, and power generated from river flows is considered unpredictable.

The ever-increasing demand for power is now met through the construction of plants that utilize scarcer or more expensive fuels, such as oil, gas, coal, and nuclear material. This trend is generally expected to increase sharply during the coming decade. Solar energy, the burning of solid wastes, and geothermal energy may, when fully developed, satisfy a portion of America's power needs, but they will probably not become major fuel sources for some time.

A crucial credit factor studied by investors and bond analysts has been a power project's type of fuel supply and fuel mixes. Most analysts feel that a utility that has a diversity, or mix, of different fuel sources is far stronger than one that relies on a particular type of fuel, such as hydroelectricity, nuclear material, coal, or oil. A mix provides flexibility; it enables management to cope with any eventual fuel cost changes or fuel shortages.

Rates

Customer revenues, both individual and corporate, are vital to credit analysis because they must be judged to be sufficient to meet all operating expenses and debt service. Because a bond's term to maturity can extend up to 30 years or so, the track record of the rate increases needed to keep pace with inflation is critical. The projected rate increase schedule and evidence of customer willingness to accept future rate increases are also highly important. A realistic schedule of rate increases is critical where there appears the likelihood of failure to control or recoup costs. Because it is possible that municipalities will set inadequate rates and then fail to revise them at frequent intervals, the costs per customer could increase soon after being set. As a result, rates must be competitive, but they must also leave room for adequate increases that may be needed later. There must also be an ability and a willingness to raise them as quickly as necessary.

Most states allow municipally owned utilities to raise rates without requiring approval from a regulatory body, provided that the purpose of an increase is to permit the utility to continue to cover fully the costs of furnishing service. Nevertheless, some municipalities face state or local restrictions on charges. Yet because self-regulation has prevailed in most states and for most public utilities, it has established a general assurance of revenue flow to pay increased costs required for debt service charges. The independence of such public utilities in setting and raising their own rates could be in jeopardy. Indeed, pressure for outside regulatory bodies to put a cap on rate increases has risen because of escalations in electricity rates. This pressure is now expected to undermine what for decades has been a significant strength of the municipal utilities issuing bonds, namely, their independent ability to raise rates on their own initiative.

Power Supply Contracts

Power supply contracts that extend over the total life of the bonds are obviously preferred by investors to short-term or weak supply contracts. In spite of such long-term contracts, recent experience has shown that utilities cannot be certain of every eventuality. Bond analysts today are especially interested in seeing interlocking arrangements between utilities, or *interties*, in case of any emergency. These interties are expected to guarantee continuity of service, or long-term reliability. Power must be able to be purchased cheaply or at very competitive rates, if necessary, and excess power must be able to be readily sold. These contracts must be in place or be covenanted to be in place, together with power sales, purchase, and transmission agreements. Fuel adjustment clauses in certain contracts, to pay for increased fuel costs, should be easily activated.

Major investors virtually require evidence that the different participants (i.e., the power wholesalers, distributors, buyers, sellers, and producers) are all fully "locked into" any complicated financing arrangements. In other words, their prime focus is on the amount of emergency protection secured by contract. Thus the power sales contracts must appear strong and unquestionably enforceable. In some important cases, certain contracts for payments made by the participants were ruled to be invalid. It is important, therefore, that contracts be validated to the fullest extent possible under law.

More specifically, most contracts for power are of one or two types. *Take-or-pay contracts* guarantee that the purchasers will pay for the power whether or not the power is provided or the facility is operating. *Take-and-pay contracts* require a purchaser to pay only for the power that is received. Take-or-pay contracts, when properly validated, are generally considered to provide better security than take-and-pay agreements, but there are cases where take-and-pay contracts could be of a quality equivalent to or better than certain take-or-pay arrangements.

A final note must be said about contracts in general. A contract may legally be sound and binding and it may truly be enforceable. The analyst, however, should evaluate the political climate in which the agency operates and have some feeling for the willingness of the local governments of general jurisdiction or the participants or the power purchasers to make good on their commitments under these contracts. For most investors and analysts, this is a difficult part of the analysis, but it is certainly not an impossible one.

Other Legal Considerations

Debt service coverage and other legal considerations are as important in the area of public power as they are with most other revenue bonds. With joint action agencies, however, debt service coverage cannot be high because they are cost-of-service enterprises. Revenues are expected to cover debt service, operating, and maintenance charges, with a sufficient amount left over for a margin; the remainder is usually credited to the next years' payments to be made by the participants. The rate covenant is usually $1.1\times$ (times) to $1.2\times$, and the additional bonds test usually has historical and future ratio requirements.

Most contracts are either take-or-pay or take-and-pay. Some contracts make the participants liable only for their required amount of payments, which is termed a *several agreement*. Others are *joint and several*, which make the participants liable for their pro rata share of the costs, plus an amount in proportion to their own pro rata share that must be paid on a defaulting participant's share; this is called the *step-up* feature. There are other joint and several agreements that have limited step-up provisions, whereby the participants are liable for a defaulting participant's payments, but only up to a certain percentage of their own payments or a set percentage overall. Payments made by participants should be operating expenses of their electric systems and thus usually come before payments of their own debt service. The financings can either be *closed-end*, which involves the reliance on the power purchaser's credit over the life of the project, or *open-end*, which involves reliance on the power purchaser's credit only during the initial stage of the project.

Depending upon the kind of financing and the type of project, closed-end or open-end financing can have both positive and negative aspects to it.

Case Studies
The Municipal Electric Authority of Georgia*

In 1975 the state legislature of Georgia created the Municipal Electric Authority of Georgia (MEAG), which has been providing substantially all the energy requirements and power for 47 participants since 1977. The participants, which comprise 46 cities and 1 county, are all located in Georgia. MEAG has ownership interests in two coal-fired plants, Plant Wansley and Plant Scherer, and two nuclear plants, Plant Vogtle and Plant Hatch, all constructed by the Georgia Power Company. Each plant is composed of two units. Approximately 51 percent of the plants' total capacity is nuclear and 48 percent is coal, with a combined total capacity of 1545 megawatts (MW). In 1984 the service area of the participants had a total population of approximately 495,000, which was 8.5 percent of the state's population. Total customers increased from approximately 223,000 in 1980 to about 236,000 in 1984.

Participants make payments on their obligations through take-or-pay contracts. Certain Georgia courts have affirmed that the participants' obligations under these contracts are valid and that they were authorized to enter into these contracts. Payments made by the participants are treated as operating expenses of their electric systems. If payments are not made by the participant's electric systems, the obligations are secured by the full faith and credit of the participants, which include the ability to levy ad valorem taxes in their local governments of general jurisdiction. Each participant has agreed to charge and collect rates sufficient to meet its payments to MEAG under its contractual obligations. There is a sell-back arrangement whereby MEAG receives revenues from the sale of its power back to Georgia Power Company at certain times on a take-or-pay basis. Revenues from purchases are then credited to the accounts of the participants.

MEAG's cost of power was budgeted to be 3.9 cents per kilowatthour in 1984 and 5.2 cents per kilowatthour in 1988. Projected peak demand is expected to increase from 1247 MW in 1985 to 1750 MW in 1996. Projected energy requirements in thousands of megawatthours is estimated to increase from 5892 in 1985 to 8626 in 1996. In 1984, total electricity generated and received in millions of kilowatthours was 62,457, and sales of electricity in millions of kilowatthours totaled 59,055, with residential customers purchasing 11,549, commercial customers purchasing 10,902, and industrial customers purchasing 18,863; sales for resale were 17,399, and other sales totaled 342. Electrical revenues in thousands of dollars totaled $3,132,880 in 1984. The compound annual growth rate from the mid-1970s to the

---

* Data from Official Statement of $650,000,000 Municipal Electric Authority of Georgia, Power Revenue Bonds, Series K, dated May 1, 1985.

mid-1980s was 3.9 percent, and the compound annual growth rate from the mid-1980s to the mid-1990s was projected to be 3.5 percent.

City of San Antonio, Texas: Electric and Gas Systems Revenue Improvement Bonds*

The overall program for the city's electric and gas systems included the site development and construction of generating units, distribution and transmission lines, and other improvements to the city's electric and gas systems. The city's major generating facilities included 12 natural-gas units having a combined capacity of 2400 MW and two 418-MW coal-fired generating units, for a combined total of 3236 MW. All these units are capable of operating on fuel oil. The electric system served a territory consisting substantially of all of Bexar County and small portions of certain adjacent counties. Electricity was also sold at wholesale to other cities. There were other contractual arrangements in the form of power sales agreements between the City Public Service Board of San Antonio (CPS) and other entities.

For the electric system, there were approximately 363,100 residential customers and 40,688 commercial and industrial customers, for a total customer base (including others) of 413,842. Sales in kilowatthours (kWh) to residential customers totaled $3.5 billion, sales to commercial and industrial customers $4.1 billion, and sales to public authorities $1.25 billion. These sales, together with sales to other entities, resulted in total sales in kilowatthours of $9.1 billion. The gas system had approximately 258,664 residential customers, 18,130 commercial customers, 244 industrial customers, and 1981 public authorities customers, so that the total customer base was 279,019. Total sales in thousand cubic feet (mcf) for residential users was approximately $13.6 million, for commercial users $7.2 million, for industrial users $3.0 million, and for public authorities about $1.7 million. Total sales in mcf was $25.5 million. The typical residential gas and electric bills of six comparative Texas cities for 500 kWh of electric service and for 6000 cubic feet of gas revealed that San Antonio ranked second to the least expensive in total bill costs of $67.48, with the cheapest being $66.09 and the most expensive being $80.95. In 1985 the net kilowatt (kW) generation was 9,774,125,100 kW, which was an 8.7 percent increase over the previous year; the maximum demand was 2,210,000 kW, which was a 2.89 percent increase over the previous year, and the average demand (which was an average of the monthly peak demands) was 1,723,000 kW, with a 50.35 percent load factor.

In 1985 net revenues totaled $324,137,470, with actual principal and interest requirements on the Old Series Bonds of $16,498,031, with payments on the New Series Bonds of $129,894,634, and with total principal and interest payments of $146,392,665. The total amount of bonds outstanding in 1985 was $1,729,110,000, actual debt service coverage was 2.21× (times), and coverage with the additional bonds was 1.78×. Over recent years, debt as a percentage of net plant averaged approximately 70.1 percent. In 1990, peak

---

* Data from Official Statement of $150,000,000 City of San Antonio, Texas, Electric and Gas Systems Revenue Improvement Bonds, New Series 1985-A, dated April 1, 1985.

demand was projected to be 2677 MW, with a total of $11.5 million in kilowatt sales. Debt service coverage for that year was expected to be 1.95×. The estimated capital expenditures for the construction program for gas was $11,662,000 in 1986 and $14,982,000 in 1990. For the electric system, capital expenditures were to drop from $428,146,000 to $331,964,000 for the same time period.

The bonds were payable solely from and secured by a lien on and pledge of net revenues of the city's gas and electric systems, subject to any other prior liens of the pledge to the Old Series Bonds. The city covenanted to maintain gas and electrical rates and charges that would be sufficient to pay the maintenance and operating expenses of the system, to pay all debt service requirements, and to maintain required reserves. At the time of the issuance, the City of Austin was a 16 percent owner of the South Texas Project, Central Power and Light Company was a 25.2 percent owner, Houston Lighting and Power Company was a 30.8 percent owner, and the CPS Board of San Antonio was a 28 percent owner. The project involved the construction of two 1250-MW nuclear generating stations.

NOTE: For an analysis of the WPPSS situation, see the following, among other bibliographic references too numerous to detail here: U.S. House of Representatives, Committee on Interior and Insular Affairs, Subcommittee on Mining, Forest Management, and Bonneville Power Administration, "WPPSS Bond Default: Who Pays?", Oversight Hearing held on January 26, 1984, Washington, D. C.: U.S. Government Printing Office, 1985.

8
Housing Bonds

Americans spend more than 25 percent of their annual income on renting or purchasing homes or apartments. Each year, spending for housing represents the largest segment of disposable income to be spent upon any one commodity; the purchase of a house or apartment is usually considered the largest investment a person will ever make.

Rents and the costs of homes and apartments have risen sharply over the past 15 years. Prices have increased to such an extent that many families fear they can no longer afford to purchase a house, or they are settling for smaller homes because of high costs. Likewise, ordinary rents in many cities have risen out of reach for many families.

For example, in the United States today there are 1.8 million new households created each year, yet simultaneously there has been a shrinkage in the number of rental units available since 1970 that has resulted in a net loss of 20,000 units annually. This loss has occurred primarily because of the declining production of new buildings, the abandonment and foreclosure of older apartments, and the conversion into cooperatives or condominiums of many sought-after units.

The key result of this shrinkage is that the government finds itself called upon to finance two-thirds of all rental units now being built. In fact, in some cities the government has become practically the only financier of new rental buildings. For example, in New York City during the 1970s virtually no new rental buildings were built at all that were not backed by some form of federal government financing, federally insured mortgages, and/or tax abatement. New private production has virtually reached a standstill in some areas because of very high interest rates and the increasingly long preconstruction time required. Because very little building has taken place, rental units are scarce, and those available have escalated in price.

This difficulty of affording today's rents or house prices is one fundamental reason why federal, state, and local governments have provided massive financial support through a whole variety of grants, subsidies, loans, and guarantees designed to ensure that American families can find adequate homes. This public policy of governmental support is multifaceted, and it encompasses special tax benefits for mortgage payments and special regulations for savings banks and lending institutions. It accounts in part for the whole collection of government housing agencies at all levels of government.

Housing revenue bonds exist in a wide variety of forms. The major divisions are between those for single-family homes and those for multifamily homes; those which have federal insurance and those which do not; and those which encompass a single housing project and those which involve a pool or whole portfolio of different projects in different areas. There are also some fundamental differences as to exactly which public entity is the issuer of the bonds: a city, a local housing agency, a state, or some other public agency. The owner of the housing project may be a profit-making corporation, a nonprofit enterprise, or a government housing agency.

In bond issues for multifamily homes there is a crucial distinction between issues which have federal insurance and those which do not. Those with federal insurance tend to be rated higher than those without.

Traditionally, the single-family portfolios were also divided into those which contained mortgages insured by the Federal Housing Administration (FHA) or guaranteed by the Veterans Administration (VA) and those which did not. The FHA and VA issues received higher ratings because of the deep coverage afforded the bondholder, and the nonfederally insured or nonguaranteed issues were rated lower, unless they happened to carry a state moral obligation pledge. Recently, however, the use of various types of private mortgage insurance has become more pervasive, particularly as a result of the explosive growth and creative structure of single-family mortgage bonds that are locally issued, resulting in higher ratings.

In years past, the federal government established a large number of housing programs, which promoted the tremendous growth of tax-exempt housing bonds in the late 1970s and early 1980s. Now, however, the Tax Reform Act of 1986 has curtailed some major programs and has restricted the growth of others in a variety of ways. Nevertheless, there are billions of such housing bonds bought and sold on a daily basis requiring the kind of analysis presented in this chapter. Perhaps different types of housing bonds will be issued after 1986.

Four Types of Bonds

There are essentially four major types of municipal revenue bonds, although there are many additional subclassifications that tend to make this market appear extraordinarily complex. We will give a brief summary of each of the four types and then discuss in detail their credit aspects.

Direct Loan Programs. These involve developers receiving a direct mortgage loan from a state housing finance agency (or other public agency) to pay for building new multiunit apartment buildings. The programs are designed to finance large portfolios of units for low- to moderate-income families or for the elderly, who receive federal rent subsidies.

Mortgage Purchase Bonds. They provide single-family (or sometimes multifamily) homes for low- and moderate-income families to be financed by mortgage money. The proceeds from the sale of these housing revenue bonds are used to buy mortgages from savings and lending institutions who originate new mortgage loans.

Local Housing Authority Bonds Issued under Section 8-11(b). The U.S. Housing Act of 1937 provides low- or moderate-income tenants, whether families or elderly couples or individuals, with multiunit apartment buildings. Unlike direct loan programs, bonds under Section 8-11(b) are indirect financings. They receive no direct financing from the federal government but instead only a comprehensive rent subsidy package. Their other distinction is that they are permitted to have an extraordinarily wide range of issuers.

Loans-to-Lenders Programs. These loans involve bonds generally issued by state housing or mortgage finance agencies and are quite similar to mortgage-backed bonds in the private housing market. In essence, loans-to-lenders programs use bond proceeds to make collateralized loans to lending institutions, which in turn make mortgage loans that are payable from loan repayments by the lending institution. Loans-to-lenders programs have been declining recently as states have shifted to mortgage purchase programs.

Loans-to-lenders bonds can be collateralized by pools of mortgages, by government securities, or by both. They are fully collateralized issues. In such financings there is generally a provision that 150 percent of the loan value be held in escrow (in mortgages or securities), and if there is ever a default on that loan, the trustee need only take the portfolio and liquidate it to make good on the loan. As a result, loans-to-lenders bonds tend to be very secure bonds. While there are a number of risks in the real estate, economics, and management of this type of program, these risks tend to be offset by the very strong collateral.

Direct Loan Program Bonds

Under direct loan programs, developers receive a direct mortgage loan from a state housing finance agency (or a public agency) or from some other issuer to pay for building the new housing. The programs are designed to finance portfolios of multiunit apartment buildings for the elderly or for low- to moderate-income families who receive federal rent subsidies.

The bonds are usually secured by, and interest and principal paid from, payments on mortgages, part or all of which is paid from federal subsidies. Occasionally, an additional backup credit is provided by the state government's moral obligation pledge of appropriations if and when the debt service reserve fund ever becomes deficient. Although some analysts stress that the primary security on the bonds is mortgage payments, and therefore that the actual portolio must be assessed, others insist that the state government's moral pledge is what is critical. The latter use an automatic formula based on the state's GO credit (when a moral obligation pledge is included) to determine the worth of these housing bonds.

As mentioned earlier, the crucial distinction to be made concerning the direct loan programs is between those which are federally insured and those which are not. While the credit of federally insured housing programs is strong and the analysis of their bonds is often thought simple, they are not 100 percent guaranteed in all cases. For example, Section 221(d)(3) of the U.S. Housing Act of 1937 pays 99 percent of the principal of the mortgage. The same is true of Section 221(d)(4). The direct loan programs that are not insured by the federal government are far more difficult to evaluate because the investor must carefully consider the nature of the federal rent subsidy, the worth of the state government's moral pledge, the underlying security of the real estate and housing units themselves, and, finally, the caliber of the management of the state housing agency. Each of these programs must be analyzed on a case-by-case basis.

In evaluating the mortgage portfolio in direct loan programs, it is not feasible for an analyst to examine each mortgage unless the portfolio is very small. Therefore, under these circumstances, particularly if additional mortgages can be added, the credit evaluation focuses on the process used by the agency in underwriting the projects. The evaluation determines (1) if the systems and procedures are sound and are followed and (2) if the size and competence of the staff are adequate.

Another approach considers the balance and composition of the portfolio. Important factors include geographic diversity (inner city versus suburban or rural area), type of project (family versus the elderly), type of subsidy, and underlying state or local economic conditions. Some investors have developed a bias in favor of projects for the elderly and in favor of those which are subsidized according to Section 8-11(b).

Mortgage Purchase Bonds

The proceeds from the sale of these housing revenue bonds are used to buy mortgages from savings and loan institutions or other institutions. Once again, the bonds' principal and interest payments come from mortgage payments. State housing agencies originally organized these mortgage purchase bonds, but in the last 10 years they have begun to be issued by cities, local agencies, and counties.

The distinctions between the different types of mortgage purchase bonds have to do primarily with whether they are used to finance new construction on a new site or to fund established housing developments and whether there are small, isolated, and concentrated groups of mortgages or large, highly diversified pools of mortgages. The small, geographically concentrated pool of mortgages calls for a more specific analysis, whereas the larger, more highly diversified pool of mortgages requires an actuarial, or statistical, approach to the portfolio risks.

In the simplest terms, four factors provide an analytical checklist for these bonds: assets, cash flow, management, and legal protection. These factors are not usually independent; instead, they are interrelated, and therefore the investor or bond analyst should balance one against the other. For example, poorer assets, real estate, local economics, and demographics of the area where a housing project is to be built can be offset by greater insurance and/or more conservative cash flow assumptions. Since the housing assets have to be protected and the cash flow has to be balanced, there is usually not an either-or form of analysis but a weighing of different strengths and weaknesses.

Assets

One general approach is to consider asset protection as inherent in the composition of the mortgage portfolio. However, many of the pools of mortgages can include low- and middle-class houses in marginal areas or neighborhoods that are, or have been, on the decline. Thus much of the analysis of asset protection focuses on both the primary and secondary tiers of insurance, on supplemental insurance policies, and on mortgage reserve funds that are built up from cash. In a general recession, these two approaches are used to determine the kinds of storms the bonds can weather and the kind of protection they have—either to prevent default or to fall back upon in case the prices of houses should deflate.

Federal insurance and guarantees are regarded as affording the strongest protection; with the different types of private insurance, the quality of the insurance company must be considered. The financial strength of the private insurance companies varies widely, and the company providing the insurance may have an impact on the bond rating.

Reserve funds are another source of protection. Unlike insurance that affords protection against loss of principal, such as from default, the reserves are designed to protect against temporary cash shortfalls, such as from delinquency in mortgage payments or delays in the payment of insurance claims.

The amounts and types of insurance and reserves are determined by the characteristics of the issue. The more marginal the neighborhood in which the housing is being built and the lower the median income of those who will own the houses, the greater the need for stronger and greater numbers of reserve funds and backup forms of insurance. It is necessary to consider the extent to which this pool of mortgages has a delinquency and foreclosure rate, whether it is higher or lower than the national average, and whether it is trending up or down. In established mortgage purchase programs for single-family homes, the track record of the portfolio is important. The larger the contribution of equity in the front end by the mortgagor, the better the performance. If the portfolio is restricted to 20 percent equity and 80 percent loan/value ratio, this is good protection for that pool of mortgages. In contrast, if the equity is only 5 percent and the loan/value ratio is 95 percent, this will be a negative factor.

Bond analysts and investors must weigh the different techniques of evaluating asset protection to see which is most appropriate for a given portfolio. While insurance, reserve funds, and real estate value can each be viewed separately, it may be helpful to consider their support of each other. It is not just the amount of insurance that is important but the type, range, and protection offered.

The types of insurance used for housing revenue bonds can be divided into three broad categories: (1) *credit* insurance against losses stemming from default by the mortgagor, such as FHA or private mortgage insurance; (2) *hazard* insurance, such as fire or storm coverage, which protects against various natural and people-made disasters; and (3) *performance* insurance against nonperformance, omission, or fraud on the part of an agent or contractor.

Since the various policies are quite specific as to what situations are covered and the amounts of protection afforded, and since payment may be contingent upon or interrelated with the payment of another policy, the result is a complex multidimensional web that must be closely examined.

For example, the following insurance coverage will be found in many single-family programs: Each mortgagor's property is protected by a normal homeowner's policy, the individual mortgages are insured by a federal agency or private firm, and the mortgage portfolio is also insured against losses stemming from default. Payment on the portfolio insurance policy is made after payment on the individual insurance policy, and both the individual and portfolio insurance policies generally stipulate that if there has been a hazard loss, the property must be repaired with the hazard insurance proceeds before payment can be made on a default claim. Some hazards, such as earthquakes, are not covered by normal homeowners' policies. Therefore, if an earthquake destroyed a property in the portfolio and the mortgagor defaulted on the payment of the mortgage, unless there is supplemental protection, there would be no insurance coverage. Therefore, the supplemental, or special hazard, policy was introduced to cover such situations.

Cash Flow

The most difficult and complicated part of the credit analysis for mortgage purchase bonds is estimating the cash flow over the life of the bonds. The cash flow for housing bonds is structured in a fundamentally distinct way. While public power bonds or water and sewer bonds have a relatively stable cash flow, the cash flow of housing bonds is difficult to predict. This difficulty stems from the uncertainty as to when, if, or in what numbers homeowners will decide to prepay their mortgages.

It is uncertain to what extent management will have to tap those prepayments for cash flows, or exactly which funds will be available to pay all expenses. In contrast to simply running out trend lines, which is the practice for evaluating electric utility bonds and most other bonds, the analysis of housing bonds depends upon what are chosen as the basic assumptions. These assumptions include what the mortgage repayment schedule will be, what the bond repayment schedule should look like, and what the amortization on a monthly basis is going to be. From each of these assumptions the analyst estimates what the spread between the mortgage repayments and bond repayments will be (and thus the income from interest and arbitrage) and what the expenses and servicing fees will total. Although this figuring is now performed by bond analysis on calculators and computers, it is still a complex operation. It is made more complicated by the need to go through different models, or scenarios, of what would happen if a certain percentage of the mortgages were prepaid, or terminated, prior to the scheduled maturity date.

In general, the prepayments are tracked to the history of mortgages insured according to Section 203 of the Federal Housing Act. It has been found that mortgages are prepaid more often between the second and fifth years; the peak, for example, comes in the third year. From the FHA, which keeps detailed statistics on early terminations due to defaults or sales of houses as homeowners move, bond analysts develop their assumptions about how likely the prepayment of mortgages is.

The average life of mortgages has been decreasing substantially. Within the last 25 years it has decreased from 12 years to approximately 8 years. This means that an ever-increasing number of homeowners are prepaying very early, and thus a very large turnover in mortgage portfolios is taking place. Usually, the prepayment estimate is stated as a fixed percentage of the FHA's experience: 75 percent of FHA is a figure commonly used by many analysts. The FHA average tends to be a very conservative number, and so if the average goes below that 75 percent, the investor or analyst can be comfortable.

The simplest way to structure the analyses is to assume *no* prepayment of mortgages whatsoever. However, this approach fails to take into consideration the actual life of the mortgages. The actual life will, in all likelihood, be much shorter than the nominal life based on the scheduled amortization. The problem with this approach is that the market prices from the average life of the bonds outstanding are based upon the term and serial maturity, and this would result in a higher interest differential on these bonds. If only the printed schedule of bond maturities is used and if it is assumed that only a fixed amount of the principal payments will be coming in on the mortgages on the basis of the scheduled amortization, the average life will tend to look longer than it actually is.

The other approach is to assume that a certain number of mortgages will be prepaid and to assume further that this additional cash flow above scheduled amortization will be available to pay debt service. The serial (short-term) maturities can then be increased and the term (long-term) maturities decreased. This will shorten the average life of the bonds and therefore decrease the interest rate.

Either one of these two prepayment assumptions can result in very real problems. If principal repayments come in behind schedule, the housing agency may simply not have enough cash to pay on the bonds when they mature. Such a shortfall can lead to default. Alternatively, the housing agency might dip into its reserves, miss an interest payment, or in various other ways find itself limited. For example, if an agency has to liquidate a debt service reserve fund, it may have its interest earnings reduced, and this leads to many other complications.

However, if the bond structure is based on an assumption of no prepayments, then another problem develops, for if the mortgage is, in fact, prepayed, the assumed earnings are lost and are not available to repay nonasset bonds, which are used to pay the cost of bond issuance and other expenses. In the simplest terms, there is a double-edged sword: If very conservative prepayment assumptions are made, a problem might arise if prepayments come in too early; and if they come in too late, the necessary cash may not be available. One typical problem is that if prepayments come in too early during a period of low interest rates, the managers are not able to reinvest them at an interest rate high enough to cover the remaining expenses on the bonds.

Historically, this variation in prepayments and its sensitivity to a whole host of different factors usually lead to conservative assumptions by many analysts. Most bond analysts test all the cash flow assumptions that have been worked out in detail by the independent financial advisers of the bond issuers. Any municipal issuer who moves very far from the 75-percent-of-FHA prepayment experience by assuming heavy prepayment is seriously questioned. As a result, wherever actual prepayments or projections run decidedly behind or far ahead of the schedule of the assumed levels, investors should be wary.

Finally, the demand for mortgage money at the moment can be a crucial factor in assessing the cash flow and asset value of a particular set of bonds backed by a particular pool of mortgages. Also, the level of commitment fees and liquidated damages, which are used to assure timely delivery of new mortgages, is considered an extra check of cash flow.

Management

The requirements for management capability vary among all four types of housing finance programs. For example, loans to lenders can be run by one person, really, for all that is necessary is to obtain a few certifications at the end of the year. The bonds are fully collateralized, and therefore if anything goes wrong, the trustee bank just turns to the portfolio and liquidates part or all of the collateral to satisfy whatever emergency financial claims are presented.

The management of a mortgage purchase program for single-family homes, in contrast, requires a more sophisticated approach. This requirement is especially valid today because of the greater difficulty in first projecting the cash flow and then managing it each period despite the uncertain conditions of early or late schedules of mortgage prepayment.

When the management of the housing agency is dealing with multi-family housing, whether under direct loan programs or under Section 8-11(b) programs, that management's capability becomes critical in importance to the real creditworthiness of the bonds. This is because the managers of multifamily agencies are really acting almost as bankers, making the loans, no longer just as distant financial intermediaries. The agency, itself, is to be managing the mortgage portfolios and overseeing the management of the projects for 40 years. The housing agency does not usually manage the properties directly. It only monitors. Only if the private management company is removed does the housing agency get directly involved in management.

In general, if the mortgage prepayment is at a rate less than anticipated for single-family issues, then an inexperienced management of a housing agency can find itself in difficulties in handling its cash flow. Therefore, month-to-month monitoring of its position is of crucial importance, and a very experienced and capable group of managers is required. In multifamily portfolios the management is directly in the real estate business. It must review plans, construction loans, rentals, etc. For multifamily direct loan programs, the housing agency managers must have sufficient management oversight and control over architectural design, construction engineering, legal problems, and permits and must have sophisticated financial staffs that are used to dealing with federal and state government bureaucracies.

Today the caliber of management varies greatly among the approximately 40 different state housing finance agencies. It ranges even more among the local housing agencies. Investors should therefore be well aware of whether the housing program that administers their bonds is run by a management tending to one of these extremes or the other. The origin of mortgages, their servicing, and period-by-period cash flow management vary enormously from one program to the next.

If, as in most cases, housing portfolios of single-family issues have several lending institutions acting as servicers of the mortgages, then bond analysts are particularly anxious about seeing that a clear mechanism exists for coordinating the different lenders, making sure that lenders meet their contractual obligations, and keeping the cash flows in order.

The Section 8 Subsidy Program

Since 1937 we have seen about 40 federal housing programs encompassing a dizzying array of names and numbers. Nevertheless, the U.S. Housing Act of 1937 remains America's basic piece of housing legislation. The Section 8 amendment to this act was a primary housing assistance program for low- and moderate-income families. Although the program has been phased out by the government, there are enough of these bonds traded in the secondary market to warrant our attention.

The Section 8 program evolved from and replaced many earlier programs: the Section 221(d) and Section 236 interest-subsidy programs, the rent supplement program, and the Section 23 leased housing program.

Section 8's most widely used predecessor program was Section 236, a program introduced in the late 1960s when interest rates were considered by the federal government to be too high and were thought to be discouraging housing production. Thus the government decided to introduce a program to subsidize interest rates to 1 percent. (Later this was increased to 3 percent.) This subsidy yielded a tremendous cash flow and gave the housing market an initial benefit. However, inflation and increasing operating costs hit the program very hard, and because it was a fixed subsidy program, its directors ultimately had to raise rents in order to cover these new expenses. The result was that the administrators of the program came to tread a very fine line between failing to cover increasing costs and raising rents so high that it would force out people or cause rent strikes. One reason Section 236 was a fixed subsidy was that its designers had assumed that tenants' incomes would rise roughly at the rate of inflation and thus cover all expenses. This assumption was incorrect, and many problems ensued because Section 236 was so inflexible.

Out of the experience of the difficulties of Section 236 was developed the new Section 8 program under the Housing and Community Development Act of 1974 to ensure that if expenses increased faster than tenants' incomes, the federal rent subsidies would increase correspondingly. Yet it also provided that if the tenants' incomes increased more than the rate of inflation, the tenants would not automatically be relieved of their apartments because they no longer qualified for residence on the grounds of narrowly limited income. Section 8 is thus a very flexible subsidy which moves with the tenants' incomes and which increases with inflation. It is also a very comprehensive subsidy covering all the costs associated with projects' operating costs as well as debt service costs.

The Section 8 subsidy functions in the following manner: It is the difference between a government-approved contract rent (which cannot exceed a published fair-market rent for the area) and what a tenant can afford. For example, if the rent is $400 per month and the tenant can only pay $100 as 25 percent of his or her monthly salary, then the government pays the difference ($300) as part of a contract that is guaranteed for a 20- to 40-year period. If the tenant had no income, then the federal government would pay the full rent, i.e., $400 per month. Although the tenant is required to pay somewhere between 15 and 25 percent of family income, this amount is usually 25 percent, except under special circumstances. Indeed, the experience to date is that the federal government ends up paying about 70 percent of the contract rents in a given project. Under Section 8 the lowest 40 percent of the U.S. population is always eligible for the program, and therefore it will not become inoperative if inflation pushes everyone into higher-income brackets.

While there are many undoubted advantages of Section 8 programs over their predecessors, there are some problems that they present to the investor and the bond analyst as far as credit evaluation is concerned. First and most important, the Department of Housing and Urban Development (HUD), which administers Section 8, retains the right to withdraw the subsidy from a project under certain circumstances. If a project experiences extended vacancies or if the units, for whatever reason, do not meet HUD's standards for "safe and sanitary housing" (the guidelines are very specific), then HUD retains the right to determine whether it will continue the subsidy. Because HUD retains this right, investors and bond analysts must examine each new project on its own merits.

The second primary reason for the need to examine the credit of these projects is the great range of differences in the projects themselves: their caliber of managers, their reserves, forms of insurance and legal protections for the bondholder, the cost estimates, the strength of the trust indenture, the site of the project, and the demand of people to live in it.

Obviously, if a project is to be located next to a swamp, a slum, a dump, heavy industry, or an airport, there will be questions raised about the habitability of the units. However, the demand for housing today is so strong because of the scarcity of rentable units that it is easy to mistake the present circumstances for a permanent demand throughout the 20- to 40-year life of the bonds. Such long-term demand may well not occur, and so each project's individual characteristics must be assessed. Alternative housing must be taken into account, as should be the probability of a scarcity or an overabundance of future rentable units in an area. Vacancy of rental units is the major concern here, despite the partial government guarantees of backup support. This concern is great because HUD retains the right to terminate subsidies if the vacancies last longer than 1 year. However, HUD does guarantee 80 percent of the contract rent for the first 60 days of vacancy and also guarantees to pay debt service on that vacant rental unit for a whole year after that.

Therefore, in addition to its flexibility, the Section 8 program offers certain extra guarantees and special features to avoid the problems and inadequacies of Section 236 and earlier programs. The financial community has come to regard Section 8 as a strong program, especially because of this flexibility and collection of extra guarantees. It is concerned not with public housing in the old-fashioned way but mainly with privately owned property, usually with equity syndication. That is to say, although these projects are issued by state or local governmental authorities, they can be owned by private owners or nonprofit organizations.

For the Section 8 programs administered by state housing finance agencies, the fair-market rents are established by HUD, which sets rents for a whole variety of market areas throughout the country and which designates what rent is acceptable for each type of unit. During the life of the bond contract, the total of collected rent is kept in a reserve that HUD can use for adjustments in its subsidy allotments and for increasing operating expenses (should that become necessary). HUD, according to its regulations, is required to adjust annually the contract rents, and the state agencies can apply for hardship increases for taxes, fuel, etc., to hasten other rent adjustments.

Section 8-11(b)

Section 8-11(b) provides for 100 percent of the financing on Section 8 projects and thus can only be used for multifamily apartment buildings. Section 8-11(b) includes an especially broad range of issuers that come, in general, under the heading of public housing agencies but include cities, districts, and nonprofit corporations.

Section 8-11(b) financings essentially deal with an independent source of tax exemption from the Internal Revenue Code's famous Section 103. The purpose of Section 8-11(b) is quite specific and should not be confused with other programs or tax exemptions. Under Section 8-11(b), bonds must be for permanent financing, while short-term notes can be for construction financing. The bond proceeds can be used to cover the development cost of a project, 1-year debt service, capitalized interest (which is usually the negative arbitrage of the issuing body during the construction period), and expenses of issuance.

Section 8-11(b) financings appear in many forms: (1) insured projects of the FHA; (2) projects guaranteed by some government, government agency, or authority; (3) uninsured financings; and (4) financings that are really tax-exempt mortgages and not tax-exempt bonds at all. There are many subdivisions within each of these categories relating to the different ways of structuring both the mortgages and the cash flow.

Once again, those issues with federal insurance are considered by far the strongest credits; those issues which have some other government guarantee are the next strongest; and so forth. These bonds are backed in a variety of other forms. And some states virtually issue a GO bond whose proceeds are deposited into an insurance fund that can issue mortgages.

HUD regulates these Section 8-11(b) bonds rather tightly and has successively stiffened its rules on fees, interest rates that will be paid, and arbitrage profits that will be permitted. These restrictions and many others placed by HUD are argued by numerous critics to be far too restrictive: they make projects unnecessarily difficult, if not impossible, to undertake. Most uninsured financings of Section 8-11(b) were originally undertaken as private placements. These placements tended to have considerably higher yields and originally went unrated. Today there has been a move to attempt to secure a rating for them and to sell them publicly.

Because these projects, whether publicly or privately owned and whether insured or uninsured, must be financed entirely within the budget of the contract rent, it is important to assess whether the financial feasibility study appears reasonable. Therefore, it is important that the local housing authority, which issued the bonds in the first place, be strong enough financially, sufficiently well managed, and permanent enough to carry the ultimate responsibility for the specific housing projects and for the payment on the bonds' principal and interest "in a timely fashion."

Legal Protections

Legal protections are in some ways more important for housing bonds than for many other types because of their complexity and sometimes profit-generating nature. Legal protections must include a debt service reserve fund equal to or greater than the maximum annual debt service. The underlying security should be a gross revenue pledge (not restricted), and before including interest income or other nonrental revenue, the rents alone should be sufficient for paying debt service, maintenance, and operating expenses. All taxes, insurance premiums, and fuel and electrical bills should be paid out of escrow accounts to ensure that funds are available on time to pay all such vitally important bills.

Although FHA insurance for Section 8-11(b) projects covers 99 percent of the principal amount outstanding on the mortgage, investors must be alert to the following problem: Not only is the remaining 1 percent not federally insured, but other expenses, for costs of issuing the bonds and for accrued interest on the bonds, may not be covered. Therefore, the issuer should make it very clear that other insurance, reserve funds, or backing (in the form of letters of credit, government securities, or a separate issue of subordinate debentures) has been specifically set up and allocated to take care of what is commonly known as "the shortfall." It is obviously important that such reserves should be tapped only in the case of a mortgage default to pay off the bonds and to prevent their being used up in advance of a mortgage default. For this reason, both these reserves and the reserve for debt service should be accompanied by a guarantee that the funds will always be maintained at full value, in case of any sudden need at any time in the future.

Indentures: Closed-End versus Open-End

One of the most important provisions of the trust indenture, or resolution, in a housing revenue bond is whether or not additional mortgages can be added to the portfolio, either through the issuance of an additional series of bonds or through the purchase of new mortgages (with the proceeds of mortgages that have been prepaid). Those resolutions which prohibit the issuance of additional bonds and which restrict the use of prepayments to the early retirement of bonds are called *closed-end*, and those resolutions which allow the addition of mortgages to the portfolio are called *open-end*. Each type has its advantages and disadvantages and is better suited to different applications.

The advantage of the open-end approach is that the portfolio may be strengthened. As new mortgages are added, the portfolio grows and becomes more geographically diverse, and the impact of the default of one mortgage is lessened. The disadvantage of the open-end indenture, or resolution, is that instead of its being strengthened, the portfolio may be weakened or diluted at a later date by poor underwriting decisions or management.

The advantage of the closed-end approach, therefore, is that the quality and composition of the portfolio is fixed: "What you see is what you get." To many investors, this is comforting, and to the analysts, the portfolio and cash flow are more susceptible to analysis. To some, another appealing characteristic of closed-end programs is that they are less complex in structure. For example, in single-family issues, the cash flow of closed-end indentures, or resolutions, is greatly simplified by the application of prepayments to the retirement of bonds and the prohibition on the issuance of new bonds. Open-end programs, with their changing interest rates and maturities on mortgages purchased with prepayments or new bonds, have a complexity that calls for a sophisticated, computer-assisted, and ongoing management capability.

The choice between these two approaches is, to an extent, a subjective one. There are, however, certain considerations and caveats in approaching this choice. For example, the use of an open-end approach is better suited to issuers with an ongoing program and a staff, such as state housing finance agencies. Issuers who envision a onetime or infrequent issuance or who have limited or nonexistent staffing capabilities and rely on outside administrators are better suited to closed-end indentures, or resolutions. Some investment bankers, credit analysts, investors, and issuers also feel that closed-end indentures, or resolutions, are better suited to multifamily programs, in which the quality of the mortgages in the portfolio is more important than the quantity. However, single-family programs may be better suited to the open-end approach: These issues are approached more on a quantitative, or "actuarial," basis, and the size of the portfolio itself is a factor to consider.

Because of the complexity in the open-end indentures, single-family programs, which typically allow reinvestment of prepayments on the mortgages, require sophisticated managers at the housing agency. Under an open-end indenture, the agency can issue subsequent series of bonds, so investors have to worry about the effect of the new bond issues upon the security of their prior bonds. Investors or bond analysts must consider whether an agency's management has the expertise to determine short- and long-range cash flow patterns.

In the case of an open-end indenture, therefore, it is important that the housing agency's staff has a proven track record of cash flow management and has shown itself able to use a considerable degree of discretion in making decisions on the reinvestment of prepayments. Since many housing agency managers originate from savings and loan institutions or mortgage banking backgrounds, it is also important to gauge whether the housing agency's staff is large enough and sophisticated enough to test its different cash flow assumptions and projections on a computer.

The Section 8-11(b) issues have generally been structured with closed-end indentures. Since these issues also generally involve only one housing project, which is the only source of revenue to pay off the bonds, the rating agencies and investors look to a feasibility study to provide information on the quality of this very limited "portfolio."

The financial feasibility study for closed-end financings of Section 8-11(b) issues should be prepared by a reputable and nationally known independent firm. In the case of real estate ventures, such as these, the financial feasibility study should forecast 2 years of operations of the project once it is built. The forecast should include all reserves and their funding, the working capital for covering debt service, specific projected balance sheets, income statements, and flow-of-funds statements. If available, the feasibility study should include a market study of future levels of occupancy, "rent up," and, in general, the forecasted demand and rate of delinquency. If no feasibility study has been made, or if the issuing public authority refuses to make a study available, such conduct should tell the investor something about the management and, in many cases, discourage investment in the bonds.

Moral Obligation Bonds

We have already mentioned moral obligation bonds in various parts of this book. We touch on them again because they are a particularly important factor in the housing bond market.

Moral obligation bonds are not backed by a state government's full faith and credit or its taxing power, as are that same state's GO bonds. Nevertheless, moral obligation bonds have a kind of pledge of support from the state government in case the bonds default. While there are, by now, a number of different specific types in different states, the general concept of moral obligation bonds remains the same as at their inception; that is, moral obligation bonds were issued as a way to get around the tightening restrictions by taxpayers and legislators on issuing debt requiring voter approval and full faith and credit and taxing power guarantees. In brief, they enabled many states to issue debt to finance projects; under traditional financing schemes they would have been prohibited by law. A dispute still continues concerning the merits of moral obligation bonds. Some claim that the bonds are a vitally important financing vehicle, that they enable states to expand their debt capacity for necessary programs and avoid the constraints of archaic laws and restrictions. Others argue against the continuance of the moral obligation bonds because they commit citizens to vast extra-debt obligations without allowing the citizens the right of voter approval.

The unfortunate notoriety of the financing of moral obligation bonds, which occurred when the New York Urban Development Corporation (UDC) defaulted, brought this whole question under public scrutiny. (In fact, UDC's notes had not received the moral obligation pledge of support from the state; only the UDC bonds had.) New York State did make good on the defaulted notes, which suggested that the state was trying to protect the moral obligation bonds and thereby to maintain its own access to the municipal bond market. The state's making good also indicated that the state recognized these bonds as having a public purpose, namely, the building of housing and other projects. Meeting the bond payments further indicated that the legislature had the authority to make state appropriations in that way and, indeed, that these bonds could be considered an integral part of state government finance. Not only have state governments in various instances backed up moral obligation issues when they were required to, but they have also done so well in advance of when they had to—and at times when there was not even a moral obligation pledge.

Certain analysts have reached a kind of standing policy with respect to rating moral obligation bonds, declaring that they will rate them one full category below that same state's GO bonds. This provides a floor, and, in a few cases, the underlying strength of a portfolio behind a bond has led them even to rate moral obligation bonds a bit higher than the one full category below the GO bonds.

Local Mortgage Bonds for Single-Family Housing

The Residential Mortgage Subsidy Bond Act of 1980 placed certain restrictions on single-family financings, and this type of financing will be limited in the future. In any event, local issues attempted to take advantage of recent financing structures in the private sector, where pass-through securities and mortgage-backed bonds had become familiar. The pass-through securities, which are not bonds, were employed, for example, in the use of a portfolio of mortgages to back up a bond.

Local housing financing was used to take this structure of the pass-through certificate and graft onto it the mortgage purchase program, which had been used for many years in the municipal bond field of financing. By taking advantage of the tax-exempt feature, the interest rate was a considerable advantage and offered the opportunity to arbitrage the spread between the mortgage payments and the bond payments. It thus provided a greater flexibility in the issuers' cash flow and provided a larger market of investors to interest in these new types of bonds. By grafting these two types of securities together, the investors had created a stronger security than is usually seen in the tax-exempt market. This strength was derived from the additional security provided by the structured insurance program (including the primary mortgage insurance, pool insurance, and hazard and loss types of insurance), from the specific restrictions on the portfolio used in the closed-end indenture, from the prohibition against prepayments of the mortgage, and from mortgage reserve funds and debt service reserves. Finally, all this security was placed in back of a pass-through certificate type of financing with the very important advantages of an interest rate spread that offered clear opportunities for arbitrage and a strong cash flow. It was the familiar mortgage purchase program from the municipal housing revenue bonds market but dressed up with very strong and very attractive features. It was little wonder that the early issues created a new financing wave that would spread rapidly throughout the country.

Case Studies
The Ohio Housing Finance Agency: Single-Family Mortgage Revenue Bonds*

The Ohio Housing Finance Agency was created for the purpose of providing financing to acquire, construct, rehabilitate, or improve owner-occupied single-family housing and multiunit housing. The bonds of this issue were to provide funds for qualified persons to purchase or rehabilitate 1- to 4-unit owner-occupied residences through the purchase by the agency of mortgage loans made to such persons. Commitments were entered into by the agency to purchase mortgage loans from qualified mortgage lenders in a certain amount at a set interest rate. Each lender would service its own mortgage loans or assign the servicing function to another qualified lender or the administrator. Each mortgage loan would be for no more than 70 percent of the lesser of the sales price or the original appraised value of the residence, but the ratio could be higher for mortgage loans insured by private mortgage insurance or by the FHA or guaranteed by the VA. With mortgage insurance or guarantees, the loan/value ratio could be increased up to 95 percent, and such insurance was required to remain in force until the mortgage loan was reduced to 62 percent of the lesser of the sales price or the original appraised value of the related residence.

Each mortgagor was required to maintain standard hazard insurance providing fire and extended coverage, and in certain areas flood insurance was mandatory. There was a mortgage pool insurance policy issued by the Mortgage Guarantee Insurance Company (MGIC) that provided secondary coverage against mortgagor defaults up to a certain limitation. The pool insurance policy provided that payments would be made to the agency on mortgage loans that were two or more payments delinquent under certain circumstances. In addition, there was a special hazard insurance policy that provided secondary coverage against physical damage to the residences, subject to limitations.

The foreclosure and delinquency rates of three similar programs issued by the agency were as follows: Delinquencies of 30 days or more averaged approximately 3.0 to 3.7 percent of the total number of loans, delinquencies

---

* Data from Official Statement of $62,000,000 Ohio Housing Finance Agency, Single-Family Mortgage Revenue Bonds, Series C, dated September 15, 1985.

of 60 days or more averaged 0.64 to 0.91 percent of the number of loans, and loans 90 days or more delinquent represented 0.44 to 0.56 percent of the total number of loans for the comparable programs. Foreclosure rates ran from 0.12 to 1.1 percent of the loans provided by similar programs of the agency.

The Florida Housing Finance Agency: Multi-Family Housing Revenue Bonds*

The proceeds of this bond issue were to provide the agency with funds to make loans for the construction and permanent financing of four multifamily housing developments to be occupied by persons or families of low, moderate, and middle income. Each property was to be owned, managed, and operated as a residential rental project. At least 20 percent of each development's units were to be occupied by individuals of low or moderate income. Each indenture for bond issues of the four projects provided funds to finance a mortgage loan from the agency to a limited partnership in Florida in order to provide financing for the acquisition, construction, and equipping of a multifamily residential development. The loan agreement provided that the developer should make payments sufficient to pay the principal and interest on the bonds, together with certain expenses. The payments were secured by a mortgage and security agreement, and the agency assigned its interest in the mortgage to the trustee as security for the bonds, with the exception of the agency's right to foreclose the mortgage, among other rights remedies. The four projects were expected to have 45 buildings with 1118 units. Construction for each project was estimated to be completed at different times from mid-1987 to the early part of 1988.

* Data from Official Statement of $58,145,000 Florida Housing Finance Agency, Multi-Family Bonds, $13,660,000 1985 Series LL (Village Place Project), $21,170,000 1985 Series MM (Buena Vista Project), $5,750,000 1985 Series NN (South Pointe Project), $17,565,000 1985 Series OO (Oaks at Mill Creek Project), dated November 20, 1985.

9
Hospital Bonds

The American health care services industry has seen phenomenal growth over the last two decades. The great increases in the provision of health services and the cost of such services have been fueled by three interrelated events. The first was the rapid improvement in the quality of health service provided most Americans through new medical technology, more effective drugs, and the advent of advanced medical diagnostic and treatment techniques. At the same time, spiraling inflation and a dramatic rise in construction costs nationwide made up-to-date hospital equipment and modernization programs exceedingly expensive. These two events fostered the growth of health insurance plans, both governmental and nongovernmental, forcing hospitals to rely to a great extent on reimbursement for health costs from third parties. As a consequence of these events, hospitals were forced to move from financing their operations largely through charitable contributions and internally generated funds to financing them through the issuance of debt. Almost 80 percent of all such debt was issued through municipal bonds.

With this deluge of municipal bonds issued for hospitals came a new but relatively untraditional type of revenue bond to analyze. Indeed, the evaluation of hospital bonds has aspects that are truly unique to the field of revenue bond analysis in three highly significant and visible areas. First of all, unlike traditional revenue-type enterprises, hospitals recover the vast majority of their costs through insurers or third parties whose policies for reimbursement are, in many cases, government-regulated and subject to change by federal and state authorities and by private and commercial insurers. Second, hospitals are, by their very nature, more like corporate enterprises than are most other projects employing revenue bonds, and as a result, ratio analysis plays a somewhat larger role than with most other bonds. Finally, with a hospital as a corporate-type enterprise, its management and trustees assume a significant role in the enterprise, and their relations with the medical staff and health care professionals are of prime importance. To be sure, hospitals do not occupy the monopoly-type role that other revenue enterprises do, and thus employer-employee relations are more critical in attracting staff and, in turn, patients. Furthermore, the dynamics of these relations and the quality of management and staff are more easily determined because feasibility consultants spend significant amounts of time garnering this data, and it very often is contained in the bond issue's official statement.

Hospital Financing Vehicles

Municipal bonds are issued by all different types of health care facilities and are monitored in certain ways by surrounding governments. State and municipal hospitals and nonprofit hospitals are the largest issuers of municipal hospital bonds. Almost 50 percent of all hospitals in the United States are organized by nonprofit, religious, or voluntary organizations, and these organizations may issue municipal hospital bonds. Such municipal hospital bonds are issued through or by states, state agencies, local governments of general jurisdiction, municipal hospitals, health care authorities, or nonprofit corporations under Internal Revenue Service guidelines.

Other hospitals, such as those run by the federal government, do not finance their facilities through the issuance of municipal bonds, and private proprietary hospitals can only issue up to $10 million in municipal bonds.

A major part of the process of issuing municipal hospital bonds is the *certificate-of-need* process. The certificate is required by the National Health Planning and Resources Development Act of 1974 as well as by third-party reimbursers. Issued by states, local health systems agencies, or other planning boards, the certificate of need generally provides some assurance that the geographic service area will not be overbedded. Consultants are often employed by the hospital to help it through the certificate-of-need process.

Lease and Loan Agreements

For a period of time, most hospitals issued bonds via leasing arrangements with the issuing entity. Today, the loan method of financing is the one generally employed by hospitals. Payments made by the hospital under both financing mechanisms are approximately equivalent to bond principal and interest payments and are structured to pay such payments as they come due.

Lease Financing

In a straight lease arrangement, the hospital is bought by the issuer with the bond proceeds, and then the facility is leased to the hospital organization. Another leasing arrangement allows the hospital to be leased to the issuer, and then the facility is subleased back to the hospital. Under both arrangements, the hospital supplies an unconditional guarantee for the lease payments. Lease financing includes a transfer of title.

Loan Financing

This type of financing involves loan payments made by the hospital to the issuer in return for bond proceed monies. Additional security for the loan is a mortgage on the facilities, on which the trustee can foreclose in the event of default. The value of a hospital as an asset in the event of default is questionable, but at least the mortgage on the facilities prevents establishing other senior liens.

Third-Party Reimbursement

With spiraling increases in health care costs and increased reliance on outside financing sources, hospitals have been forced to depend on third-party reimbursements for their financial livelihood. Today, approximately 90 percent of the revenues of most hospitals come from such reimbursement programs, including private health insurance, Blue Cross, Medicare, and Medicaid. Commercial insurance is an important source of reimbursement revenue for many hospitals, but the program has large differences in coverage, rates, and reimbursement formulas. Blue Cross reimbursement plans pay anywhere from full charges to cost-of-service expenses. Federal government reimbursements to hospitals come from two programs: Medicare and Medicaid.

Medicare and Medicaid were created by Title XVIII and Title XIX of the Social Security Act. Medicare is a program of the federal government that provides health insurance to the elderly and to certain disabled individuals. Medicaid is both a federal and state health program that benefits persons of low income. In the past, payments from these programs covered the cost of care plus the reimbursement of interest payments and depreciation. Today they would cover less than the general total cost. Both programs are undergoing changes that will alter the way reimbursement is made to hospitals. Under the Tax, Equity, and Fiscal Responsibility Act of 1982 (TEFRA), Medicare payments by late 1986 will be related only to the patient's diagnosis and treatment, and such payments will no longer take into account hospital costs. Since 1982, the federal government has also decreased the amount of monies provided to states for Medicaid payments. States must therefore provide enough support for patient treatment or certain hospitals will be under increased financial pressure. Complicating matters is the fact that each state approaches this problem somewhat differently.

The Credit Analysis of Hospital Bonds

As noted at the beginning of this chapter, the credit analysis of hospital bonds is unique in three areas. The first has to do with the fact that hospitals depend in large part on third-party reimbursements for revenues. Second, because of the nature of a hospital as a corporate-type entity, ratio analysis is somewhat more important with hospitals than with other revenue-type enterprises. Finally, it is to some extent easier and more important than with other revenue enterprises to discern the ability of the hospital's management and directors and their relationships to the major employees in the hospital itself, such as doctors and administrators. It should also be noted that hospitals generally carry lower ratings than do most other revenue bonds taken as a group. Those with lesser ability to get to the market sometimes receive insurance through the FHA. Nevertheless, three general categories are as important in the analysis of hospital bonds as they are in the analysis of other revenue bonds: (1) the demand for the hospital, (2) its financial operations, and (3) the legal provisions that secure the bonds. An additional category has to do with an analysis of the hospital generally and of its staff, its management, and the services it provides. Most of this information is used in the projections made by the feasibility consultants; as a result, it is appropriate to discuss the hospital after the demand evaluation, but before the financial analysis area.

Demand for the Hospital

Critical to the security of hospital bonds is the requirement that there be a demand for the facility or for its enlargement in the service area. Unlike other revenue bond projects, hospitals do not occupy a monopoly over a given area, so it is very important that the competitiveness of the hospital be analyzed in relation to other facilities in the service area that compete for the same group of patients. Usually, the feasibility study breaks down the hospital's service area into two parts: (1) the primary service area from which the large majority of patients are drawn for the hospital and (2) the secondary service area which provides additional patients to the hospital and which may overlap the service areas of other hospitals. A comparative analysis should be made of projected expansions by other hospitals, especially when they involve increases in beds and additions of specialty areas. This is sometimes done through a study of the certificates of need that are in process. An analysis of the cost of service among various hospitals in the service area should be made, principally among those hospitals located in the primary service area of the hospital under study. In a larger sense, a general demographic trend should be discerned in the hospital's service area, including both historical and projected increases in population, industrial growth, commercial expansion, and employment. What analysts and investors should look for is at least a stable situation; that is, the hospital should have a history of attracting patients, which would subsequently lead to a high occupancy rate at the hospital, and the growth of other hospitals in the service area should be modest. To be sure, the hospital must have maintained its market share of patients and must be projected to do so. Expansions of other hospitals, especially in services in which the hospital under study specializes, are viewed negatively. A rise in the hopital's costs relative to other hospitals in the area is also seen as a potential difficulty. It should be stressed that the demand study in the case of hospitals is very important because of the geographic diversity of service areas and the inability to control or force patients to enter a hospital and pay for its services.

The Hospital Itself

A study of the hospital itself should generally cover three categories: (1) the historical and projected trends of inpatient utilization, (2) the medical staff and hospital administration, and (3) the reimbursement procedures of the hospital and the forecasted number of patients of each reimbursement category.

An analysis should be made of the historical and projected trends of inpatient utilization of the hospital, as well as of its competition, in the areas in which the hospital offers a significant amount of services. Usually these include medical-surgical areas, pediatrics, and psychiatric units. The analysis for each area should include beds in service, admissions, and average length of stay. Absolutely critical to the evaluation is the percentage of occupancy for all these areas, both historical and projected. Occupancy rates that have been known to be very positive have been in the range of 95 percent. Very often hospital bond issues pay for modernization programs which will decrease the number of beds that the hospital provides for a single service that has not had a high occupancy and which will increase beds for another service that has had a high occupancy and is projected to have an increased occupancy. This is seen as a revenue-producing measure. Also, the trends in emergency, ancillary, and outpatient services should be monitored.

A study should be done of the medical staff by age, board certification, specialty, and number of admissions. Positive characteristics for a hospital include the following: its medical staff is young, it has a large percentage of board-certified physicians, it has doctors whose specialties are diverse, and not just a few of its doctors account for most of its admissions. There should also be an active physician recruitment program. Very often the medical staff is asked to answer a wide-ranging questionnaire, and the results are often contained in the feasibility study. From these it is relatively easy to determine whether or not the medical staff views the hospital positively and whether there is a good working relationship between the medical staff and management.

An evaluation and analysis should be made of how the hospital is reimbursed from third parties. The percentage, both historical and projected, of Medicare, Medicaid, Blue Cross, commercial insurance, and self-pay should be noted. There should be a diversity of payment and, if possible, a high relative percentage of insurance that is not government-related. An assessment should be made of the ability of the hospital to work with the state in its reimbursement procedures, largely because approximately 90 percent of a hospital's budget has traditionally come from third-party reimbursements. In addition, it is important today for the hospital to have malpractice insurance; generally, the hospital should carry approximately $1 million for each occurrence and somewhere from $3 million to $5 million for the total occurrences for a year. If there are any teaching programs at the hospital, or if it is a teaching hospital, that fact should be discussed in the official statement. Teaching facilities are generally viewed positively because they draw both patients and physicians from areas beyond the hospital's primary and secondary service areas.

Financial Analysis

In general, hospitals usually present their financials for 5 years before the anticipated sale date of the bonds issue and also projected for 5 years thereafter. Included in the financial statements are the balance sheet, statements of changes in financial position, and the statement of changes in the fund balance. Forming the basis of these financial statements are the historical and forecasted revenues and expenditures of the hospital and the net operating income before depreciation, amortization, and interest expense. Usually, net income is not very high because hospitals operate on a cost-based system, but there should not be large, unrecoverable losses. Also, the extent to which a hospital is dependent on nonoperating income should be noted; a hospital should not be too reliant on revenue from this source. Particular note should be taken, in the case of hospitals, of accounts receivable and of the hospital's ability to cover them when they loom large. It is also very important for an analysis to be done of the hospital's cost per bed in private, semiprivate, and intensive care in relation to its competition.

Ratio analysis includes debt service coverage, debt per bed, debt to plant, debt to capitalization, operating margin, and gross revenues as a percentage of net income. Historical debt service coverage is calculated by net income plus depreciation, plus interest expense divided by future maximum annual debt service. In some cases, hospitals could cover their future debt service in this way by $1.0\times$ (times), but this is not usually the case. A more useful measurement may be the debt service coverage ratio on a projected basis, which is equivalent to net income divided by maximum annual debt service, calculated after the project is completed and operating, and the forecast is therefore more reliable. The ratio of debt per bed was used in the past as an important standard of creditworthiness, but because of (1) the high cost of equipment, (2) most hospitals' involvement in a large amount of outpatient facilities, and (3) the skyrocketing costs of modernization, this ratio may not be a useful measurement in today's health care world. The hospital's operating margin is more significant because it consists of gross revenues as a percentage of net income and is considered a measure of a hospital's fundamental ability to earn revenues. Finally, the hospital's ratio of net plant and equipment to long-term debt is considered to be of some importance because it emphasizes balance sheet strength or weakness.

Ratio analysis is only a tool to be used by the analyst. In the case of hospitals, it takes on somewhat greater importance than with certain other revenue bonds because of the corporate-type ongoing nature of a hospital itself. It is not any more important in the analysis of hospital bonds than is the demand for the facility, the legal provisions of the trust indenture, or the capability of management and the hospital staff, and it will not substitute for a careful analysis of the hospital's financials. Nevertheless, an inclusive study of the financial ratios of a hospital, both historical and projected, is important in analyzing this kind of revenue bond.

Legal Provisions

As with most revenue bonds, hospital bonds typically have a series of reserve funds, a rate covenant, a test for additional bonds, and a required minimum debt service coverage. Debt service coverage is usually calculated on a net basis because a hospital must be operating and adequately maintained for it to be a continuing revenue-generating source to pay the interest and principal on its bonds. Rate covenants usually fall between $1.0\times$ and $1.25\times$, but hospitals seeking good investment grade ratings should have debt service coverage well above that ratio.

Unique to hospital bonds is the establishment of a depreciation reserve fund. This reserve fund is a way of ensuring that hospitals have funds on hand in the later years of a bond issue to pay the large amount of principal due. The need occurs because bond issues are generally structured with high interest payments in the earlier years and low interest payments in the later years, with principal payments moving from low to high over the same period of time, much the same as for most home mortgages. Yet third-party payers make payments based on a depreciation schedule's set yearly amount. As a result, there is likely to be a shortfall between the required principal payment and the amount of depreciation expense during the life of the bonds. The depreciation reserve fund is designed to cover that shortfall.

Multihospital Systems

One growing trend in the hospital industry is the emergence of *multihospital systems*, which are groups of hospitals joined together either by management or ownership and using some type of shared financial arrangement or systematic use of services. Just a few years ago, multihospital systems comprised a very small proportion of all hospitals nationwide. Now, however, it seems that the growth of these systems is becoming one of the major trends in health care today, and some analysts predict that the majority of hospitals will be members of multihospital systems within 10 to 15 years. There are approximately 10 major multihospital systems in the United States today. The average number of hospitals per system is about 10, with about 2200 beds in each system. The debt service coverage for most of these systems is approximately 3.0×. A few of the systems carry comparatively high-quality ratings for hospitals.

Multihospital systems possess a number of unusual characteristics that enter into the credit analysis of their bonds. Very often a multihospital system occupies a dominant market share in a given geographic area; this is a signal of strength for the hospital system, all other factors being equal. In other instances there is a certain amount of geographic dispersion of the hospital system's facilities; as a result, the analysis of demand must center on each particular facility and its competitiveness in its given market. Certain multihospital systems have a single large, very strong facility, with other smaller hospitals in the same area or in other geographic areas; in this case an analysis must be done of the strength of the major hospital and of the extent to which it is made either stronger or weaker by the other facilities in the multihospital system. Even when hospitals of a large system are comparable in financial strength, each hospital in the system must be analyzed individually as well as in terms of its impact on the system as a whole. Generally speaking, however, the diversity of facilities and revenue streams offered by multihospital systems is rated as a positive characteristic of such hospitals. Multihospital systems may also have management and companion services that are centralized, such as budgeting, computer operations, and buying supplies on a very large scale; therefore, combining hospitals in groups may allow for consistency in administration and for the streamlining of services to each health care delivery facility.

Hospital Equipment Loan Programs

Over recent years there has been a notable rise in the number of hospital equipment loan programs financed through municipal bonds. Usually a state or some type of public authority within a given geographic area issues bonds, the proceeds of which are loans to a number of hospitals to finance equipment. In almost all cases the hospital is of investment grade quality, or its loan obligations are guaranteed by a third party, such as a financial institution or a bond insurer. The analysis of these bonds usually involves a detailed review of their cash flow. Additionally, there should be a diversity of borrowers, and no single borrower or member of the loan pool should make up a very large percentage of the total payments under the loan agreement.

Intermountain Health Care, Inc., Hospital Bonds*

In the early part of the twentieth century, the Church of Jesus Christ of Latter-Day Saints began the acquisition and construction of hospital facilities in Utah, Idaho, and Wyoming, which were areas that did not have adequate health care facilities. In 1970 the church had 15 hospitals under its jurisdiction, all of which were operated as separate units. At that time the church established the Health Services Corporation, which was a not-for-profit corporation, to operate its hospitals. Four years later, in 1974, the church decided that the operation of hospitals was not an important aspect of its mission and divested itself of the hospitals by creating a board of trustees and renaming the Health Services Corporation as Intermountain Health Care, Inc.

Later, on January 1, 1983, Intermountain Health Care, Inc., was reorganized, and it became the parent company of its not-for-profit hospital corporations and wholly owned-for-profit health care corporations. IHC Hospitals, Inc., comprised 96.4 percent of the total assets of the entire group. Intermountain Health Care, Inc., the parent company, had 2.6 percent of the assets, and the remainder was divided among IHC Affiliated Services, Inc., IHC Professional Services, Inc., IHC Foundation, Inc., and IHC Management, Inc. Each of these entities was created to service a certain portion of the health care industry under the jurisdiction of Intermountain Health Care, Inc.

IHC Hospitals, Inc. IHC operates 23 hospitals within the states of Utah, Idaho, and Wyoming. Of the 23 hospitals, 15 are owned by IHC and comprise 84 percent of all hospital beds in the system. IHC leases two others from county or municipal governments and operates six hospitals through management contracts. All the hospitals in the system are general acute-care hospitals. Primary Children's Medical Center is the exception; it deals primarily with pediatric care in the intermountain western region, which generally includes eastern Nevada, western Colorado, and the states of Utah, Idaho, Wyoming, and Montana. In Utah, hospitals of the system represent 53 percent of all the acute-care hospital beds in the state and 55 percent of all the hospital admissions in the state. Population growth in Utah, Idaho, and Wyoming has averaged about 37 percent, substantially higher than the U.S. average of 9.4 percent.

The issuance of bonds by IHC is accomplished through a master indenture. The master indenture for all the financings has the security provisions and covenants by which IHC must abide. IHC usually issues bonds for each hospital project through the city in which the hospital is located; in turn, the city issuer lends the proceeds to IHC for the construction or renovation of the project in the given city. IHC then provides a loan note to the city and

---

* Data from Official Statement of $116,310,000 Hospital Revenue and Revenue Refunding Bonds, Series 1983, (IHC Hospitals, Inc.), (including $82,450,000 Salt Lake City, Utah; $11,360,000 Sandy City, Utah; $4,625,000 Orem City, Utah; $12,730,000 Washington County, Utah; $1,605,000 Sevier County, Utah; $2,540,000 Mt. Pleasant City, Utah); dated April 1, 1983.

makes payment on that loan note as required under the indenture. IHC's
financings are all equally secured by IHC's revenues.

System Statistics and Financials.   At the start of 1983, the 23 hospitals in
the system had 2711 licensed acute-care beds, with 233,750 admissions and
686,579 patient days. The average length of stay was 5.13 days and the
overall occupancy was 69.4 percent. The percentages of third-party
reimbursement were as follows: commercial insurance was 46.7 percent,
Medicare was 25.7 percent, Blue Cross was 13.3 percent, private payment was
9.1 percent, and Medicaid was 5.2 percent. Operating revenues totaled
$312,550,000, and operating expenses (which excluded depreciation and
interest), totaled $275,754,000. Net income from operations totaled
$36,796,000 and nonoperating income totaled $9,468,000; consequently,
income available for debt service came to $46,264,000. Debt service was
$8,413,000, and the coverage of actual debt service was 5.50× (times). The
maximum annual debt service was $19,225,000, so that historical coverage of
maximum annual debt service was 2.41×. IHC projected capital expenditures
for all of its hospitals and projects to total $221.3 million for the 4-year
period ending on December 31, 1986. IHC also had an internal policy to
maintain a debt/assets ratio that would not go above 50 percent during any
given year; it was expected that the debt/assets ratio would hover at
approximately 42 percent for 1986.

IHC's Centralized Services.   One of the key characteristics of a
multihospital system, such as the one established by IHC, is its capability to
provide an integrated system of centralized services for all its hospitals. This is
a direct result of the system's ability to mobilize staffs for assignment to
specific areas of service. An important aspect of this system created by IHC is
central purchasing. Approximately 90 percent of all monies was spent for
standard hospital supply items purchased through contracts negotiated by
IHC under a centralized procedure. The result was a large cost savings to the
hospitals.

Substantial cost savings also accrued to IHC through the system's
association with other hospitals for the purpose of establishing a mutual
insurance company to purchase hospital liability and insurance coverage for
the members of IHC. A management engineering staff providing productivity
studies was created by IHC, and it was believed that this also achieved
substantial savings systemwide. Other centralized services that generally
streamlined operations, improved service delivery, and provided centralized
procedures, all with the result of reducing costs, included: data processing,
nursing, management, personnel recruitment, financial accounting and
auditing, construction management, fund raising, and long-range planning.

The centralizing of services by IHC is not restricted to its own multihospital
system. Indeed, IHC became a member of Associated Hospital Systems, which
is a combination of 11 not-for-profit hospital systems. The association
comprises a total of 40,000 acute-care beds and over $2.3 billion of total
assets. The group was organized to provide a way of combining its purchases
so that the gross volume would help in reducing costs. As a result, IHC has
experienced a further decrease in costs related to the purchasing of supplies
and equipment.

IHC's Major Hospitals.   In 1982, five hospitals in the IHC system
collectively provided approximately 78 percent of the total patient revenue.

As of 1981, LDS Hospital, located in Salt Lake City, Utah, had 551 beds with an occupancy rate of 79.3 percent and contributed 26.8 percent of IHC's patient service revenues. Utah Valley Hospital in Provo, Utah, had 389 beds with an occupancy rate of 76.6 percent and contributed 16.0 percent of IHC patient service revenues. McKay-Dee Hospital in Ogden, Utah, had 370 beds with an occupancy rate of 73.8 percent and contributed 14.1 percent of IHC's patient service revenues. Cottonwood Hospital in Murray, Utah, had 243 beds with an occupancy rate of 79.2 percent and contributed 9.1 percent of IHC's patient service revenues. Primary Children's Medical Center in Salt Lake City had 154 beds with an occupancy rate of 74.1 percent and contributed 10.5 percent of IHC's patient service revenues.

The Bonds and Projects.   The bonds issued were both for refunding outstanding bonds and for providing new funds. Refunding bonds were issued for LDS hospital in Salt Lake City; Alta View Hospital in Sandy City, Utah; and Orem Community Hospital in Orem, Utah. Bonds previously issued for the hospitals in Sandy City and Orem provided monies for the construction of two new hospitals, while funds for LDS hospital in Salt Lake City were used to provide construction financing for a new hospital facility and the renovation of certain other facilities of the hospital. Bonds were also issued to provide new funding for three hospital projects; they were the Dixie Medical Center in St. George City of Washington County, which required remodeling and expansion, a similar operation for the Sevier Valley Hospital in Richfield City of Sevier County, and the construction of a new hospital for Sanpete Valley Hospital in Mt. Pleasant City of Sanpete County.

Kentucky Development Finance Authority: St. Joseph Hospital Project*

The Kentucky Development Finance Authority issued the bonds for the St. Joseph Hospital project. The hospital was a division of the Nazareth Literary & Benevolent Institution (the corporation), which was a Kentucky not-for-profit corporation formed in 1829 and providing health care since 1876. The corporation operated general acute-care hospital facilities in the United States and overseas, including eight hospitals that had a total of 2406 beds. Five of the facilities were located in Kentucky and had 1285 beds, or 53.4 percent of the total bed capacity. The proceeds of the issue were lent to the corporation, and payment on the loan was made by the corporation in amounts sufficient to pay principal and interest on the bonds from revenues solely from St. Joseph Hospital. The loan agreement provided for a mortgage on the site of the hospital and a pledge of gross revenues. The project included the new construction of about 87,000 square feet, including four new additions for the hospital, and the improvement and renovation of about 80,000 square feet of the hospital's facility.

The Hospital and the Service Area.   The hospital is located on 14 acres in Lexington, Kentucky, and is approximately 324,000 gross square feet. The bed capacity of the hospital would increase under the project from 436 to 468

* Data from Official Statement of $23,600,000 Kentucky Development Finance Authority, Hospital Revenue Bonds (St. Joseph Hospital Project), dated May 1, 1981.

beds. The hospital's medical-surgical unit had a 341-bed capacity with an occupancy rate of 90.55 percent, the pediatric unit had 47 beds with an occupancy rate of 65.22 percent, and the psychiatric section of the hospital had 48 beds with an occupancy rate of 79.97 percent. Average occupancy for the hospital was approximately 86.7 percent in 1981, which was expected to increase to 89.2 percent in 1986. The hospital had 1192 full-time personnel, which was projected to increase to 1318 in 1985–1986. Of the hospital's 228 active and associate staff members, 169 were board-certified. St. Joseph Hospital's room rates were substantially lower than the rates of hospitals in its primary service area. The hospital's third-party reimbursement payers and the percentages they comprised of total third-party revenues were as follows: Medicare was 39.2 percent, Medicaid was 5.4 percent, Blue Cross was 25.7 percent, commercial insurance was 20.9 percent, and self-pay was 8.8 percent. It was forecasted that in 1986 Medicare would rise to 51.6 percent, Medicaid would be 6.7 percent, Blue Cross would be 20.0 percent, commercial insurance would be 16.3 percent, and self-pay would be 6.9 percent.

The hospital's primary service area, Fayette County, accounted for 31 percent of the patient discharges, and the secondary service area accounted for approximately 50 percent of the patient discharges. Population in the primary service area was expected to increase from 203,000 in 1980 to 223,400 in 1990, registering an increase of approximately 10 percent. The secondary service area, for the same time period, was expected to register a population increase of 7.81 percent, with population rising from 752,000 in 1980 to approximately 811,000 in 1990. Competing hospitals in the primary service area included Central Baptist, Good Samaritan Hospital, and University Hospital. Central Baptist had 297 beds with an average occupancy rate of 78.8 percent, Good Samaritan Hospital had 298 beds with an average occupancy rate of 80.5 percent, and University Hospital had 466 beds with an average occupancy rate of 81.5 percent. The total number of beds in the service area was 1497 with an average occupancy rate of 82.6 percent.

Financial Forecast. It was forecasted that total net revenues for the fiscal years ending in 1985 and 1986 were to be $6,041,000 and $6,086,000, respectively, with debt service coverage requirements in those years totaling $3,136,000 and $3,124,000, respectively. As a result, the debt service coverage ratio was projected to be 1.93× (times) and 1.95× for the 1985 and 1986 fiscal years. There was a rate covenant whereby the corporation agreed to fix charges and collect rates and fees for the use of the hospital that would produce net revenues available for debt service equal to at least 1.10× the maximum amount of principal and interest.

NOTE: This chapter was written by Stephen P. Rappaport in a report entitled "An Investor's Guide to Hospital Bonds" at Prudential-Bache Securities Inc., 1986. Reprinted by permission.

10
Water and Wastewater Bonds

Water, wastewater treatment, and also sewer bonds have been a mainstay of state and local debt issuance and certainly represent the most basic public services needed by any society. They are generally issued for the purpose of building or extending a water or a sewer system to benefit residential and industrial customers within a single municipality or within a region encompassing a number of local governments. Depending upon state statutes, the municipality may issue its own GO bonds for this purpose, it may create a special taxing district, or it may issue municipal revenue bonds. Most communities, however, are reluctant to issue GO bonds or create a special taxing district, as they had in the past, to finance a purpose that has a clear revenue-earning potential from user charges. More important, a new GO bond issue could force a municipality to hold an election, and it could use up borrowing capacity unless the bonds were clearly self-supporting. As a result, today when communities need to borrow for so many other purposes, most municipalities will devise a way in which they can issue revenue bonds whose debt service will be repaid by user charges or water and sewer rates.

Water and sewer revenue bonds tend, in general, to be thought of as among the safest municipal investments because people must have water and sewer services. However, ratings vary from the highest grade for systems in long-established, stable service areas to lower grades for systems that are being newly constructed or rapidly extended. Water bonds are usually more highly regarded than sewer bonds and sometimes command a higher rating than the GO bonds of the same municipality.

An Overview

There are at least four types of bonds in the water and sewer category: (1) solely water revenue, (2) solely sewer revenue, (3) combined water and sewer revenues, and (4) water or sewage treatment authorities or districts where the taxing power is used and more than one municipality in a region is involved. Nevertheless, whether the project's revenue source is primarily user fees or special tax assessments, the general approach to credit analysis remains substantially similar.

Water and sewer systems, like public power utilities, are usually monopoly operations with virtual control over these essential services. They also often have control over rate making without regulation. Where the facility is an established water and sewer system that has held a monopoly-type position for years or decades, the risks for the investor are usually thought to be small in buying such bonds issued to update, improve, or enlarge the system. However, the risks of start-up situations involving new construction are greater because of the uncertainty about whether customers will actually hook up rather than use their own wells and septic systems, whether new population will actually move into the area at all, or whether the projected new industrial or commercial firms will be lured into the area to expand their businesses. Predicting with accuracy the number of customers, the timing of their connection to the system, their amount of water use, and thus the actual operating cost of the newly constructed facility for water supply or sewer treatment is problematic. Together with these uncertainties are always the usual problems involved in any sizable construction project, such as lengthy delays or expensive cost overruns.

User Charges and Connection Fees

Two basic revenue streams are critical for analyzing water and sewer bonds: (1) user charges and (2) connection fees. Although user charges are usually quite uniform, whether by flat rate assessment or by meter reading of actual use, connection fees are unpredictable. Bonds dependent upon large amounts of revenue projected from connection charges should be more carefully analyzed than when the revenue is anticipated from user fees. A 'far higher debt service coverage level is expected in cases where bonds are secured by connection fees. Once customers are hooked up to the system, rate increases tend not to affect usage to any great extent, and hence, over the years, bonds with large economically strong service areas have rightly maintained and improved their credit quality. For many decades, municipalities did not have the legal power to force property owners to connect to their system because homeowners could insist on supplying their own water and their own septic system. However, recently a number of states have enacted new laws requiring that property owners in certain areas connect to the systems. This reinforced the municipality's legal right to charge annual fees for its services.

The soaring rate of capital construction costs has meant that the financing of water and sewer systems has become increasingly difficult because of customer resistance. To keep these debt charges down, many water and sewer authorities have decided to increase the initial assessment fee on each prospective user of the system. The municipalities or water and sewer authorities also have increased the charges for connecting each new customer to the system and for installing the water and sewer line that is connected to the house. Both assessment fees and connecting fees provide up-front operating capital to fund interest payments and to lower the amount of debt that the system must incur for a new bond issue. Assessment fees can be paid by the property owner either immediately or at the end of the construction period, when the new water or sewer system is complete. To ensure that the assessment charges are paid, the municipality usually has a lien upon the homeowners' property in case of nonpayment.

In contrast, the connection fee usually cannot be made subject to a lien. Instead, a "notice to connect" is sent to the property owner. It states that in order to be connected to the water and sewer system, the property owner must acquire a "permit to connect." This permit requires prepayment of the connection charge. Both connection and assessment charges are one-time fees; therefore, annual user charges usually represent the bulk of the new or rapidly growing revenue of the water and sewer authority.

Federal and State Involvement

Upgrading water and sewer systems to meet federally mandated standards can be extremely expensive, costing $100 million to $300 million for a moderate-size city. The work also requires substantial amounts of lead time for construction and installation. Under the Clean Water Act of 1972 and its amendments, the federal government is committed to providing capital grants to cover up to 55 percent of the total construction costs needed to build any municipality's sewer system. In addition, state governments also provide capital grants of up to 15 percent for water and sewer projects. This means that the municipality or authority that needs to build a new system or substantially upgrade an old one can acquire a large percentage of the construction costs from the federal and state governments, but only if certain standards, deadlines, and inspection criteria are met.

For instance, the federal government, and sometimes state governments, tend to become involved in the rate structure of a municipality's water and sewer system in an effort to ensure that local industries, which are the major users of water, pay their fair share. In this way, they influence the regulation of rates because grants are provided only if rates are considered adequate and industry pays its proportion of the costs. The federal government therefore makes its payments on a staggered basis. All during construction, certain requirements set by the government must be met. First, a plan must be developed. Then the water and sewer authority must set a rate structure and submit it to the government when construction is 50 percent complete. When the construction is 75 to 80 percent complete, the federal government insists upon approving the rate structure. Finally, the government requires that the municipality provide, in advance of operation, a complete engineer's guide to the operation of the whole water system.

The federal government also requires each corporation in the locality to repay its proportionate share of the federal grant over time. Municipal water and sewer rates are expected to fully reflect the repayment of government grants by major industrial users, and the water and sewer system itself is required to repay 50 percent of this amount to the government. The balance may go into the general fund of the system and be used for operations and for debt service. In any event, the analyst or investor must be certain that commitments have been made for project grant monies.

Project Economics

Once again, demand is highly important to the evaluation of bonds issued for water and sewer purposes. An economic analysis of the service area forms the basis of demand studies showing projected population and industrial growth. An analysis must be made of the historical growth of the system's customers and their projected growth, which includes individual, industrial, and commercial users. Demand should also be assessed from the perspective of the ability of the system to raise rates and still remain competitive. Therefore, net debt statistics of the service area should be evaluated, including debt per capita, debt as a percentage of personal income, debt as a percentage of full real estate valuation, and all overlapping and underlying debt ratios. This would give a complete picture of the ability of the municipality and its populace to pay for water and wastewater services.

Financial Analysis

Historical and projected operating results, including revenues and expenditures, are the foundation of a system's financial analysis. The system should have a diverse customer base, and sales by customer and type of customer under all usage conditions should be evaluated. The financial strength of the customers should be assessed, and a ratio analysis should be performed for all customers.

Because water and sewer revenue bonds are really cost-of-service enterprises, the rate covenant has traditionally been set low, usually $1.1\times$ (times) to $1.20\times$, which would produce more than enough revenues to pay operating and maintenance expenses and debt service. In the case of a fully guaranteed municipal revenue bond (with the pledge of taxing power, if needed) for a new or expanded water and sewer system, the rate covenant may provide that rates produce sufficient amounts to ensure the payment of principal and interest after operating and maintenance costs, but it may not require the maintenance of a separate debt service reserve fund. The first 5 years of the operation of a new water and sewer system are critical. If the debt service payments are made regularly without reliance on monies in the reserve funds or a municipality's guarantee, if any, the facility will probably continue to meet its obligations. The rate structure itself should be competitive and flexible, and the requirements for additional debt should be well regulated because of the low coverage requirements.

The System

Critical to the analysis of water and sewer bonds is some appraisal of the entire system. This is usually done by the engineer. The age, condition, capacity, and adequacy of the reservoir and of the storage, pumping, and treatment facilities must be assessed. The water supply contract, if any, the degree of external dependence, and the adequacy of available water are important factors. Sewage treatment and water supply contracts should be executed and should run for the term of the bond issue. Future capital improvements and construction should be feasible as projected by the consulting engineer.

Case Studies
The Suffolk County Water Authority*

The Suffolk County Water Authority was established to acquire, construct, maintain, and operate a water supply and distribution system in Suffolk County, New York. The county's freshwater supply comes from rainfall and surface water that percolate through the soil and result in underground reservoirs in the authority's service area. High-capacity wells are then drilled to reclaim this water. The authority serves approximately 850,000 people in Suffolk County, which represent about 75 percent of the county provided with public water supply, or approximately 66 percent of the county's total population. The service areas of the authority include the municipalities of Babylon, Bayshore, East Hampton, Huntington, Patchogue, Port Jefferson, Smithtown, and Westhampton. The authority has 382 active wells and 159 pumping plants with a total daily capacity of 563,638,000 gallons. There are 58 storage facilities in the service area with a capacity of 56,708,000 gallons, and in total, the authority has 250,544 active services. It has approximately 3700 miles of mains in use.

Total revenue for 1984 was $43,479,351, with operating expenses totaling $23,966,977. Total debt service was $9,687,213, so that the coverage of outstanding debt by net revenues was 2.01× (times). Debt service coverage was projected to average approximately 1.73× from 1985 through 1989. The authority had a rate covenant so that net revenues would produce 120 percent of the amount required to pay the aggregate of interest, principal, and other payments for the following year. A rate increase of approximately 18 percent was put into effect on May 1, 1982, with previous rate increases running approximately every 2 to 3 years since 1973.

Suffolk County contains approximately 930 square miles and covers about two-thirds of Long Island on its eastern end. The population of Suffolk County rose from 1,116,672 in 1970 to 1,296,539 as of January 1, 1983, registering a 16 percent increase—as opposed to an outflow in New York State of 3.8 percent and a population rise in the United States of 11.4 percent. County unemployment hovered at 6.8 percent, while New York State unemployment was at 8.6 percent and unemployment in the United States was approximately 9.6 percent. The county's four largest employers are the New York Telephone Company, Fairchild Republic Company, Brookhaven National Laboratory, and the Grumman Aerospace Corporation. Agriculture and fishing are important to the economy of the county. The county's property is divided among residential, commercial, and industrial uses in proportions of 65, 25, and 10 percent, respectively.

---

* Data from Official Statement of $18,000,000 Suffolk County Water Authority, New York, Water Works Revenue Bonds, Series U, dated February 1, 1985.

The Cape May County Municipal Utilities Authority: Sewer Revenue Bonds*

The Cape May County Municipal Utilities Authority was created to help abate water pollution in Cape May County and to provide wastewater treatment for the region by constructing and operating regional wastewater treatment facilities. These facilities included pumping stations, treatment plants, gravity interceptors, force mains, composting facilities, and ocean outfall. The county is located in the mid-Atlantic region of the United States at the southern end of New Jersey, which is a peninsula of 454 square miles bordered by the Atlantic Ocean on the east and Delaware Bay on the west. The year-round population of the county in 1985 was 95,718, with the summer population burgeoning to 593,856 individuals.

The authority designed a comprehensive water pollution control project on a multiregional basis to solve the wastewater management problems of the county. The project included a series of regional networks so that the participant municipalities could enact their local sewerage collection systems. The participants' wastewater was conveyed, treated, and disposed of by each service region. A centralized sludge-composting facility was established so that wastewater sludge from the service regions could be treated. The authority provided service to 16 municipalities, including certain sewage districts. The service regions of the authority were: Ocean City Service Region, Cape May Service Region, Wildwood/Lower Service Region, and the Seven Mile Beach/Middle Service Region.

Service agreements with the municipalities in the county allowed for the authority to provide wholesale treatment services while the municipalities operated and maintained their local collection systems for commercial, industrial, and residential use. The agreement itself obligated the municipalities to pay user charges to the authority based on the volume of wastewater and municipality discharges; this would become effective when the authority provided services to a municipality. Additionally, the county was required to make up any deficiencies in annual revenue of the authority if such revenue proved insufficient to cover current operation and maintenance cost, debt service requirements, and other related expenses.

In 1985 the total cost for the entire project was slated to be $361,601,000. Federal and state grants for the project were projected to be $181,171,000. The total cost for the portion of the project advanced partly from this bond issue was slated to be $136,950,000, with $92,500,000 coming from this bond issue and $44,450,000 from federal grants. Debt service coverage in 1984 was 1.31× (times), and projected coverage from 1985 through 1989 averaged approximately 1.19×. The treatment charge of the Cape May County Municipal Utilities Authority was $102 per equivalent dwelling unit, an amount equal to the quantity of wastewater discharged by average single-family residents. This compared favorably to fees charged by other similar municipal authorities in the general area.

* Data from Official Statement of $92,730,000 The Cape May County Municipal Utilities Authority, Cape May County, New Jersey, County Agreement Sewer Revenue Bonds, Series 1985, dated August 1, 1985.

11

Transportation Bonds

Transportation bonds led America into the municipal bond market through securities issued first for port facilities and then for larger issues for toll roads and related facilities, such as bridges and tunnels. Indeed, in the early years of America's expanding transportation networks, ports of entry located at major seaways began the soon-to-be-stepped-up process of municipal bond issuance through the use of the public authority device. At first, port bonds were issued primarily for shipping- and cargo-related purposes. Later, as ports expanded their operations, large umbrella-type port authorities subsumed a variety of transportation facilities under their jurisdiction. For instance, the Port Authority of New York and New Jersey, with about $3 billion in outstanding debt obligations, comprises such diverse facilities as the World Trade Center; Kennedy, LaGuardia, and Newark airports; and Manhattan's major bridges and tunnels.

Concurrent with the increase in bonds issued for port facilities came the increase in toll road bonds issued for the nation's rapidly expanding highway systems. In hindsight, it might be worth noting that highway revenue bonds, with some notable exceptions, have been the most successful of all revenue bonds issued. Related to toll road financing, bonds issued for bridges and tunnels were also among the earlier tax-exempt vehicles sold in the securities markets. Finally, as technological progress gained momentum and the need and frequency for fast long-distance travel became important, bonds issued for airports came center stage in the ongoing evolution of transportation financing—and

144

later outstripped, in size and number, the issuance of bonds for ports, toll roads, bridges, and tunnels. As a result, the following evaluation of transportation bonds begins with airport bonds and then discusses bonds issued for toll roads and port facilities.

Airport Revenue Bonds

The evolution in the analysis of airport financing seems to parallel the changing nature of the airline industry, its regulation, and the surges in demand for airline travel. Indeed, factors affecting the airline industry have changed the emphasis of analysis from the financial viability of the airline carriers to the underpinnings of demand for the airport facility itself. To be sure, the nature of tax-exempt airport financing was changed partly by the Airline Deregulation Act of 1978 and the contributing effect it had on the financial viability of many carriers. This act generally permitted airlines greater flexibility in service, including setting fare rates, and movement in and out of scheduled routes. The idea behind the act was to allow the market to operate in a free fashion, but the actual result may have been to move certain carriers toward financial distress, which was fueled by a somewhat problematic national economy. As a result, the study of bonds issued for airports involves at least a working knowledge of airlines as corporate entities and of events affecting the airline industry.

Use Agreements

For years, use agreements were the principal security of airport revenue bonds. At the time of their widespread use, the airlines using them were financially sound, in most cases. Regardless, airline payments under use agreements are composed of terminal rentals and landing fees, and the contracts run for the life of the bond issue. Airlines make payments on their contracts with airports in one of two ways: Payments either may or may not take into account the amount of concession and other revenue generated by the airport's facilities. In the first instance, the airlines make payments in amounts sufficient to comply with rate covenants and to cover debt service levels. The second case, however, mandates specific levels of payment by the airlines so that either surplus revenues may be generated or there may even be operational losses.

Today, use agreements may be less significant for a number of reasons. Among them are that airlines are generally not as financially sound as they once were and that use agreements are sometimes for a period often shorter than the bond issue or are not even used at all.

Moreover, in some instances airlines may prefer to drop service rather than to pay for a losing operation. Nevertheless, use agreements do provide an additional measure of security when coupled with strong demand for the airport.

Demand for the Airport

As a result of the foregoing, the quality of any particular airport revenue bond is more dependent on demand than on any other factor. Yet in the case of airports, assessing demand is somewhat complicated because of different types of airports, the varied character of their service areas, and the diversity of carriers. Airports that are hubs or home bases for certain airlines tend to have more financial strength than those which are not. Airports that are origination and destination facilities also tend to be stronger, but they are more dependent on the economy than are connecting airports, which are not generally considered to have as strong security characteristics. Airports used primarily for their surrounding tourist attractions are usually considered to be less creditworthy than those used principally for business travel, but this may not always be the case. Furthermore, many airports may be used for any combination of the above, which makes the credit analysis of them particularly cumbersome.

The key to the analysis of airport revenue bonds is the number of enplanements, both historical and projected. The less dependent an airport is on a very small number of carriers, the better. Similarly, the less an airport is dependent on a few airlines comprising a disproportionately large percentage of enplanements, the better the quality of the airport revenue bond. Historical and projected air cargo loads should also be reviewed. Some attention should also be paid to the ability of the support facilities to handle the projected passenger load. As with all user-type capital projects, there should be a demonstrated need for the facility, and competition for the service of the facility should be limited.

Demographics are highly important to the analysis of airport bonds because they will usually impact demand significantly. The general trend of the service area's economy should be studied to note sweeping trends, such as the inflow or outflow of industry or the movement to a service-oriented economic base. Projected population growth of the area is important, as are the trends of industrial growth, employment, and per capita income.

Airport Finance

The financial analysis of airport revenue bonds may take one of two forms.

The first method should focus on a review of the airport's historical financials, including its audits. A detailed study of the airport's historical and forecasted revenue and expenditure patterns should be made, including a consideration of the effect the new facilities will have on the airport's balance sheet and income statement. As part of this analysis, the airport's financial ratios should be studied to make sure that there are no aberrations and that projected debt service coverage is somewhat above the rate covenant. For airports, however, ratios other than the debt service coverage ratio seem to be less useful than for other revenue enterprises because of the various ways in which airports account for their revenues, expenditures, and interest expenses.

Airports are also issued tax-exempt bonds secured by payments from a specific airline. This is the second form of airport bond analysis; compared to the first, it involves less municipal analysis. While demand factors cannot be ignored in the analysis of these bonds, the primary source of payment is the airline itself. As a result, a corporate financial analysis of the airline involved in the project is usually completed.

Toll Road and Special Transportation Tax Revenue Bonds

There are essentially two kinds of highway revenue bonds. One type is payable by tolls from users of the facilities, and the other is payable from special taxes, including those levied on gasoline and other fuel purchases, drivers' licenses and registrations, and highway fines. In some instances, highway funds have been established with some combination of revenues from various funding sources. The fund may be established by a state's constitution or by statutory means, and pledges for bond payments from the highway fund can be first or second lien. Some states pledge their general obligation for payment of the bonds so that the bond effectively has a double-barreled type of security.

Bonds issued for toll roads require an analysis of demand presented by the feasibility study. An evaluation should be made of the trends of traffic as well as of the planned expansion or construction of competing highways or alternative means of transportation. The diversion of traffic by the construction of bridges and tunnels that would compete with the path of highway traffic should be analyzed. In addition, an economic evaluation of the service area should be completed with a view toward ascertaining population growth and movement and the potential for the continued need of the highway. The costs of future capital construction should also be studied in light of estimated demand and projected revenues. The ability to raise tolls must also be carefully considered in light of competing roads.

For special transportation tax revenue bonds, more emphasis should be placed on the analysis of the history, diversity, and projected revenues from the taxes slated to pay for the bonds. Any major historical decreases or increases in revenue should be taken into account as well as the potential for the future enhancement or dilution of major revenue streams. Diversity of revenue sources is important because undue reliance on one particular revenue stream may pose potential problems if there are difficulties with raising that revenue in later years.

Bonds for Port Facilities

Evaluating the security behind bonds issued for port facilities is usually more complex than it initially appears. Of primary importance is the competitive environment of the port and the demand for the port's facilities. Evaluation then must be made both of the general trends in the amount of cargo and other such items handled by the facility and of the ability of the port to regulate charges for the use of its facilities. An evaluation should be made of the port's historical and projected financial operations and of its future capital plans. The revenues of the port facility should be diverse, and the economy of the service area should be growing at a fair rate, or at least its growth should be stabilized. It is also important to analyze the financial stability of the companies and other entities using the port. As mentioned at the beginning of this chapter, many municipal bonds issued by so-called ports are secured by very large transportation systems with diversified revenues derived from a large number of different sources, such as bridges, tunnels, airports, and office buildings. Therefore, a detailed evaluation of each revenue system and a sensitivity analysis for the group as a whole are required, and these should cover various economic circumstances.

Case Studies
The New Jersey Turnpike Authority*

The New Jersey Turnpike Authority was created to construct, maintain, repair, and operate turnpike projects in New Jersey. The proceeds of this were to provide financing for the 1985–1990 widening program and constituted the largest long-term bond issue ever brought to market up to

---

* Data from Official Statement of $2,000,000,000 New Jersey Turnpike Authority, Turnpike Revenue Bonds, 1985 Series, B-Model Multi-Term, Format, Mode/Bonds, dated November 21, 1985.

that time. The project included the addition of two and three lanes in either direction at certain points along the turnpike. It was anticipated that the expansion of the turnpike would alleviate capacity constraints projected to occur from 1985 to 1995. In 1985 the total length of the main-line turnpike was approximately 118 miles. It had 28 interchanges that connected the turnpike with major traffic arteries and other centers of population and had 13 operating service areas providing gasoline and restaurant services in either direction. It was anticipated that the widening program would be completed by November 15, 1990.

In 1979, annual vehicle miles on the turnpike totaled 2,803,773,003, which increased to 3,442,060,842 in 1984. Total vehicles on the turnpike in 1979 were 121,179,478, and in 1984 were 156,698,876. In 1984, net operating revenues before interest and other charges came to $86,398,000. In making the toll and concession revenue projections, it was estimated that across-the-board toll increases of 40 percent would be made on July 1, 1986, another 40 percent increase would be made on January 1, 1990, and a 20 percent increase would be effective on January 1, 1992. In addition, revenues collected from the New Jersey Sports and Exposition Authority would be increased in 1986, 1990, and 1992 in proportion to the toll increases placed in effect during those years.

Projected debt service coverage on the 1985 bonds in 1990 was 1.59× (times), in 1992 was 1.53×, and in 1995 was 1.52×. Debt service coverage on all the authority's bonds was expected to be 1.20× in 1990, 1.20× in 1992, and 1.21× in 1995. Total operating revenues were projected to be $170,588,000 in 1985 and estimated to be $439,459,000 in 1995. Net revenues were projected to be $334,345,000 in 1995. The authority covenanted to fix and collect such tolls that net revenues would be at least equal to the greater of either (1) the aggregate debt service on the bonds, maintenance reserve payments, state payments, and special project reserve payments or (2) 1.20× the aggregate debt service on the bonds. The 1985 bonds were priority bonds, payable from and secured by a lien and pledge of net revenues of the turnpike. The lien and pledge were senior to refunding bonds and were on a parity with the lien and pledge for any additional parity bonds to be issued under the resolution.

Stapleton International Airport of Denver, Colorado*

Denver's Stapleton International Airport, operated since 1929, is one of the six most widely used airports in the United States today. The others are Kennedy International Airport and LaGuardia Airport, both in New York; Newark Airport in New Jersey; Atlanta Airport in Georgia; and O'Hare Airport in Chicago. The airport is also one of the 24 large hubs in the U.S. airport transportation system. In 1983 the airport ranked seventh worldwide in terms of total passenger traffic and was the principal airport in the Rocky Mountain region. The airport serves the six-county Denver-Boulder Consolidated Metropolitan Statistical Area (CMSA), which accounts for

* Data from Official Statement of $253,815,000 City and County of Denver, Colorado, Airport Revenue Bonds, Series 1985, dated November 1, 1985.

one-half of Colorado's population, and is located 6 miles east of downtown Denver. The population of this CMSA was approximately 1,721,000 in 1982 and was forecasted to rise to 1,919,000 in 1990. The proceeds of this issue will be used by the city to finance improvements at the airport and also to finance part of the acquisition of land for a new airport to be constructed by 1995 to meet the existing and projected demand for airport facilities in the Denver region.

Total enplaned passengers in 1979 were 9,896,968, which rose to approximately 13,736,415 in 1984. About 80 percent of the total enplaned passengers had been a function of the operations of United Airlines, Frontier Airlines, and Continental Airlines. Nineteen other airlines registered between 0.1 and about 2.5 percent of all the other passengers enplaning at the airport. Total takeoffs and landings increased from 486,300 in 1979 to 515,489 in 1984. Approximately 59 percent of the passengers using the airport's services were connecting from one flight to another.

Payment of the bonds was from net revenues of the airport. The city agreed to fix and collect charges so that gross revenues in any fiscal year, together with available funds, would be sufficient to provide for the operation and maintenance expenses for the year and to provide for the greater of (1) an amount not less than 125 percent of the aggregate debt service requirements for such year or (2) the amount needed to make the cash contributions into all the accounts. Coverage of debt service was estimated at about 2.38× for the outstanding bonds in 1984. It was projected that debt service coverage would be 1.85× in 1986 and 1.75× in 1990, when total enplaned passengers were expected to be 18,660,000.

NOTE: This chapter was written by Stephen P. Rappaport in a paper entitled "Transportation Bonds: A Comprehensive Analysis" at Prudential-Bache Securities Inc., 1986. Reprinted by permission.

12

Resource Recovery and Solid Waste Bonds

Most people have long realized that over the courses of their lives there are a number of daily occurrences which they take for granted and on which they do not spend large amounts of their time pondering. One important item that certainly fits this bill is their garbage and waste and the collection and disposal of it. For a long time, refuse collections were easily handled by private carters and some municipalities; much was dispensed appropriately in landfills or taken out to sea, and the rest was incinerated through municipal or private incinerators. Not surprisingly, the disposal of solid waste in America, now estimated to be 500,000 tons daily, has come to present major problems to states, cities, and localities nationwide. To be sure, this trend is likely to continue. The situation is largely the result of the closing of landfills, tighter standards for pollution control, ecological damage, and the age and incapacity of many incinerators. This problem has collided with the financial re-trenching of many state and local governments, and it has thus become a problem of local origin and local solution.

One feasible answer to the problem of waste disposal is to convert it into energy to be subsequently sold. This conversion process is known generally as *resource recovery* and is now taking hold in America, although it has been largely the province of European technology and achievements over many years. Nevertheless, the construction of re-source recovery plants to burn garbage and waste and subsequently to sell energy is not only technologically complex but also financially complicated. America's local governments have met this problem with the issuance of debt for the purpose of constructing these plants. As a result, resource recovery municipal bonds have been catapulted onto the investment scene in the East Coast and midwestern regions and will probably take hold all around the country in a short period of time.

During 1985, approximately $2.0 billion worth of resource recovery bonds for 20 tax-exempt financings was outstanding. As a project type of financing, the structuring of resource recovery bond issues is extremely complex and is probably one of the most creative and interesting types of financings in which investment bankers can become involved. Consequently, the process of understanding them and making the appropriate evaluations as to the creditworthiness of these entities is comparatively complex. This stems in large part from the number of "players" involved in the financing and from the fact that some of them are corporate entities. What seems to make the evaluation of resource recovery bonds even more difficult is the way that discussions of them have been presented; that is, discussions have focused on those certain characteristics of a revenue bond which are considered to be critical in determining the creditworthiness of the issuing or guaranteeing entity, which generally include legal, economic, administrative, and financial factors. However, analyzing a resource recovery bond in this way surely makes the matter more difficult, less interesting, and less useful. It is much easier, it seems, to present a general sketch of what happens in the total project and then to study each part of it in order to understand what is crucial to the process at each of its stages. Evaluating the security aspects of a resource recovery project in this way provides the analyst and investor with a better understanding of what is important to bond security at each stage of the process. As a result, it is probably best to begin with a very brief discussion of exactly what is involved in these projects.

Essentially, a resource recovery project is a closed system with three critical parts to it: (1) Waste must be provided from the municipality to the resource recovery facility; (2) the facility must be built, it must be tested, and it must operate for the life of the bond issue; and (3) from the facility must come energy to be sold for the life of the bond issue. At each one of these stages there are contracts that are critical to the revenue projections (which we will examine in this chapter). This kind of project has had some success in America. Indeed, there have been a handful of projects that have issued tax-exempt debt, but the earlier ones have not been as successful as anticipated. The more recent ones have received sound ratings for a variety of reasons, and these projects seem to be either on their way to completion or operating. Interestingly, one of the key problems in achieving a successful financing has not been the financial or technological difficulties that have been encountered in the past, but political problems from constituents in a particular jurisdiction who need the plant, and who want it, but who do not want it located near them. Ultimately, because other choices for the disposal of waste may be virtually nonexistent, resource recovery plants may in fact have to be constructed near residential areas, regardless of the residents' wishes.

System Inputs:
The Municipality

First and foremost, the municipality that is in need of a better waste disposal system must be capable of preparing and sending solid waste to the resource recovery plant. Furthermore, it must have the necessary quantity of solid waste, produced steadily on a yearly basis, to haul to the plant for conversion into steam or electric power. Project revenues are derived from this disposal system through the payment by the municipality and other haulers of so-called tipping fees for every ton of garbage carted to the site; usually, the tipping (or disposal) fees account for a wide-ranging percentage of the revenues slated to pay off the bonds issued to construct the resource recovery plant. The municipality should have the ability to control the waste flow so that there is no strong competition from others who are able under law to compete for hauling the waste, perhaps at a lower price. The municipality must also keep its disposal fees competitive, although this can potentially give rise to an antitrust problem. In order for the municipality not to fall victim to charges of monopolism, it has usually been held that the local government must be following some kind of state edict that allows it to control the flow of waste within its governmental jurisdiction.

Additionally, there must be a contractual agreement that commits the municipality to bring the waste to the resource recovery facility in a certain amount: an amount that will allow the generation of a sufficient amount of revenue through tipping fees. This contract is usually written so that the municipality is liable for the payment of the tipping fee even if the resource recovery plant is not operational or garbage is not delivered in the amount specified. Moreover, the investor should be aware of the willingness of the community to abide by these contractual relationships. This is an unquantifiable aspect of the analysis.

The analyst or investor must also be able to calculate the ability of the municipality to make these payments. A general evaluation must be made of the local government, just as one would usually make in analyzing a general obligation bond. This evaluation should include a thorough economic appraisal, covering such areas as population growth, employment trends, real estate valuations, and industrial growth. Similarly, a financial analysis should be undertaken covering revenue and expenditure patterns. A debt analysis should also be performed, including historical and projected debt-related ratios. Payments on the disposal contracts generally come from the operating budget, so the size of the payment in relation to the total budget should be noted. Finally, assessments must be made as to the extent to which the community and its political leaders support the construction of the plant and the need for the plant as the only real available alternative for waste disposal.

Finally, the disposal fee and rate structure should be carefully analyzed. Tipping fees should be able to be increased as expenses rise because they are a portion of the total revenues that must be used to pay for the operating and maintenance costs of the project and for debt service. A rate covenant must also be in effect so that total revenues cover debt service by a specified percentage. Revenues include both tipping fees and monies from sales of electricity. If there are excess monies generated by the project because net revenues are higher than anticipated, the financial rewards should be provided to the community and the corporate sponsor as economic incentives.

The Resource Recovery Plant

The next step in the analysis of resource recovery bonds is the evaluation of the plant itself—its construction, operation, and management—and of the guarantees brought to bear by the builder and operator for its performance.

Resource recovery plants today basically use one of two specific types of technology. One is the *mass burning* technology, and the other is a system termed *refuse-derived fuel*. In general, the mass burning operation has had a much better success rate and is an easier system to operate. Major items are removed from the waste, such as automobile parts and the like, and the refuse is then sent to a boiler, which turns the thermal energy into steam; the steam may be used for heating or may be turned into electricity through a conversion process. This system has had wide use in countries outside of the United States. The refuse-derived fuel system involves a much more detailed sorting process and shredding operation and has not had the success that mass burning has had.

In terms of evaluating plant size, one of the principal difficulties facing builders of these plants is what has been called the *scale-up problem*: plants built in the United States have had to be much larger than the ones in Europe. Because of the larger plant size, certain technological and engineering problems have resulted that were not encountered in the smaller European operations. Problems have also occurred in the United States because of the different composition of refuse.

In terms of evaluating plant management, it is important to note that the more experienced the builder-operator is, the more comfortable an analyst or investor should be with the bond issue. It is also better to have as the owner-operator a corporate entity that has had experience with resource recovery than it is to have an inexperienced corporate or municipal entity.

Especially critical to a successful resource recovery financing are the guarantees and insurance provided for all stages of the project. There should be a guarantee provided by the corporate builder for completion of the plant and for its operation in the desired fashion; this entails an analysis of the financial capability of the company to provide adequately for these guarantees. There should also be some type of insurance to cover items not covered in the original construction contract. Additionally, it is very important to have preformance guarantees as well as business interruption insurance. All necessary insurance and guarantees can have a variety of provisions and arrangements, and a careful study of them is therefore required. Insurance policies should run through the maturity of the bonds. Among the operational problems associated with resource recovery plants are pollution, corrosion, capacity failures, and residue deposits. Very often the builder involved in the project provides an equity participation, which in the past has averaged about 30 percent of the investment in the project. Tax benefits, such as depreciation, investment tax credits, and energy tax credits, have in the past been important items, any one of which the equity investor would consider as a trade-off for participation. As noted earlier, sharing excess revenues is a very important inducement for the company involved in the project.

System Outputs: Energy Sales

In the same way that an analyst evaluates the potential sale of power in the public power arena, the market for energy from the resource recovery facility, its price, and the kinds of sales contracts must be thoroughly analyzed in the case of resource recovery bonds. The price of the energy produced from the project must be regulated and must be competitive. A strong market should be available, and sales should not be dependent on a buyer who has options to buy from a large number of competitive sources. Contracts with the purchasers must be studied for their ability and willingness to pay. This may include an analysis of a utility buyer from a corporate standpoint and an analysis of the company's obligation to buy the energy at a specified price over a long period of time. Such an analysis includes an evaluation of the status of the company's payment as it ranks in its general indebtedness or within its liability structure. The contracts in these instances are usually take-and-pay, in which the buyers of the energy from the resource recovery plant purchase the energy at a specified price, if the energy is available.

Guarantees and the Feasibility Study

Because of the complicated nature of resource recovery plants, the number of contracts involved, and plants' track records over recent years, a municipality may desire to provide some kind of guarantee for the bonds of the project. It is usually more useful, from the standpoint of bond security, to have a local government rather than a corporate entity guarantee the debt. Public as opposed to private ownership is also encouraged.

One of the more unique aspects of resource recovery projects is the way the feasibility study and projected financial operations are presented. The study, usually completed by a nationally recognized firm, provides a series of economic and financial scenarios covering cases ranging from the best projected revenues from tipping fees and energy sales to the worst case under poor economic circumstances. This sensitivity-type analysis could also include other variations on this theme. Because of the difficulty of predicting financial and economic circumstances over long periods of time in the life of a resource recovery plant, the worst-case scenario should allow for payment of the debt service on the bonds.

Solid Waste Bonds

As a precursor to the development of a resource recovery facility, bonds may be issued for the disposal of solid waste to cover the costs of landfills, transfer stations, and the acquisition of a site for the resource recovery facility. Bonds for solid waste may also be issued when a resource recovery facility is not in the offing. Debt service on the bonds is usually payable from tipping fees charged by the issuer and paid to those which dispose of their waste at the site. There must be little competition for waste disposal in the general geographic area, and the tipping fees charged must be competitive so that use of the facility will continue. The feasibility consultants must project that adequate solid waste will be available so that delivery will continue and adequate revenues will be produced from the tipping fees. There must be an economic analysis of the municipality that will provide the solid waste to this facility, including various employment trends, population growth, industrial strength, and so forth, as noted earlier in this chapter. A financial evaluation must be done of those carting the waste to the facility and of their ability and willingness to make payments on the debt. This type of evaluation is very much the same kind that is done for the first stage of a resource recovery project.

Case Study

Hillsborough County, Florida: Solid Waste and Resource Recovery Project*

History of the Project. Hillsborough County had studied the application of waste to energy technology to meet its specific needs over a number of years beginning in 1977, when local governments—Hillsborough County and the cities of Tampa, Plant City, and Temple Terrace—signed an agreement establishing a management committee to study this problem. An evaluation was made of the possibilities for solid waste disposal in the county and of the feasibility of a project for resource recovery. In 1979 the U.S. Environmental Protection Agency (EPA) aided the efforts of these local governments with matching funds for the study of resource recovery technology. In 1981 the management committee decided that resource recovery was a viable option and that the mass burn technology would be the most economical system for Hillsborough County.

Later, on October 31, 1984, the Florida Department of Environmental Regulation caused the county to cease operating the Hillsborough Heights Sanitary Landfill. At this time the county began preparation for a new landfill serving all three cities, as well as the county, and also for the resource recovery financing, which occurred during late 1984. In addition, the county owned and operated two solid waste transfer stations and another landfill. This landfill, which was to be used for processable residue and nonprocessable waste and as an emergency backup disposal site for the resource recovery facility, was approximately 180 acres on a site of 1100 acres and was located in the southeast corner of the county. At this time the landfill was being used by all three cities, but it would not be used by Tampa when its own resource recovery facility opened.

---

* Data from Official Statement of $144,045,000 Hillsborough County, Florida, Solid Waste and Resource Recovery Bonds, Series 1984 A, dated December 1, 1984.

The County. The county's total land area is approximately 1100 square miles and includes three incorporated cities: Tampa, Temple Terrace, and Plant City. The county is one of Florida's most populated counties and is located in the middle of the state's west coast, in one of its most rapidly growing areas. In 1985 the population in Hillsborough County stood at 693,000, up from 250,000 in 1950. About 392,000 of that number in 1985 resided in the unincorporated portions of the county. Approximately 1 million people were projected to be living in Hillsborough County by the year 2000, with about 600,000 individuals residing within the county's unincorporated area. During the mid-1980s, government employees at all levels accounted for the largest number in employment, totaling 44,000 individuals.

The two largest property taxpayers were the General Telephone Company and the Tampa Electric Company, comprising 4.7 and 4.5 percent of the county's property taxes, respectively. No single taxpayer in the county paid more than 4.7 percent of the county's total ad valorem tax revenues. Tax collections of the county from 1981 through 1983 hovered at approximately 98 percent, and the county's fund balances in 1983 stood at $11.7 million. Countywide debt, which was payable from ad valorem taxes, totaled approximately $33.9 million in 1984, while the total direct debt of the county, which was payable from ad valorem property taxes, totaled $12.6 million. As a result, the bonded debt per capita was approximately $18.18 in 1984. Unemployment in 1983 stood at 8.1 percent, which was well below the national average of 9.6 percent. Tampa International Airport serves the county.

The Facility. The facility was one that would process solid waste and generate electricity. It was designed to process 1200 tons per day of waste and be expandable to a potential capacity of 1600 tons per day. The facility would use the mass burn technology of Martin GmbH that was presently in use at 100 Martin facilities around the world. The electricity provided by the facility would be transferred to the Tampa Electric Company (TECO), where it would be run through its distribution system. Ogden Martin Systems of Hillsborough, which was a subsidiary of Ogden Martin Systems, Inc., would design, construct, and operate the facility. This company was a subsidiary of the Ogden Corporation, which would guarantee the performance of the contractor in the design, construction, and operation of the facility. The contractor guaranteed that the facility would be operational within a given period of time and would receive fees plus 10 percent of the revenues derived from the sale of electricity produced by the facility.

It was expected that the city of Tampa would activate its resource recovery facility in 1985; thus, the financial analysis was based on the total amount of waste from Temple Terrace and Plant City less the capacity of the city of Tampa's resource recovery facility, which would become operational in July 1985. It was also anticipated that processable residue and nonprocessable waste would be delivered to the county's landfill for disposal.

Waste Control and Waste Flow. On June 30, 1983, the state legislature of Florida adopted a law that allowed the county to have exclusive control over the collection and disposal of solid waste generated within its area, and the county covenanted that it would not permit additional waste disposal facilities for the unincorporated county that would make the county unable to perform its obligation under the agreement for this project. The county agreed to deliver a minimum of 280,000 tons of processable waste to the facility during any given year. It was projected that in 1989, which would be the first full year that the facility was in operation, 350,000 tons of processable waste would be generated within the unincorporated areas of the county. It was also projected that the county could meet its guaranteed tonnage in the first year of operation by delivering only 85 percent of the available processable waste.

The Rate Covenant and Debt Service Coverage. The county covenanted to establish rates that would be not less than 110 percent of the debt service requirement for net revenues. It was estimated that it would cost each household about $7 to $9 per month to meet this revenue requirement. A comparative analysis indicated that these charges compared favorably with similar disposal charges within the county. Debt service coverage was projected to be approximately 1.12× (times) to 1.18× from 1989 through 2005. During that same time period, the estimated average user fee per ton for disposal was to drop from $51.30 to $45.56 while the debt service coverage increased somewhat.

County and TECO Payments. The county covenanted to make up any deficiency in the debt service fund from non-ad valorem tax revenue of the county or from any other legally available funds, subject to certain limitations. The county's non-ad valorem tax revenues totaled approximately $79 million in 1984 and were projected to be approximately $94.2 million in 1985. Such revenues included federal and state monies and local funds; local monies comprised the largest proportion of the non-ad valorem tax revenues. The county also covenanted to insure the facility and to acquire or cause to be acquired business interruption insurance in certain amounts. Tampa Electric Company contracted to take-and-pay for all the electricity available for sale from the facility and also agreed to construct and maintain certain interconnection facilities for the transmission of power generated by the facility.

Projected Financial Operations. Projected financial operations of the system used a base case in selected years from 1989 to 2005. System operating revenues comprised tipping fee revenues and electricity revenues. Tipping fee revenues were projected to increase from approximately $26.6 million in 1989 to $31.2 million in 2005. In a similar way, electricity revenues were projected to increase from $6.2 million to approximately $17.3 million during the same time period. As a result, total operating revenues were to increase from $32.8 million in 1989 to $48.6 million in the year 2005. Consequently, in 1989 electricity revenues were to comprise only approximately 19 percent of total system operating revenues, while in the year 2005 electricity revenues were to comprise approximately 37 percent of total operating revenues. Projected gross revenues of the entire system, which included investment earnings, were slated to increase from $34.8 million in 1989 to approximately $51.1 million in 2005. During this period, the cost of the operation and maintenance of the system was projected to rise significantly, from approximately $14.3 million to $31.3 million. As a result, net operating revenues were slated to decrease from $20.5 million in 1989 to about $19.8 million in 2005. Debt service requirements during that period were projected to drop slightly, from approximately $18.2 million to $16.8 million. Consequently, debt service coverage in 1989 was projected to be approximately 112 percent, or 1.12×, and was expected to increase through the year 2005 to 118 percent, or 1.18×. The estimated average user fee per ton for disposal through the system was projected to decrease from 1989 through 2005 from $51.30 to $45.56.

NOTE: This chapter was written by Stephen P. Rappaport in a report entitled "An Investor's Guide to Resource Recovery and Solid Waste Bonds" at Prudential-Bache Securities Inc., 1985. Reprinted by permission.

13
Education Bonds

Most students and their parents have found out some unfortunate news over different periods over the last 10 to 15 years. The news is that the cost of attending college and graduate school has far outstripped the increases in costs for most other items in their budget. Indeed, the cost of going to college for many students has become almost prohibitive. In addition, many parents with a number of children have been confronted with the possibility that they would not be able to pay the cost of their children's education even when they had thought they had made adequate provision for that expense over the years. Moreover, many students have found that even part-time jobs or summer employment do not go very far in paying even the cost of tuition, apart from the additional expense of room and board, for only 1 year of their education.

Increases in college costs have not occurred in a financial vacuum. To be sure, private institutions of higher learning have found that the costs of providing sound education (including new facilities, laboratories, dormitories, campus upkeep, and faculty salaries) have seen increases outstripping their fund drives and budget. State-supported institutions of higher learning have had similar experiences. Not surprisingly, bonds issued for colleges and universities, as well as for loans to students, have become an important part of the municipal market over the years. Nevertheless, the Tax Reform Act of 1986 will affect the issuance of such bonds. Whatever the future holds for the educational bond arena, there are enough of these bonds outstanding in the marketplace to warrant the attention of the analyst and investor.

Bonds Issued for Colleges and Universities

Demand for the School

There seems to be one factor that sets the analysis of college and university bonds apart from the evaluation of most other types of revenue bonds. It is that what may appear to be a successful institution in the past may not be the kind that survives in the future. This is partly because colleges and universities do not have a monopoly over a given geographic area or group of potential students, or customer base, as do most other revenue bonds. Private universities do not even have to submit to a process within a state for the expansion of these facilities. To be sure, there are revenue bonds issued by educational institutions which are related to a specific facility and its revenues, and there are bonds which are general obligations of the university, but the fact remains that the project and/or the university must be competitive in the future market for students. Indeed, the cost of college has gone up so dramatically that even many students taking out loans or having the ability to finance part of their education through employment are seeking an educational program that is job-oriented, or a college or university whose costs are substantially lower than might be incurred if they were to go elsewhere. In addition, there may be large groups of students nationwide who would be willing to forgo the experience of living in dormitories and might be willing to live at home to save large amounts of money for room and board. All these factors have resulted in a fiercely competitive environment for colleges and universities and have made their bonds more complex than they appear at first.

Previously, many analysts have focused on a school's perceived quality of education, on the types of students who attend the school, on the degrees, publications, and notoriety of its faculty, and on peer pressure to go to the very "best" schools. Although all these factors, if positive, would lead an analyst to expect that this would be the kind of institution that would certainly be financially solvent on an ongoing basis, the future may not be so for this type of college or university. What parents, students, and administrators of institutions of higher learning are beginning to recognize is that they are in a market which is intensely competitive and which is subject as much to the vagaries of student fads as it is to the significantly important aspect of cost and that what the institutions once were may not be an indication of what they will be. A fine school's reputation may not fade, and the quality of its education may still be superior, but the fact remains that the analyst or investor evaluating a college or university revenue bond must be concerned with the school's competitiveness in terms of attracting future students.

Financial Analysis

The financial analysis of a college or university as it relates to the evaluation of the bonds it issues may be much more detailed for a private university than for a state-supported one. For a private institution, its balance sheets, income statements, and endowment size should be analyzed. Critical in this case is a historical and projected tuition fee schedule and how it compares to like institutions within the state, the region, and the country. A similar analysis should be undertaken for state-supported institutions, but in this case the size of the endowment would not usually be very important. In the case of bonds issued for a particular project and backed by revenues solely derived from that project, such as a dormitory, a financial analysis of projected income stream should be completed. Very often, bonds secured by revenues from a specific source may be also backed by the general revenues or other unrestricted funds of the school. For private institutions, the kind and size of its fund drives are important, and future plans for funding should be evaluated with a view toward the likelihood of its fund-raising efforts.

When analyzing college and university bonds, it is critically important for the analyst or investor to make some kind of general determination as to what the future holds for the institution in terms of financial viability. This analysis is somewhat easy to do for state university systems, but for private colleges it is certainly more difficult to do because their competitive position is more likely to change over time.

Bonds for Student Loans

Municipal bonds issued for the purpose of providing loans to students had been in the marketplace for a number of years before 1981, when the volume increased well into the billions. Contrary to common perception, student loan bonds have a number of security provisions that provide additional strength above and beyond the repayments made by those who borrow the money. Additionally, student loan bonds depend more on cash flow than do many other kinds of revenue bonds, and analysts therefore focus on it. Indeed, the kinds of cash flow assumptions and scenarios that must be evaluated are not dissimilar to those kinds which the analyst must evaluate for other municipal securities, such as mortgage payment bonds.

As a result, three major areas must be evaluated when analyzing student loan revenue bonds: the program's cash flow, the insurance provided from governmental sources, and (if possible to evaluate) management's ability to undertake the program. In general, payments on student loan revenue bonds are made from three sources: repayments made on the loans by the students, monies contained in the funds established by the indenture, and insurance payments made either by the federal government (under an early program) or by the state government (which took over insurance payments in the mid-1980s).

Cash Flow

Critical to the security of student loan revenue bonds is an analysis of the cash flow of the loan portfolio, which must generate enough monies to pay the interest and principal on the bonds. The evaluation must be done under a variety of economic and interest rate assumptions. It is particularly important that the ability of the cash flow to pay for nonasset bonds, which include those costs not related to the actual student loan payments, be assured under the worst-case economic scenarios. Assumptions must be made about the average life of the loan and the projected rate at which the loans will be paid as well as about projections of delinquencies and defaults. The rate of return on the investment of income for the funds must be realistic, even under worst-case conditions. An assessment must also be made of the ability of the reserve funds to generate adequate interest income if they are used in the event that student loans are not repaid.

Insurance and Guaranteed Payments

For defaulted loans, approximately 80 to 100 percent of such payments are made through federal reinsurance, and these monies are provided to the state guarantee agency. Therefore, a review of the guarantee agency's program default record is considered important in order to ascertain the projected level of defaults as a function of the size of the portfolio of loans.

Program Administration

It is difficult for the analyst or investor to make determinations as to the quality, experience, and ability of management. Nevertheless, if the administrators of a program have had successful experience in the area of issuing bonds for student loans, then this is generally considered to be a positive indication of creditworthiness. Management should also have the ability to successfully evaluate projected cash flows and reevaluate the investment earnings so as to maintain adequate cash flow throughout the life of the program, and it should have demonstrated this ability.

Case Studies
The City University of New York*

The case presented here is especially rich in material for studying the credit analysis of municipal bonds in general and of higher-education bonds in particular. The case study is of the nation's largest locally supported system of higher education, the City University of New York (CUNY). CUNY's outstanding municipal obligations total above $1 billion, and its revenue stream is tied not only to tuition and fee income but also to financial support by both New York State and New York City. A review of this credit therefore provides a good overview of the financial character of bonds issued for higher education, especially those of government-supported institutions. In addition, and perhaps most important, this analysis of the security behind CUNY's obligations strikes at the heart of the "weakest link" theory traditionally employed by certain analysts and investors. The theory suggests that a municipal obligation whose debt service is paid from a variety of income sources can only be as secure as its weakest source of payment. Thus, a close look at the underlying security of CUNY's bonds reveals how interesting and how resilient the financial backing of certain municipal bonds may be.

Dormitory Authority of the State of New York. The Dormitory Authority is authorized to acquire property for educational and medical use and to construct such facilities through the issuance of bonds and to lease such facilities to qualifying institutions. When leased by the City University of New York, the university is responsible for the operation and maintenance of the facilities.

City University Construction Fund (CUCF). The fund is authorized to provide for the construction of facilities for all the institutions of the university. It is presently administered by a board of nine trustees chosen as follows: two are designated by the governor of New York State; four are designated by the mayor of New York City; and the chairperson of the Board of Higher Education, the chancellor of the City University, and the chairperson of the Planning Commission of the City of New York are all ex officio trustees of the fund. All trustees, except those who serve ex officio, have terms expiring at the end of the term of the elected official who appointed them.

After the trustees approve plans for the construction of a facility, the sale of tax-exempt bonds through the Dormitory Authority is arranged. The Dormitory Authority owns the facility during the period of time that the bonds are outstanding, and during this same period leases the facility to the fund for use by the City University. As a result, the fund pays to the Dormitory Authority an annual rental that is designed to cover the debt service on the bonds issued for the construction of the facility as well as to cover the Authority's administrative expenses and debt service reserve requirements.

* Data from Official Statements of $57,850,000 Dormitory Authority of the State of New York, City University Refunding Bonds, 1984 Issue, dated January 1, 1985; $48,250,000 Dormitory Authority of the State of New York, City University, Community College Issue, dated August 1, 1979; and $12,750,000 Dormitory Authority of the State of New York, City University Subordinated Community College Issue, Revenue Bonds Series 3, dated February 1, 1985.

Presently, the outstanding indebtedness related to the City University is approximately $1.1 billion, of which $700 million is for the university's senior colleges and $350 million for the community colleges. The community colleges are presently limited to the issuance of no more than $650 million, of which there is a $470 million ceiling on the total outstanding principal amount of community college bonds that are secured by a debt service reserve fund to which state funds are apportionable. Bonds may be issued above that amount that are not so secured and may not be on a parity with the bonds issued under the ceiling. The bond resolution limits the maximum annual debt service on the bonds outstanding to an amount not to exceed the aggregate amount of instructional and noninstructional fees received during the preceding fiscal year from both the senior and community colleges.

The Six Tiers of Bond Security.

1. and 2. The debt service on the outstanding bonds of CUNY is paid through annual lease rentals provided to the City University Construction Fund. The state and the city each are required to pay 50 percent of the annual rentals payable by the fund.

3. If the city fails to appropriate its 50 percent share to the fund, the state is required to pay the city's portion, which is to be taken from the next state aid payment apportioned to the city as per capita state aid for the support of local governments under Section 54 of the State Finance Law. Such monies provided to the fund from per capita state aid slated for the city are not to exceed $65 million in any one given year relating to leases of both the senior and community colleges combined. (However, the $65 million limit may not be effective if the outstanding bonds of the New York State Dormitory Authority that were issued to finance facilities through the fund are accelerated as a result of a default under the Dormitory Authority bond resolutions. All such outstanding bonds of the Dormitory Authority could then be due and payable and could have a prior claim on per capita aid to the extent of 50 percent of such principal amount.)

The payment of per capita state aid to the fund must come before such aid that is paid, if necessary, to the:

(1) New York City Housing Development Corporation
(2) New York City Transit Authority
(3) New York City Police and Pension Fund
(4) Municipal Assistance Corporation (under the Second General Bond Resolution)

4. If the funds above are not sufficient, the fund is obligated to pay annual rentals from all instructional and noninstructional fees received from the senior and community colleges for their respective debt service obligations. (Such fees from the senior colleges are subject to a prior pledge of the first $50 of tuition received from each graduate student as a result of a prior agreement between the Board of Higher Education and the Dormitory Authority executed on January 10, 1966, for the financing of CUNY's graduate center. The maximum annual debt service on these bonds is $521,063.) If this is the case, such funds will not be available for operating expenses.

5. As additional security for the bonds of CUNY's senior and community colleges, debt service reserve funds are established equal to the maximum annual debt service on each system's outstanding obligations. If such monies are used, the fund is required to include such an amount needed to replenish

the debt service reserve fund in its estimate of the amount of monies that will be required from the state and the city in the next fiscal year.

6. Finally, in the case of the community colleges, the state of New York has pledged its "moral obligation" to appropriate monies necessary to restore the debt service reserve fund to its required level under the standard deficiency makeup arrangement.

(The bonds of the senior and community colleges are issued under separate resolutions, and the sources of payment for each are not transferable.)

The Layered Effect in Theory: A Conceptual Model. One of the more intriguing aspects of the security of municipal bonds today, which is alien to corporate obligations, is introduced here as the *layered effect*, a mechanism providing increased security to certain municipal obligations. The concept is based on the increased practice of tying the security of municipal bonds to a series of "layers" (or tiers) of fund sources from which payments of the debt service on bonds can be made—sources above and beyond the traditional funds, such as the debt service reserve and capital reserve funds.

The idea behind the layered effect is that if one tier of funds is not sufficient to pay the entire debt service on the bonds, the amount of monies left to be paid after payment is made by the first tier is provided by the second tier of funds, and so forth through the other tiers of revenue sources. The use of each fund reduces the amount of debt service that must be paid by the following fund, and the series of funds, when taken together, increases the debt service coverage in the aggregate.

The argument in favor of advancing the layered-effect theory is clear: Each tier of security is not dependent on any other; if one tier of fund sources is slim or weak, the other tiers make up the difference, and the debt service may still be paid over a period of years; and when the monies from each tier are combined, the debt service coverage is increased by the size and number of tiers of security.

The layered-effect theory thus strikes at the heart of the weakest-link argument traditionally employed in municipal analysis. The latter theory suggests that the security of the bonds is generally only as strong as the weakest link of the security and can really never be stronger than the strongest source of payment for the bonds. In the weakest-link argument, the effect of the combination of funds from the many tiers is not taken into account. Under the layered effect, the additional tiers of security in fact provide additional security.

The layered effect also provides additional security under default conditions in American state and local finance, because as funds from each tier are used to pay debt service over a period of years, additional time is provided for municipalities and public authorities to work out their financial problems. During this "refinancing period," state monies may be appropriated, new agencies may be created to assume the default debt, monies from funds may be transferred where needed, and various other intergovernmental rescue programs may be implemented and even statutorily enacted. Much of the impetus behind such rescue operations is directed at preventing the impairment of the credit standing of surrounding governmental entities or similar ones nationwide as the result of a psychological spillover effect from the defaulted issuer.

The Layered Effect in Practice. *The City University of New York, both its senior and community colleges, provide landmark examples of how the layered effect works in practice.* Referring to the six tiers of bond security discussed earlier, a potential default scenario on CUNY's bonds and its effect on the payment of the debt service would be as follows:

1. If the city failed to pay its entire share of the debt service on both the senior and community college bonds (50 percent of the total debt service), the state would step in and take from the approximately $500 million in per capita state aid annually apportioned to New York City an amount equal to the city's portion of the debt service. This sum would be about $23 million for the senior colleges and $11 million for the community colleges, for a total of $34 million. *The degree of coverage is therefore obviously extensive.*

It is especially important to note that payments for the debt service on CUNY's obligations have a prior lien on state per capita aid to New York City above certain major city agencies, including the Municipal Assistance Corporation (MAC) for the City of New York.

2. *If state per capita aid was not appropriated, bond payments would be made from tuition and fee income.* With the imposition of tuition, coverage on the senior college bonds jumped from 1.8× (times) to 3.2×, and coverage on the community college bonds increased from only 0.78× to 2.2× in the first year.

In reality, then, financing the operations of the City University does not have a first claim on certain large amounts of the university's own operating income. *Interestingly, and as a result, the City University could completely cease operations and the debt service on the bonds would continue to be paid for a number of years.*

3. If student enrollment dropped substantially and tuition and fees were not increased enough to pay the debt service on the bonds, then bond payments would be made from the debt service reserve fund. Unlike most instances, the debt service reserve fund, in this case, is in fact considered to be a tier of security because if it is used to any extent, the amount of monies used is subject to repayment into the fund by the state and the city in the following year. *Thus, the debt service reserve fund is not ultimately dependent on operating income, which may have been cut off entirely.*

4. If the debt service reserve fund is not sufficient or is used, and additional monies are not forthcoming, then the state has a "moral obligation" to replenish the fund for payment of the debt service on the bonds of the community colleges. Such an arrangement is the standard deficiency makeup provision, and *it takes a certain type of government official to risk impairing the entire credit standing of New York as well as that of its revenue authorities for failing to pay approximately $11 million.* In the case of New York State, it would be $11 million as compared to a total budget of almost $13 billion.

New Hampshire Higher Education and Health Facilities Authority: Student Loan Revenue Bonds*

The New Hampshire Higher Education and Health Facilities Authority was created to help certain New Hampshire nonprofit institutions construct

---

* Data from Official Statement of $26,000,000 New Hampshire Higher Education and Health Facilities Authority, Student Loan Revenue Bonds, New Hampshire Higher Education Assistance Foundation 1985 Issue, Series A, dated October 1, 1985.

higher-education and nonprofit health care facilities, finance and refinance those projects, and also provide student loan financing. The New Hampshire Higher Education Assistance Foundation is a private nonprofit corporation organized in 1962 by the New Hampshire Association of Savings Banks and the New Hampshire Bankers Association to help students pay for their higher education by guaranteeing low-interest loans. Originally, the foundation guaranteed loans through its higher-education loan plan. Later, in 1965, the foundation received greater federal financial assistance through programs of the Higher Education Act of 1965, which embodied the Guaranteed Student Loans (GSL) and the Parent Loans for Undergraduate Students (PLUS). The foundation had guaranteed 106,000 loans with approximately an aggregate value of $220 million through 93 lending institutions; the average loan size was $2100. The foundation had a 4.7 percent default rate for loans guaranteed under the federal loan programs. Another plan, the Alternative Loan Program for Parents and Students (ALPS), had loaned over $17 million to borrowers under its first program, with a total of 2730 loans and an average loan size of $6200. The default rate under this program was less than 0.1 percent. The bond issue discussed here was for the alternative loan program.

The authority lent the proceeds of the bonds to the foundation for the student loan program known as ALPS II. The foundation used the proceeds to make loans to students. All revenues from the loan program went to pay debt service on the bonds. Under this issue, the loan program would make loan monies available to those who were not able to secure them under the Higher Education Act of 1965. The New Hampshire Higher Education Assistance Foundation projected that loan demand would be sufficient to make use of all the revenues available in the program fund. The foundation had an annual loan demand of over $10 million under its first ALPS program, with about 7500 inquiries about the program from potential borrowers. Estimated loan demand for this bond issue was projected to be $11 million annually over the following 3 years. Loan servicing was to be done by Educational Loan Services, Inc. (ELSI), a Massachusetts corporation owned by the Massachusetts Higher Education Assistance Corporation (MHEAC). Five banks, through the Participating Banks Agreement, agreed to purchase the student loans based upon a certain percentage of each bank's participation in the program and with certain terms and conditions regulating their purchases.

NOTES: This chapter was written by Stephen P. Rappaport in a paper entitled "Evaluating Municipal Bonds Issued for Education" at Prudential-Bache Securities Inc., 1986. Reprinted by permission.

The case study of the City University of New York was written by Stephen P. Rappaport in a report entitled "A New View of the City University of New York's Bonds" at Thomson McKinnon Securities Inc., 1979. Reprinted by permission.

14

Industrial Development Revenue Bonds and Pollution Control Bonds

Industrial development revenue bonds and pollution control bonds are really corporate bonds disguised to look like municipal bonds. Although each is officially a type of municipal revenue bond, they differ from the other types of bonds discussed in previous chapters that have the direct backing of a municipality or public authority. In contrast, pollution control bonds and industrial development bonds are backed solely by the corporation (not by any governmental unit at all) and as such are actually corporate credits; they are nominally structured as municipal bonds in order to qualify for issuance under Section 103 of the 1954 Internal Revenue Code, which deals with tax exemption. The Tax Reform Act of 1986 is designed to restrict their issuance, but there are enough bonds outstanding that were issued under earlier rules to warrant a discussion of them as they presently exist in the municipal marketplace. The present tense will therefore be used in this chapter.

Both types of bonds offer substantial cost savings to the corporation, and this is, unquestionably, their central attraction. Indeed, because these bonds pay interest on a tax-free basis, they almost invariably carry a coupon of at least 2 percent (200 basis points) lower than the corporation's general indebtedness, and they generally carry a coupon of about 3.5 percent (350 basis points) lower than the corporation's regular bonds, whose interest would be fully taxable.

The proceeds from the sale of these bonds are used to construct industrial or commercial facilities, to purchase equipment, or to purchase or construct pollution control devices, which are then usually leased to the corporation. Both industrial development revenue bonds and pollution control bonds can be structured as a municipal (1) lease, (2) installment sale, or (3) loan to the corporation. State law determines which way they must be structured, not the Internal Revenue Code. It is crucial to note that these lease, loan, or installment sale payments from the corporation are specifically structured to cover all the costs of servicing the municipal bonds that have been issued, including all principal and interest payments.

Genesis of Industrial Development Bonds

Industrial development bonds actually had their genesis 50 years ago in American state and local finance as offshoots of lease financings. Indeed, through a 1936 Mississippi industrial development program termed "Balance Agriculture with Industry," the state authorized the first American industrial development revenue bonds. They were issued by the city of Durant for the construction of a Realsilk Hosiery Mill factory. This effort was designed to draw industry into communities for employment and economic benefits through the use of tax-exempt financing. The financing is accomplished by a municipal entity that issues bonds to build and operate an industrial plant. The security of the plant is in the lease payments made by the corporation to the municipal issuer; the lease payments are equivalent to the debt service payments on the bonds. To be sure, this did not take a fast hold in American finance: only Kentucky and Mississippi sanctioned the use of such industrial leasing schemes. By 1950 lease contracts between different governmental entities were becoming commonplace.

Industrial leasing, however, as might have been expected, engendered charges that such financings constituted an abuse of the tax exemption. The issue came center stage early in leasing history when in 1938 a Mississippi court held, in the case of *Abritton v. City of Winona*, that the construction of plants and the subsequent leasing to private industry served "public purpose" objectives and that the bonds employed should therefore be "tax-exempt." The case was never appealed to the Supreme Court, presumably because of its earlier ruling in *Union Lime Co. v. Chicago–Northwestern Railway Co.* (1914), which made it a matter of future policy that the Supreme Court would not review decisions by a state court concerning what that government considered to be a promotion of "public purposes" as defined in its state legislation. Beginning in 1954, the IRS also formally supported the tax-exempt status of industrial development bonds.

From 1950 to 1968 industrial development financing finally began to catch on as leasing arrangements between corporations and governments gained state approval. By 1968 local governments had received authorizations for such financing in 40 states. During this early period, the total dollar volume of industrial development revenue financing jumped dramatically from $1 million to $1.5 billion annually, increasing from 0.1 percent of all municipal issues to almost 10 percent of the total volume. This dramatic percentage increase outran the multiple increases registered by every other municipal security issued for any other purpose.

Nevertheless, as industrial lease financing became overwhelmingly popular, Congress reacted swiftly to what was perceived to be an abuse of the tax exemption. This was despite court decisions and IRS rulings, too numerous to detail here, which concluded that industrial leasing arrangements provided "public purpose" objectives and that those bonds should be tax-exempt. As a consequence, Congress in 1969 limited the exemption to industrial-leasing issues under $1 million (or, for certain cases, up to $5 million), except for specified purposes such as pollution control, and the volume fell dramatically. Although erratic, the growth of industrial development bonds has resumed, but thus far the bonds have not returned to the striking level of 1968.

It should be stressed, however, that the total number of industrial development bonds issued increased through the early 1980s because of a 1978 regulation that raised the limit of industrial development bonds from $5 million to $10 million for certain projects. Since a corporation could finance up to $10 million with such bonds for each plant it has in different municipalities by using different municipal issuers, it was able to greatly increase its financing from this source in a relatively short space of time. In today's period of high interest rates, corporations and commercial businesses are intensifying their search for ways to issue such bonds as one simple means to reduce their total cost of net interest.

Types of Industrial Development Bonds

Section 103 of the 1954 Internal Revenue Code provides for two types of industrial development bonds.

Unlimited Size. Although unlimited in size, this type of bond is *restricted in the use of its proceeds* to the following: convention facilities; sports and trade shows; airports, wharfs, and docks; air and water pollution facilities; and sewage and solid waste disposal. Also, a few miscellaneous projects are allowed.

Limited Size. Although limited in size, this type of industrial development bond has an *unrestricted use of proceeds*. Under this heading are included the two so-called small-issue exemptions: (1) $1 million and (2) $10 million. The category of up to $10 million in tax-exempt bonds keys directly off the level of capital expenditures that the corporation has made. The $1 million does not.

Under the $1 million restriction, the capital expenditures that the bonds may finance include the acquisition of land or the construction on or acquisition of depreciable property for use by a company. Under the $10 million exemption, a municipality may borrow up to that total amount for the benefit of a corporation *if* that corporation has not exceeded and will not exceed that amount in capital expenditures over a 6-year period beginning 3 years prior to the issuance of the bonds.

If a corporation violates the restrictions on industrial revenue bonds, the IRS removes the tax exemption on interest received by bondholders. Those bondholders could always sue for damages "to make them whole" for this breaking of its covenants by the corporation. However, because the reliance on court suits for damages in such cases would be, inevitably, both costly and time-consuming, there occurred between 1975 and 1977 a general movement toward the adoption of a "special mandatory call" to avoid the need for such lawsuits. By 1979 this mandatory call had crept into most industrial development bond issues.

Although there are many variations on the form of a mandatory call, in general, if the bonds become taxable because the corporation violates a covenant in its lease, loan agreement, or installment sale agreement and such violation causes interest on the bonds to become taxable, then the corporation must immediately redeem the bonds at par.

Pollution Control Bonds

Coming in the wake of the Clean Air Act of 1970 and the Water Pollution Control Act of 1972, the first recorded financing of a pollution control issue was underwritten in 1971–1972. As with the case of industrial leasing, the pollution control issues were accomplished not only by governments alone but also through leasing, loan, or installment sale arrangements between governments and corporations.

The 1977 amendments to the Clean Air Act of 1970 postponed the deadline of the original legislation that required all areas of the nation to have attained ambient air standards by mid-1977. But those amendments tightened up on penalties for abuse, making noncompliance far more expensive than compliance. For the nation's governments, the deadline was extended to 1983, except for cities, such as New York, with severe carbon monoxide problems, which were allowed until 1988. State progress would be monitored through revised implementation plans for pollution control to be submitted in 1979 and 1982. Industries were given the option for 3-year delays in compliance, through permission from the state or the EPA. These delays would allow them to operate from stationary sources to pollution even though emission standards were violated. Penalty assessments were calculated to be not less than the entire cost of constructing, operating, and maintaining the pollution control facility. For violations of the act, the new law authorized the courts to impose civil penalties of up to $25,000 per day with the possibility of criminal sanctions for knowing violations of the delayed compliance penalty provisions.

The thrust of the 1977 amendments to the Water Pollution Control Act of 1972 closely resembled the "clean air" amendments: The deadline for swimmable and fishable waters was extended. In 1972 Congress set mid-1977 as the deadline for the installation by both governments and industries of the "best practical" treatment facilities for fluid wastes. It also shifted by 1 year (1983 to 1984) the time limit for the institution of the "best available technology" (BAT), with a 1985 goal of "zero discharge" of pollutants into the nation's waters. By the time the act's original deadline came, however, the compliance rate of municipalities had reached only 30 percent. Municipalities were outstripped markedly by industries, which registered an 85 percent rate of compliance. In the 1980s, most of the deadline requirements were extended.

Similarly, the cost to industries of pollution control has been anything but cheap. Businesses have spent about $4.0 billion each year on the construction of treatment facilities, an additional $5.0 billion on the operation and maintenance of those facilities, and almost $4.0 billion on the capital costs of interest and depreciation, all in an effort to meet the federal pollution standards. Making matters worse for industries and government, the EPA, which was endowed with the prerogatives of enforcement of the new legislation, instituted a stiff program of compliance.

Advantages of Tax-Exempt Financing for Corporations: Pre-1986 Tax Reform

In addition to the obvious tax advantage for corporations using industrial development bonds, there are a number of other important advantages. Before noting them, however, it should be stressed that tax exemption is the main advantage. During the 25- to 30-year term to maturity of the bonds, the 2 to 3.5 percent interest cost savings over taxable corporate bonds makes tax-exempt bond financing the least expensive method of financing a project in most cases, as noted earlier.

Another advantage is that tax-exempt bond financing allows for special arrangements for the corporation to depreciate the facility (of which it is the owner for tax purposes). Different methods of depreciation are allowed. One such method is covered by Section 169 of the 1954 Internal Revenue Code, as amended, and provides for a 60-month period over which to amortize the cost of the facility. If a corporation elects to depreciate by using Section 169 and elects to use tax-exempt financing for the facility, then it is restricted to an investment tax credit of 5 percent.

If the corporation does not use tax-exempt financing, it may take an investment tax credit of 10 percent. Therefore, the corporation's method of financing will depend on what is more advantageous: a higher rate of depreciation or a higher investment tax credit. It should be noted that there are cases where the value of conventional accelerated depreciation is greater than that of depreciation allowed by Section 169. If the corporation decides to use Section 167 rather than Section 169, its investment tax credit will vary depending on the life of the facility. The range of investment tax credit under Section 167 is generally between 5 and 10 percent.

There are three other major benefits for corporations from financing with tax-exempt municipal bonds. First, when the bonds have been fully paid for, the corporation usually is granted the right to purchase the facility for a nominal sum. Second, in contrast to most corporate securities offerings, which require extensive measures to satisfy the registration requirements of the Securities and Exchange Commission (SEC) under the Securities Act of 1933, the industrial revenue bonds, because they are "municipals," are exempt from such SEC registration. In many instances, they are also exempt from state registration requirements under specific state blue-sky laws. Third, it should be noted that according to certain state laws, some states will allow the governmental unit issuing the industrial revenue bonds to be treated as the owner of the facility, and the new plant, facilities, equipment, or land may be partly or totally exempt from local property taxes or sales taxes.

The Status of the Lease

One of the most critical aspects of analyzing the credit of leasing schemes for industrial development and pollution control is the status of the lease in bankruptcy. In most rental agreements, the lease comes in the form of either a lease-purchase contract or an installment-purchase contract. Under the lease agreement, the rentals paid by the company to the municipality are designed to sufficiently service the debt or the principal and interest on the bonds. When the lease term has ended, the corporate lessee may purchase the facility. The defect in this contract, however, is that the receiver retains the option to terminate the lease in the event of bankruptcy. As a result, in reality, the lease constitutes a subordinate corporate credit and thus is rated one notch below the company's senior debt (as opposed to a loan agreement).

Corporate guarantees of payment under both types of leases, however, render the bonds general obligations of the company that are on a par with the company's senior debt. In the lease-purchase contract, the guarantee may come (1) through a corporate pledge of payment on the rental contract that a company subsidiary has entered into with the municipal entity or (2) through a corporate guarantee to the receiver. With the installment-purchase agreement, the company may assume title to the facility after construction is completed or when the bonds mature. Under this arrangement, the company's obligation to pay the purchase price of the facility, with sufficient interest to cover the debt service, yields a rating which is equivalent to that of the company's senior debt.

State Governments and Industrial Development Bonds

In order to issue industrial development bonds, a municipality must, in addition to qualifying under the various federal laws discussed thus far, meet certain state government specifications. State laws, for example, often require proof that the proposed facilities will result in a net economic benefit to the community, whether they are for new industrial plants, land, or motels. Corporations are expected to demonstrate a public purpose that will be served by the tax-exempt financing of these new facilities. Increased employment for workers of the region, increased trade for local merchants, increased access of local economic interests to broader foreign or national markets, and the rescue of the industrial base of a declining community are typical of the public purposes that corporations usually advance to support their applications for state government permission to use tax-exempt municipal financing.

State statutes, in addition to setting out this public purpose, are also important in specifying the exact form of authorization required for such a municipal issuance. The forms of authorization vary a good deal, and each one should be examined separately and carefully. Such statutes will also stipulate whether or not there will be an interest rate limit on the bonds, and they will specify the maximum maturity schedule permissible for these bonds and the exact manner of sale—whether a private offering or a public offering. Many states allow such private sales, but some do not. Furthermore, some states impose a ceiling on the total volume of industrial development revenue bonds or pollution control bonds that can be issued without the approval of the state legislature. States also set up state commissions, state authorities, or other statewide bodies in some cases, and these must pass on the acceptability of each proposed project for industrial development bond financing. The entities vary from state to state, but generally, in effect, they establish other preconditions.

Case Studies

Payments made for the debt service on industrial development revenue bonds and pollution control bonds are usually made by companies. Therefore, for the analysis of these bonds, an evaluation of the corporate enterprise must be made, which is another whole area of securities analysis. As a result, the cases presented here will be in a discussion-type format. It is sufficient to state that there are important corporate financial ratios and indicators for analytical purposes: the pretax fixed-charge coverage, cash flow to long-term debt, pretax return on total capital invested, and long-term debt to capitalization, among others. Where there is a group of companies involved in the facility, the analyst must evaluate each company's percentage of ownership and its ability to make the required payments. Frequently, an industry analysis is also required to evaluate the company's projected financial operations.

One of the largest and most important issuers of pollution control bonds has been the Gulf Coast Waste Disposal Authority (GCWDA), which is a conservation and reclamation district in Texas established to control water pollution and to provide waste treatment and disposal systems in the counties of Harris, Galveston, and Chambers. Under the Texas Clean Air Financing Act, the GCWDA also has power to issue bonds for air pollution control facilities. A number of major companies have issued bonds through the GCWDA for pollution control financing during the 1980s. Among them have been the Exxon Corporation, the Diamond Shamrock Corporation, the Amoco Oil Company, and the Amoco Chemicals Company. Information about these corporations and financings may be ascertained from their respective official statements and annual reports.

The GCWDA has issued pollution control bonds for a number of interesting projects for these companies over recent years. The Exxon Corporation, which is engaged in the exploration, production, and sale of crude oil and natural gas as well as in the manufacturing of petroleum products, has issued bonds through the GCWDA. One project was specifically designed to remove the "rotten-egg smell" of hydrogen sulfide gas from atmospheric discharges by the plants and to treat wastewater and rainwater contaminated with sulfur compounds and hydrocarbons. The Diamond Shamrock Corporation, which also issued bonds through the GCWDA, is a company involved in energy (including oil, natural gas, and coal) and chemicals. The Amoco Oil Company and the Amoco Chemicals Company, which are subsidiaries of the Standard Oil Company of Indiana (an integrated petroleum, mining, and chemical company), issued environmental improvement bonds. The Amoco Oil Company and the Amoco Chemical Company jointly and severally agreed to make payments for the project under an installment sale agreement, which made such payments effectively equivalent to the senior unsecured debt of the Standard Oil Company because it unconditionally guaranteed the debt of the project.

Certain companies issue pollution control revenue bonds and solid waste disposal bonds in joint issues. The Dow Chemical Company issued such bonds through Midland County, Michigan. The company is a manufacturer and seller of chemicals, metals, and plastic materials as well as of pharmaceutical, agricultural, and consumer products. It is important to note that a corporation often has a choice of different methods of tax-exempt municipal financing, which, for example, include specifying an improvement as a pollution control bond or as a solid waste facility. In many cases, the rules about whether a project strictly qualifies is determined by various governmental bodies, but it is the corporation that chooses the particular method of financing, and it is critical to examine the advantages and disadvantages of each. These two methods of financing, namely, pollution control and solid waste issues, are each governed by a separate set of tax regulations. Pollution control bonds are also subject to the *incremental cost rule,* which states that the cost of a pollution control facility eligible for tax-exempt financing is reduced by the extent to which a company derives economic benefit from that facility by, for example, generating steam or using some other source of power.

Most big companies issue pollution control bonds in the form of installment sale contracts, with the payments constituting "unconditional obligations" of the company that rank on a par with the company's senior unsecured debt. Very often certain well-established companies are permitted to issue debentures, which constitute a form of senior debt. Payments for pollution control facilities would then rank on a par with the company's debentures. To be sure, first mortgage bonds are secured debt, having a lien on the facilities. Most major companies, however, have "negative pledge clauses" in their issuing statutes that prohibit them from issuing first mortgage debt in any meaningful amount, which is usually 5 percent of the net tangible assets of the company. As a result, the bonds issued under such circumstances rank, in the event of bankruptcy, just about as high in relation to the company's other outstanding debt as is possible. Certain other kinds of these bonds may be secured by lease rentals; in bankruptcy, the status of these leases is usually equivalent to the company's subordinate debt unless there is a separate guarantee by the company for payment of the lease. In such a situation, the lease payments issued would be equivalent to the company's senior unsecured debt.

Some very large companies have issued industrial development revenue bonds or economic development bonds in small amounts. The K mart Corporation has issued economic development corporation bonds through the township of Lenox, Michigan. K mart, a large retail seller of general merchandise, sold goods through K mart, Kresge, and Jupiter stores. The developer of the project would make payments on the bonds, and the project would be leased to the K mart Corporation. The company would provide an unconditional guarantee to make payments. A standard type of corporate analysis would have to be performed for such bonds secured by companies. The bonds would also be secured by a first mortgage on the facilities. The company's payments would be approximately equivalent to its senior debt.

PART 4

Financing State and Local Infrastructure Needs

15
Bonds for Infrastructure Purposes

The goal of public finance in the 1980s and beyond is surely to repair America's infrastructure, given what some believe to be the continuing need for much better government capital facilities. In general terms, the word *infrastructure* is usually considered to mean bridges, tunnels, highways, water and sewer projects, and a whole vast array of other public service–type enterprises. To most observers, therefore, it is very difficult to distinguish the real meaning of *infrastructure* from the kinds of projects that have traditionally been financed with municipal bonds over the years. There are, however, major differences. Indeed, many of the public services that are considered to be in the infrastructure category have previously been financed with state and local appropriations and bonds of the general obligation variety. Infrastructure financing takes a somewhat different form. Such services are generally financed through revenue bonds, but their financing also includes a whole host of sometimes ingenious mechanisms of paying for these public enterprises that make the financing structure a hybrid-type entity.

Creative infrastructure financing may assume several forms. A major technique involves pledging a state's credit in a variety of ways for local issuers who are unable to come into the market by themselves. This is usually done through state bond banks or similar agencies, such as local government development authorities. Additionally, certain state, local, or public authority revenues may be diverted, under new statutes, to provide funding for general infrastructure improvements. Furthermore, new special taxes may be enacted so that the infrastructure improvements or new financings can be secured by such limited-obligation-type debt. Some states have embarked on trust fund–type enterprises, which include escrowing surplus revenue from other enterprises as well as obtaining state and federal grant monies to pay the costs of infrastructure improvements throughout the state. Other states have embarked on large public-building programs, which are either paid for through leases-rentals paid directly to service the bonds or, in some cases, paid in an appropriations-type allotment to state agencies, which then pay rentals equivalent to bond principal and interest payments. Very often local governments have been involved in state-created building authorities whereby local governments pay their percentage share of leases-rentals, or if they default on their payments, state monies intended for local governments are diverted for payment of the bonds. Bankers have also designed state infrastructure banks with a wide variety of funding sources, to the extent that there seems to be a different type of bank for every particular state's needs. Another area that has been investigated is privatization, which allows private enterprises to become involved in providing government services on a fee-type arrangement; federal legislation, however, may affect the potential widespread use of privatization. Various kinds of credit enhancements, such as insurance or bank lines or letters of credit, have also been widely employed. Municipal leasing has also become a major factor in infrastructure financing.

Related to these financing structures has been a wide variety of market-related debt mechanisms that seek to provide low-cost financing to states and localities based on a vast array of types of floating and fixed rate debt, some with demand features. These have been grafted onto the infrastructure mechanisms, but some, in fact, have been a necessary part of state and local debt financing over recent years. There has also been a greater use of short-term municipal debt instruments, such as municipal notes.

It is critical to acknowledge, however, that these new financing structures present a whole new array of credit analysis questions to the analyst and investor. Many of these have to do with the potential liability of a state once these financing structures for large multi-billion dollar programs are overlayed on a state's debt structure or placed within the structure's various layers. Additionally, at one time, insurance and letters of credit were considered by most analysts and investors to be gilt-edged arrangements because the credit ratings were usually at the highest level. Recently, however, there have been a large number of downgrades in ratings by the rating agencies of banks supplying letters of credit, and certain insurance companies involved in the general municipal bond insurance field are beginning to weather financial difficulties. Not surprisingly, therefore, the analysis of any of these kinds of financing mechanisms and credit support facilities must be dealt with on a case-by-case basis.

Building Authorities and Bond Banks

Building authorities are among the major financing vehicles employed by governments to provide infrastructure-type services. State and local building authorities have employed a leasing concept to acquire, construct, or rent office space for their agencies. Usually, such payments are made through rental payments payable by state building authorities. Such payments are either included as line items in a state's budget, or if there are local governments involved, municipalities make payments equivalent to their proportionate share of bond principal and interest payments. In certain instances, appropriations at the state and local level have gone directly to state agencies, and then the state agencies themselves make rental payments singly, or as a member of a pool, which are used to pay principal and interest payments on the bonds.

Over recent years a number of states have found that their localities have desperately needed to provide certain government services for their population or to enlarge those services or even improve them. Very often such localities have not been capable of entering the debt markets at reasonable interest rates because they have been unable to secure investment-grade ratings. Their problem has been partly solved through the establishment of state-created municipal bond banks, which issue debt on behalf of a number of localities and loan this money to the local governments. The municipalities then provide monies for payment on the loan, and these monies go to secure and pay off the bonds. As a result, the states can provide money to the localities at interest rates far below what they could get if they entered the market themselves. There is a certain degree of diversification of risk in this kind of pooled bond bank concept, and this diversification forms the basis of bond security. As a backup security, in most instances the state withholds state aid that would normally go to the locality in an amount sufficient to pay the locality's share of bond payments if it does not make payments on its proportionate share of the loans. As a result, most bond banks are rated one category below their respective states, but there are notable exceptions to the principle. The quality of a bond bank's obligations also depends on the number of localities involved in the bond bank, the size of a locality's payment in relation to its general budget, the ability of these localities to make payments on the loans provided by the state, the amount of state aid money flowing to the localities, and the percentage of the loan pool for which the localities are liable as a function of their credit rating or perceived quality.

Somewhat similar to a bond bank concept for funding infrastructure projects are state infrastructure banks that enter the market on behalf of localities. Proposals for state infrastructure banks include concepts whereby state appropriations and federal grants are used to lower the interest costs on any borrowing. In these instances the federal government would have to approve the use of categorical grants for infrastructure purposes within a state. Federal monies would also be used as a reserve for a state's infrastructure bank borrowing and other capitalization purposes. Local governments would then have to relinquish control over their federal grants, but they might thus be able to gain more money at lower costs for large projects than they could finance by themselves.

Credit Enhancements

Municipal Bond Insurance

One of the most important developments in the field of municipal bonds was the introduction some time ago of municipal bond insurance, yet only recently has a tremendous rush to the market of new municipal issues carrying municipal bond insurance in substantial amounts occurred. At the present time, municipal bond insurance can be used to insure primary and secondary issues, bond funds and unit investment trusts, bond portfolios, certain maturities, and reserve funds of bond issues as well as to insure other credit enhancement techniques, such as letters of credit. The insurance policies usually guarantee timely payment of principal and interest, and there is usually no acceleration of the payments in present insurance clauses and no premiums on calls that are paid. There are a number of municipal bond insurers. Some of them are combinations of other insurance companies, and others just insure municipal bonds. The insurers include the American Municipal Bond Assurance Corporation (AMBAC), the Municipal Bond Insurance Association (MBIA), Industrial Development Bond Insurance (IDBI), Health Industry Bond Insurance (HIBI), the Financial Guarantee Insurance Company (FGIC), and Bond Investors Guarantee (BIG).

When rating agencies have rated bonds secured by municipal bond insurance, these bonds have usually been rated "triple-A". However, some insurance companies participating in these municipal bond insurance programs have experienced financial problems; thus, while no one can be certain whether such problems may continue, it is certainly worth monitoring not only those insurance companies which have experienced problems but also all other companies involved in municipal bond insurance programs. It is sufficient to suggest, however, that municipal bond insurance does provide another layer of security for municipal bond issues—which should imply to the investor and the analyst that the bonds are better secured than if they were solely dependent on their own revenue stream or tax structure.

Lines of Credit and Letters of Credit

Banks provide both of these facilities to municipal bond issuers for a fee, and both are generally considered to improve the rating on the debt to the triple-A (Aaa/AAA) level. [Recently, however, some banks have had their guarantees through lines or letters of credit dropped to the double-A (Aa/AA) category because the bank's rating has been lowered.] A *line of credit* provides a guarantee in the sense of liquidity so that the issuer can meet future bond payments, such as when put option bonds are issued. A *letter of credit* is different, for it is a pledge of the bank's credit to make principal and interest payments on the bonds even if the issuer is in default. Some analysts suggest that a major difference between these two credit facilities is that the letter of credit is available only for a specified time period, whereas a line of credit is usually issued for the entire term of the bond issue. The analysis of bank-related debt, however, can be quite complex.

Leasing

One of the more interesting corporate concepts grafted onto municipal bonds over recent years has been that of leasing as a way to finance the purchase of equipment and the acquisition of real property by states, municipalities, and even certain revenue authorities without impairing the issuer's credit standing. This has usually been accomplished through a lease-purchase-type agreement, which some analysts consider similar to an installment sales contract. Leases come in a variety of forms, but usually a governmental entity issues bonds, and the user of the facility or equipment leases it from the issuer. Lease payments are usually equivalent to bond principal and interest payments over the life of a lease, and with the last lease payment and an additional small payment, the user takes title to the equipment. The use of the concept has seen widespread growth, partly because a lease is not treated as general debt on a municipality's or state's balance sheets, but rather is considered only a contingent liability. Leasing, therefore, does not increase the municipality's debt ratios, and it also avoids the necessity for bond referendums or constitutional-type approval. As a result, however, most leases are not rated as highly as the governmental entity's senior or general obligation debt, but there are variations in the relative ratings of leases. In some cases, however, leases are also secured by the entity's senior debt, the lease may have a long term, and the investor may have remedies, in the event of default, which are similar to those of an investor who invests in the entity's senior debt. Such leases are usually rated as high as the entity's senior debt.

Leases have a number of characteristics that must be considered by analysts and investors when evaluating the creditworthiness of lease obligations. In most cases, lease payments are usually made subject to annual appropriations. Some assessment must be made as to the desire of a legislative body or municipal government to make these annual appropriations. The lease should usually have a covenant that includes a request for appropriations in the entity's annual budget for payment of the lease during the following year. Also, the length of the lease should be the same as the term of the bond issue. In addition, an analysis should be made of the entity's history in honoring similar lease payments. The piece of equipment or the building should be considered an essential service of the entity leasing it, and the more essential it is, the better the quality of the obligation.

Many have argued that a nonsubstitution clause in the covenants of a lease obligation is very important to the security of the lease; however, it may not be as critical as many investors and analysts believe. Nonsubstitution clauses state in effect that the lessee cannot lease, purchase, or use a similar piece of equipment for at least 30 days to a year or more in the event of nonappropriation by the state or local government of lease payments. Yet even without the piece of equipment, there may be ways for a lessee to get around the intent of the nonappropriation clause and obtain the same service, or the service could be suspended for a time until the nonsubstitution clause is terminated or runs out. If an entity desires to prepay lease obligations and thus terminate the lease, such payments would be equivalent to the outstanding principal balance of the lease.

An analysis should be made of the entity leasing the equipment and of the equipment itself. There should be some assessment as to whether or not the leased equipment will be obsolete technologically in a short period of time or anytime before the final lease payment is due. This evaluation would entail some kind of corporate-type analysis of similar kinds of equipment and, if possible, the technological stages at which similar equipment is being developed by other companies. Moreover, the company providing the equipment should be analyzed because the equipment would be in operation over the length of the lease period. Therefore, proper maintenance, servicing, and parts may have to be made available to the lessor by the company. Usually, however, the entity covenants to maintain the piece of equipment in good operating condition and to provide for service payments and insurance. Also critical is a credit analysis of the municipality or state leasing the piece of equipment. This entails a general obligation–type bond analysis with special attention to the state or municipality's amount of contingent liabilities, such as other lease obligations.

Case Studies

The State of Connecticut's Special Tax Obligation Bonds: Transportation Infrastructure Purposes*

The state's Transportation Infrastructure Program was a 10-year project that included generally the construction and rehabilitation of the state's transit facilities. The program, which would be administered by the state's department of transportation, would increase the department's capital needs substantially at the expected average rate of more than $550 million per year over the 10-year period. The program specifically included: completing the interstate highway system, making improvements to the state's primary and secondary roads, constructing substitute highway projects for which the federal Interstate Transfer Program funds were available, rehabilitating and replacing state and local bridges, improving bus and commuter rail operations, making capital improvements to the Bradley International Airport as well as five state-owned airports and certain municipal airports, resurfacing and restoring the state's highway system, repairing maintenance garages, and expanding and improving the department's administrative facilities and safety programs. The 10-year project was projected to cost $5,574.4 million, which comprised $3,332.9 million of federal money, $1,557.5 million of bond monies, $504.1 million of appropriations, and $179.9 million in monies from other sources. Total bond issuance over this period was projected to be $1,848.1 million.

Revenues to cover the state's share of the infrastructure program were expected to come from motor fuel taxes; motor vehicle receipts; motor vehicle–related licenses, permits, and fees; and other transportation-related revenues. After providing for debt service requirements, the balance of the receipts could be applied to payments for the state's general obligation bonds and for annual budgeted expenses of the transportation department. Such revenues were subject to a prior statutory pledge for payment of the Expressway Bonds, of which approximately $67,535,000 were outstanding.

In 1984 motor vehicle fuel taxes totaled $205.6 million; motor vehicle receipts totaled $79.5 million; and license, permit, and fee revenue totaled

---

* Data from Official Statement of $125,000,000 State of Connecticut, Special Tax Obligation Bonds, Transportation Infrastructure Purposes, 1984 Series A, dated September 15, 1984.

$39.3 million. Total revenue was $324.4 million. It was projected that by 1994 motor fuel tax revenues would rise to $358.3 million; motor vehicle receipts revenues would increase to $174.0 million; and license, permit, and fee revenue would increase to $128.1 million. Total revenue would increase to $715.0 million in 1994, which also included interest income and UMTA grants from the Urban Mass Transit Administration. Aggregate debt service coverage for the bonds and projected additional bonds to be issued would be 3.3× (times) in 1994, down from approximately 5.1× in 1988 and 6.4× in 1987. The state covenanted to charge, impose, raise, levy, and collect and apply the pledged revenues in amounts necessary to pay debt service requirements so that net revenues, after reserve requirements, would be equal to 2.0× the principal and interest requirements on bonds and notes outstanding.

The Maine Municipal Bond Bank*

The Maine Municipal Bond Bank was created to provide access to the capital markets for governmental units to make public improvements. The bank assisted governments in financing by issuing its own obligations and making funds available at reduced interest costs and on more favorable terms through loans. The loans were made pursuant to loan agreements between the bond bank and certain local governments. This was accomplished by the purchase of the governmental units' bonds by the bond bank. The governmental units would service their municipal bonds by levying ad valorem taxes or collecting rates, charges, or assessments.

The bank is able to purchase municipal bonds of governmental units; these include bonds of counties, cities, towns, school administrative districts, community school districts, and other quasi-municipal corporations within the state, except for those bonds and notes issued under the Revenue Producing Municipal Facilities Act or the Municipal Securities Approval Act of the state. Additional security for the bonds is the state's appropriation of monies sufficient to restore the debt service reserve fund to the required amount, upon certification to the governor by the chairperson of the bank of the amount needed. There was approximately $504,800,000 of bonds issued, of which $286,705,000 was outstanding, with approximately 382 municipal bond issues purchased by the bank.

Kentucky State Property and Building Commission†

The commission is empowered to acquire real estate and to construct and equip building and other projects for any state agency and to issue revenue bonds to provide financing for such purposes. For payments of the

---

* Data from Official Statement of $22,660,000 Maine Municipal Bond Bank, 1985 Series C Refunding Bonds, dated December 1, 1985.

† Data from Official Statement of $44,195,000 Commonwealth of Kentucky, State Property and Building Commission Revenue Bonds, Project No. 32 (Second Series), dated November 1, 1985.

revenue bonds, the commission is authorized to execute lease agreements with state agencies and to use these payments made to the commission to make principal and interest payments on the commission's revenue bonds.

The bonds of this issue were used to fund various cabinet projects, to refund the commission's revenue bond Project No. 32, and to provide for the cost of issuance and fund reserves. The bonds are not secured by a lien on the properties of the project, but are secured and payable solely from the revenues derived from rental payments of the lessee under the lease. The lease is between the commission and the lessee and it relates to the project. The lessee will lease the project from the commission and will pay rentals to the commission during renewable biennial terms. Such lease payments will provide funds sufficient to pay the principal and interest, any additional sums, and the premium, if any, on the bonds that are due. The lessee has been granted by the commission the exclusive option to renew the lease for successive renewal terms of 2 years until the time when the bonds are no longer outstanding. The commission is prohibited from entering into lease obligations extended beyond the biennial budget period, and each lease is automatically renewed unless written notice is given by the lessee.

The lessee has covenanted in the lease that when appropriations bills are prepared for the general assembly, it will include the required appropriations for that biennial period to enable the lessee to make the rental payments required to the commission. The commission has covenanted that it will apply such lease monies for payment of principal and interest on the bonds. Appropriations for the rental payments under the lease are subject to the approval of each successive biennial session of the Kentucky General Assembly. There is no assurance that any of the appropriations will be made in the future general assembly sessions or that such appropriations will not be reduced or eliminated by the governor, if such appropriations are made in an effort to balance the budget.

The total population of Kentucky is approximately 3,723,000. The state is the leading state in total tonnage of coal produced. Tobacco is a major crop of the state, the state's manufacturing mix is diversified, and horse breeding plays an important part in the state's economy. Total debt outstanding was $3,697,000,000 in 1985, and the total amount of outstanding appropriation-supported debt was $2,103,265,000, or 37 percent of the total debt. The state has a diversified tax system consisting of eight general classifications of revenue sources. In 1985 the state had an undesignated general fund balance of $41.3 million and an undesignated combined major fund balance of $323.6 million.

NOTE: Part 4 (Chaps. 15 and 16) was written by Stephen P. Rappaport in a paper entitled "Financial Alternatives for State and Local Infrastructure Needs" at Prudential-Bache Securities Inc., 1986. Reprinted by permission.

16

Bonds with Market-Related Financing Options

Municipal Notes

Since the mid-1970s, short-term municipal notes have become an increasingly important part of the municipal debt market. There are eight basic kinds of short-term obligations: tax anticipation notes (TANs), revenue anticipation notes (RANs), tax and revenue anticipation notes (TRANs), grant anticipation notes (GANs), bond anticipation notes (BANs), project notes, construction loan notes, and commercial paper. TANs are issued in anticipation of the receipt of tax revenues; RANs are issued with the anticipation that they will be paid from future revenues, which are usually state or federal aid. Very often these two kinds of note issues can be combined in the form of TRANs. GANs are issued in anticipation of federal or state grant monies for a project and are provided to a municipality or state. BANs are usually issued to provide short-term financing in anticipation of long-term or permanent bond financing because of the inability to calculate the total construction cost of a project in its early stages. Project notes have been issued by the U.S. Department of Housing and Urban Development to fund local housing and urban renewal projects. Construction loan notes are issued to provide short-term financing for construction projects, usually in the multifamily housing area. Commercial paper is used in the municipal market for large construction programs and generally to reduce borrowing costs.

In general, notes are issued for a period of 90 days to 1 year, and their credit analysis depends on the ability of the government to pay off the notes through forthcoming monies or to reenter the debt market by either rolling over the notes or funding them into a long-term bond issue. In today's market, securities can still be called "notes" and be issued for a period of up to 3 years. With the length of note terms increasing, many analysts and investors have tried to discern whether or not the issue may really be called a note or is actually a bond, and sometimes the nomenclature gives rise to additional questions. In general, many analysts argue that if market access becomes significantly important for payment or refinancing, the instrument is closer to a note than to a bond.

It is important to understand that most RANs and TANs cannot be rolled over, but BANs usually can be. Rolling over notes may still be a backstop for repayments as long as it is not a habitual practice. This is so because issuers have become more sophisticated and have decided on maturities of much less than a year. Issuers closely follow the direction of interest rates, which gives them some flexibility to either bond-out the notes or pay them off, and yet still borrow at a lower interest cost for the short term. The most obvious use of this technique is commercial paper.

Many analysts and investors have tried to draw conclusions about what an issuer's note rating should be, based on its bond ratings. In general, the higher the entity's bond rating, the more likely it is that its note rating will be high, but this is not a hard-and-fast rule. Many issuers who have low investment grade ratings may receive high note ratings on their TANs, for instance, and the opposite could also be the case. An entity's note rating depends in some measure on whether or not the note is secured on a parity with the issuer's long-term debt and also on how strong the issuer's cash flow projections are to pay the notes. Nevertheless, a major basis for the note rating is the issuer's general debt structure as well as its financial and economic position.

It is generally considered that tax and revenue anticipation notes secured by property tax revenues are more secure and, as a result, need less of a financial cushion than notes secured by other revenue sources. For TANs and RANs, it is highly important to determine cash availability to pay off the notes under collection rates that are very low. Evaluating cash flow statements, both historical and projected, on a monthly basis through the time the note is to mature is critical; indeed, cash flow is perhaps one of the most important determinants of the ability of an issuer to pay these notes. Yet it is difficult to find any relative benchmark on the amount of note issuance as a percentage of the city or state's budget that can be called a test of good management because of the great variations in amounts with which state and local governments of different sizes have successfully used notes in the past. There are, however, some warning signs for which the analyst or investor should look. One of them is the constant rolling over of notes, which would possibly be the result of budget deficits occurring on a yearly basis over a long period of time. Another problem would be the use of notes to fund operating expenses on a very large scale. The issuer should also have the ability to collect taxes promptly and at a sufficiently high collection rate. Usually, this is at a rate of 90 to 93 percent at the minimum.

One of the critical issues in analyzing the ratings of notes that must be refinanced, such as BANs, is the ability of the issuer, when refinancing the notes, to withstand interest rates that are substantially higher than projected at the time the original notes were brought to market. An evaluation of different interest scenarios for refinancing notes is critical in this analysis. Also important are the projected cash flow supporting the notes and the projected balance sheet of the issuer, which would be available at the time the notes are refinanced or bonded into long-term debt. BANs are also generally secured by the issuer's general obligation pledge, as is sometimes the case with TRANs, so cash flow analysis is especially important because of the potential impact on the issuer.

There is a variety of rating symbols used for rating notes and commercial paper. Moody's rates notes with the symbols MIG 1 through MIG 4 [standing for Moody's investment grade (MIG) ratings]. Standard & Poor's note ratings are slightly different than Moody's; they are SP-1+, SP-1, SP-2, and SP-3.

Commercial paper is being issued now with increasing frequency by municipalities, although it has usually been issued by corporations in an unsecured fashion. Commercial paper issues have very short maturity (usually 15 to 45 days), are backed by some kind of credit facility (such as one offered by a bank), and may in most cases be rolled over. Ratings on commercial paper should reflect not only the general evaluation of the issuer itself and the financial capability of the issuer to make payments but also the quality of the guarantor, the security of the contract, and the ability of the issuer to make payments on the credit facility backing the commercial paper, if necessary. To be sure, this type of analysis appears to be all-encompassing, but any one of these factors without strength in the other is seen to be a negative factor in relative terms. Standard & Poor's commercial paper ratings are A-1+, A-1, A-2, A-3, B, C, and D. Moody's commercial paper ratings are P-1, P-2, and P-3.

Variable Rate and Put Option Bonds

Variable rate bonds are those bonds whose yields change at various times over the life of the issue, based on a variety of their indices or percentages or on their market value. They may be adjusted on a daily, monthly, annual, or longer-term basis. Usually, the bonds have an interest rate floor and a ceiling that provide some limits for the issuer from the standpoint of paying interest and for the bondholder from the standpoint of receiving such payments. Some variable rate securities may be converted to fixed interest rates after a certain amount of time. In some cases, upon conversion, the holder has the option to *put* the bonds in some way, which means to keep the bonds at the fixed rate. This put, or demand, feature allows the investor to put the securities at any number of specified time periods, and the holder will usually receive par for the bond. The issuer must have cash flow to pay the principal and interest on the bonds if the bondholder decides to put them back to the issuer, or a type of credit enhancement facility must be in place, such as a letter of credit, to pay the bonds that are tendered; this occurs to the extent that the tendered bonds have not been remarketed. Sometimes the put may be exercised at the market value of the bonds. In other cases, these bonds may have certain call dates so that the issuer can redeem the bonds when the conditions in the market are appropriate.

The issuer's cash flow and liquidity supports are critical to the analysis. The cash flow of the issuer must be sufficient to pay the debt service under a variety of interest rate scenarios. Another concern is the issuer's ability to repay the line of credit or letter of credit if either is needed. Payment on the line or letter of credit would have some impact on the credit of the issuer.

The demand feature has given rise to new rating symbols. These put option bond issues usually carry two ratings, one for the bond issue itself and one for the put option, whether it is to the issuer or is secured by an insurance company or a bank. Standard & Poor's uses A-1+, A-1, A-2, A-3, B, C, and D for the short-term portion of the ratings. Moody's uses the symbols VMIG-1, VMIG-2, VMIG-3, and VMIG-4 for the short-term portion of demand obligations with the put option, which can originate from fixed rate and variable rate bonds.

Zero Coupon Bonds

Zero coupon bonds, or capital appreciation bonds (which also come to market under a variety of other names), are bonds which are issued at a substantial discount and which are redeemable at the total value at maturity. Such bonds have imputed semiannual coupons and a yield to maturity, both computed through the discount price. The issuer bears the risk of reinvestment, and the reinvestment rate is the same rate as that of the purchaser's bonds. The issuer must be able to make the payment on the bonds when they come due, which could be a typical type of credit concern.

Warrants

Municipal bonds have been issued with *warrants*, which guarantee that the investor can purchase an additional bond at the same interest rate and at the same price as the original issue. Credit concerns occur if investors decide to exercise their warrants in a period of declining rates and the issuer must sell bonds in large amounts at the original higher rates.

Refunded Bonds

Municipal bonds are *refunded* when new bonds are issued to pay off the old bonds, which are then secured by an escrow fund (or can also be collateralized) with maturity schedules to match payments due on the refunded bond. Refunding has been employed to save an issuer interest expense if the new bond issue's interest rate is sufficiently lower than that of the one outstanding. This technique has also been used to circumvent covenants that are restrictive (such as ones that limit additional financing) and to revamp the issuer's debt maturity schedule. Very often there is a combination of these factors involved as well as the need for new financing, which can be issued at or about the same time. Over the years, the federal government has sought limitations on this practice.

Case Study
State of California:
Revenue Anticipation Notes*

The state of California issued $2.3 billion of revenue anticipation notes to fund in part the state's cash flow management program for the fiscal year 1985–1986, which ended on June 30, 1986. Proceeds from the sale of the notes were deposited in the general fund of the state treasury. Payment of the principal and interest on the notes from unapplied monies was subject to

---

* Data from Official Statement of $2,300,000,000 State of California, 5.30% 1985 Revenue Anticipation Notes, dated August 13, 1985.

the prior claim of monies from the general fund to support education, to pay the principal and interest on the general obligation bonds of the state, and to cover the prior application of monies in the general fund transferred from the state's special funds and needed for reimbursement. The state had established the Special Fund for Economic Uncertainties, which had $1.04 billion of general fund surpluses covering the past 2 years. Principal and interest on the notes were payable from monies in the general fund for the fiscal year 1985–1986 and from certain internal borrowing by the state from the special funds.

The controller had determined that the monies in the general fund would not be sufficient to cover the payment of all appropriations by the state legislature for the fiscal year 1985–1986. Based on the controller's estimate, a demand of $2.3 billion was then drawn against appropriations made from the general fund before such income was received in the fiscal year 1985–1986. The demand for nonpayment was given to the treasurer, who registered the demand and then notified the controller of this fact. The controller then apprised the Pooled Money Investment Board (which consisted of the state's controller, the treasurer, and the director of finance) of the demand, and the board then advised the governor of the registered demand and requested a determination of whether there would be the transfer of monies from the special funds to the general fund of the state. After 5 working days' notification, the board authorized the treasurer to sell those notes of the state which represented the registered demand for $2.3 billion. Then the treasurer adopted the note resolution authorizing the issuance of the notes, payable not later than June 30, 1986, and not renewable beyond that date.

The state's fund balances, calculated on a modified accrual basis, were $490.6 million for 1983–1984 and were estimated to be $1,265 million for 1984–1985. For the fiscal year 1985–1986, fund balances were projected to be $1,054.3 million. For this fiscal year, it was estimated that about $1.04 billion from the Special Fund for Economic Uncertainties, together with $2.75 billion from other special funds, would be available to meet the cash needs of the state. The state had a $7,732,590,000 principal amount of general obligations outstanding, with $3.1 billion of authorizations unissued. It also had an $8,634,101,356 principal amount of revenue bonds outstanding, and $109,105,100 outstanding of contingent liabilities from lease purchase agreements and certificates of participation.

NOTE: Part 4 (Chaps. 15 and 16) was written by Stephen P. Rappaport in a paper entitled "Financial Alternatives for State and Local Infrastructure Needs" at Prudential-Bache Securities Inc., 1986. Reprinted by permission.

PART 5

The Structural Framework for Public Finance

17
Municipal Accounting

Introduction

In 1975 New York City's books were balanced in accordance with the financial practices of the city. In actuality, the city had accumulated a deficit of close to $5 billion. Moreover, it was incurring an unfunded pension liability that it could not foresee paying and was negotiating contractual benefits with labor unions for which it was unable to carry the financial burden. Yet the financial statements presented a picture of sound financial management. The "telephone book" financial statements provided a deluge of financial data, but the actual financial operation and position of the city were not apparent in its report to the public.

The financial emergency that struck New York City so severely in 1974–1975 shocked the financial community. How could such a crisis come about so precipitously and without warning? Why had the reporting mechanisms not revealed the deficiencies that had been building up for years? Moreover, did the problem facing New York City indicate similar problems about the financial soundness of other municipalities across the nation? Clearly, the accounting systems, the financial management, and the efficacy of that management in running municipalities were in immediate question. A strict accounting of services and practices as well as accurate, timely, and fairly presented financial pictures of cities were required. The long-neglected areas of municipal accounting and accounting standards were coming into the limelight.

The purposes of this chapter are (1) to discuss the basic theories of municipal accounting, reporting, and budgetary practices and (2) to highlight problem areas that may be encountered when reviewing a municipality's financial reports.

The Municipal Budget

Investors and bond analysts, in order to obtain even the most basic idea of how a given municipality handles its debt, must look at the municipality's budget and financial statements.

The final budget is a more important document than the accounting statements because the budget sets out all the legally authorized expenditures for that municipality. In contrast, the accounts are intended to be merely a reflection of the expenditures and receipts that were previously authorized. Obviously, it is of key importance to the analyst to check if the budget and books of account do correspond to one another, or instead appear inconsistent.

Not only is the budget system more important than the accounting system, but the budget, in effect, sets the shape and scope of the whole accounting system and lays down the specific terms of the accounts—i.e., whether the accounting will be on a cash basis or on an accrual basis is determined by the municipality's budgetary expectations.

The Budget and Budgetary Accounting

By the 1920s most of the major municipalities had, in the light of financial reforms, adopted some type of budgetary practice. Legislation was enacted on the state and local levels requiring budgets for at least the general fund of each municipality. Formal comparisons were required to be made between budgeted expenditures and actual amounts utilized. If a formal audit was not required by law, the general fund was usually accounted for by presenting a comparison of it with its adopted budget.

The budget provides a standard of measurement by which the performance of the municipality in achieving predesignated goals can be seen. With increasing controls and evolving reforms, the municipality's incorporation and use of budgets are being encouraged for most funds. The development of the budget is essentially a "political" process, which is the governmental unit's means of delineating fiscal and social policy. The timing as well as the content and format of the budget vary from municipality to municipality. Some statutes clearly define the information and structure of the budget, whereas others are vague in their specifications. The National Committee on Governmental Accounting recommends that the annual budget be prepared using the modified accrual basis of accounting; the accounting system becomes the control mechanism ensuring that revenues and expenditures are used as defined in the budget.

The Budgetary Process

The budgetary process can be looked at as a cycle. The first step is the initial preparation of the budget itself: Department heads submit programs, projects, and operating costs according to their estimated needs. Financial information is correlated, and projected program requirements based on historical data are developed. Financial officers of the municipality compile the estimated revenues and expenditures. They review the programs and departmental needs and prepare a "balanced budget" document.

The next step in the cycle is the submission of the proposed budget to the legislature; while the legislature reviews the document, public hearings are held. If necessary, in order to raise additional funds, appropriations and tax levy ordinances, such as a property tax, are drafted and adopted. Expenditures are established through an appropriations act, and an act is legislated that stipulates maximum spending authorizations. Expenditures cannot exceed the spending limit unless the act is amended. Depending on the terms of the law, appropriations not spent by the end of the fiscal year may lapse or be continued in the next year. Thus the legislature will either approve, reject, or modify the budget.

Once the budget is adopted, the next step is its implementation. The terms of the budget must be complied with, and monies are spent according to specified allocations. Interim reports may be prepared on a monthly or quarterly basis to detail the progress of the services and programs provided. Administration of the budget entails the accounting for, as well as the implementation of, revenues and personnel.

At the end of the fiscal year, financial reports are generated. This is the final step in the budgetary cycle. The financial statements are frequently audited to determine their accuracy and compliance with generally accepted accounting principles (GAAP); moreover, their compliance with legal and budgetary requirements is reviewed. Financial and statistical data are compiled for the fiscal year and summarized in many of these reports.

The budgetary cycle is an integral part of the management of a municipality. With the increasing complexity of the financial management of a governmental unit, there is a greater need for planning, and the budget is an essential tool for adequate planning and management. It is also used to evaluate the performance of the municipality.

Methods of Budgeting

Budgets can be distinguished in terms of purpose, being either operating budgets or capital budgets. The operating budget, or annual budget, applies to the general and special revenue funds and may be used for the debt service fund where it is specifically adopted. The capital budget is adopted for long-term financial planning. It is an outline of ongoing capital improvement programs (CIPs). Annual preparations for such plans will specify the necessary appropriations for the forthcoming fiscal year and will show estimates for 5 years thereafter. This budget is necessary for the analysis of proposed plans as well as the estimated means of financing such projects. Rating agencies review this document: It is considered an essential component for a well-managed municipality.

Three types of budgets are commonly used: traditional budgets, performance budgets, and program budgets. The *traditional budget* is determined by the objectives of the expenditures. The objective of this type of budget is to define accounting and administrative responsibilities and delegate them to department heads. The revenues are determined by the needed expenditures. In its basic form, the traditional budget does not provide a measure for total expenditures for specific services, duties, or activities. Prior years' expenditures are used as the basis for determining the needs in future years.

The second type of budget is the *performance budget*. It attempts to present a clearer relationship between the use of resources and the resultant services. The purpose of this type of budget is to present quantitative data concerning the "units of work" performed or the services provided, identified by organizational areas. This data can then be used as a means of measuring the work output of the departments. Moreover, it is used to determine the funding requirements.

The *program budget* is based primarily on the program of work and secondarily on the nature and purpose of the program. It is viewed as a compromise between the traditional budget and the performance budget. The program budget attempts to measure the overall cost of a program, and it tries to establish a criterion under which one program can be evaluated against another in terms of importance. One major flaw is that it may not clearly show certain information that may be necessary in order to evaluate specific operations within a program, especially when increased expenditures are involved.

In the 1960s a new approach to budgeting—the planning, programming budget system (PPBS)—was developed. Through a definition of the objectives and goals of the programs offered, this method attempts to coordinate the program, planning, and budgeting processes. The objective of PPBS is to identify the long-term consequences of current decisions in compliance with the stated objectives. Selections are made from alternative means of attaining stated objectives on the basis of a full analysis of the cost-benefit findings of each alternative. PPBS provides a *multiyear* perspective: i.e., it covers a specified number of years into the future.

PPBS is but one means in a trend toward developing a set of criteria for measuring the success of a program by quantifying the actual benefit derived from it. Another approach being developed follows the method used by the General Accounting Office (GAO) in its audits of federal agencies. Basically, the GAO sets forth three standards for evaluating performance, each being dependent on the preceding step. The guidelines used are (1) review of financial compliance, which includes the basic evaluation of compliance with budgetary and regulatory requirements; (2) evaluation of economy and efficiency, which determines those areas where revenues can be enhanced and costs reduced; and (3) evaluation of program results, whereby the program's actual results are compared with the original objectives.

Budgetary Accounting

The budget is not only a legal financial plan for the municipality but also serves as an essential element in the financial planning, control, and evaluation of the operations of the governmental unit. The book *Governmental Accounting, Auditing & Financial Reporting Standards* recommends that annual budgets be adopted by all municipalities. The annual budget should cover the fiscal year, and its basis of accounting should follow that used for the differing funds. Budgets are recommended for government funds because of the need to incorporate a control mechanism over these funds. Requirements for the use of budgets vary from state to state as well as from municipality to municipality. For financial reporting purposes, the statement of revenues and expenditures of the general fund and certain special revenue funds should have a comparison with a formal budget.

A distinction should be made between fixed budgets and flexible budgets. A *fixed budget* has a set dollar amount; a *flexible budget*, on the other hand, has a changeable dollar amount—an amount that depends on the demand for goods and/or services.

The annual budget provides control over the use of resources for the municipality. The accounting system must provide the information to show that legal requirements are being met. Budgetary accounts may be integrated into the fund accounts, but these accounts will not have an effect on either the financial position or the fund balance as shown on the financial statements.

Proprietary funds usually do not require budgets. Those which are recommended are flexible budgets, which are more like approved plans than formalized budgets. The rationale behind this type of budgeting is that since proprietary funds provide goods and services, the demand for these functions will determine the level of necessary revenues and expenses. In addition, these funds resemble private enterprises inasmuch as differing levels of expenditures are budgeted according to expected demand. Fixed budgets are usually not used for these funds, unless stipulated by law.

The types of budgets used for fiduciary funds vary according to the nature of the fund, whether it is expendable or nonexpendable. Trust funds are similar to special revenue funds and may require budgets, whereas agency funds do not require the use of budgets, since they are of a custodial nature.

Variations in the Budget

A final approved budget legally authorizes a municipality's financial managers to spend and to collect specific amounts of money during the budget period. However, although the budget is quite rigid legally, it does have some flexibility, which arises from its administrators' desire for at least a degree of discretionary control and from the administrators' desire to include reserve accounts (e.g., in case of uncollectible taxes or other revenues or unexpected expenses).

Uncertainties about the accuracy of the budget may occur because those grants or monies from federal or state governments which municipalities anticipate receiving may or may not materialize. Likewise, revenue-producing municipal enterprises that are expected to provide specific amounts of money may fail to do so. Despite these inevitable uncertainties, the proposed budget, to the extent that it can feasibly do so, should attempt to anticipate the actual expenditures and revenues.

Often the budget is changed during the fiscal year to which it applies, and so the projected budget and the final budget can differ substantially. (However, budgetary discrepancies even of major emergency proportions are not necessarily, by themselves, indicative of bad management.)

Incrementalism

Although zero-based budgeting has been discussed, practiced, and studied a good deal in Washington and elsewhere over the past two decades most state and municipal budgets are still prepared on an *incremental basis*. This means that the municipality's financial managers start by assessing their last fiscal year's budget and then forecast from that the budget for 1 or 2 years ahead. The estimates from all the municipal departments and subdepartments that are requested in order to make up the budget also tend to be based upon an assessment of the previous year's budget.

Despite this incremental growth in municipal budgets, many observers of the municipal budgetary processes have noted that financial managers repeatedly demonstrate a tendency to avoid asking for a tax increase to cover the growth in appropriations, even when they think it is needed and justified. Instead, they will attempt to get by on inadequate appropriations by resorting to emergency expenditures or by making use of deficiency reappropriations. Obviously, if over 5 or 10 years this appears to be a pattern for a particular municipality, a bond investor should become wary.

Municipal Accounting Standards

In the past the subject of municipal accounting was the primary concern of the Municipal Finance Officers Association (MFOA), formed in 1906. In 1934 the MFOA created the National Committee on Governmental Accounting (NCGA), whose purpose was to develop a standardized set of accounting principles for governmental units. The product of the NCGA was the "bible," or blue book, *Governmental Accounting, Auditing & Financial Reporting Standards* (GAAFR), which contains the generally accepted accounting principles for governmental accounting. In a recent major restatement of GAAFR, the underlying principles for governmental accounting were organized into seven major categories; (1) generally accepted accounting principles and legal compliance, (2) fund accounting, (3) fixed assets and long-term liabilities, (4) basis of accounting, (5) the budget and budgetary accounting, (6) classification and terminology, and (7) financial reporting. The purposes of the redefinition were to refine existing GAAFR principles and to provide a clearer definition of these principles and their application. The categories will be discussed in the remainder of this chapter.

Generally Accepted Accounting Principles

The entrance of the American Institute of Certified Public Accountants (AICPA) into the field of governmental accounting has been recent. In

1974 AICPA published an industry audit guide: *Audits of State and Local Governmental Units* (ASLGU). The guide incorporates GAAFR with generally accepted accounting principles (GAAP), and a certified public accountant must follow it when performing an audit of the financial statements of a municipality and in providing an opinion on them. Differences may arise between the accounting methods and reporting systems of a municipality and GAAP as a result of statutory requirements. In such instances the auditor will determine the nature and effect of the departure and comment on it.

GAAP is considered to provide only a minimum standard for accounting and reporting mechanisms; consequently, the fact that municipalities follow GAAP does not ensure the creation of financial statements of a comparable nature. Since there are also numerous variations permitted under GAAP, the accounts of 10 cities can differ greatly even though all of them were prepared in accordance with GAAP. The issue of comparability of statements in governmental accounting has been troublesome.

For the reader of financial statements, it is necessary to implement a standardized method of accounting and reporting in order to better analyze the financial reports on an equal level. Nevertheless, investors or bond analysts must keep in mind that standardized methods of accounting do not ensure the accuracy of the reporting within those statements.

New York City dramatized several of these points. With the fiscal crisis of 1974–1975, the SEC investigated the accounting practices of the city. Questions arose as to the adequacy of the accounting system, the consistency in recording transactions, and the quality of the overall reporting system. It was shown that the methods used by the city concerning the consistency, accuracy, and timely reporting of financial events were not major considerations for its actual financial practices in use. The financial picture presented during that time was not complete. Thus a true analysis of the city in relation to its ability to carry the burden of outstanding debt and issue new debt was seriously threatened. The concept of this security as a "safe investment" was jeopardized, and the SEC hearings on the crisis of New York City emphasized this fact.

Fund Accounting

A municipality, or governmental unit, is a nonprofit organization. Its purpose is to provide those services which are determined by the needs of the community, within legislative and political constraints on the local, state, and federal levels. Unlike a private business enterprise, the municipality does not derive revenue from the goods produced and/or the services provided. Revenues are received from tax levies, grants, appropriations, and revenue-sharing programs. There are exceptions to this, such as a water and sewer facility, which receives revenues from rates charged to its users. Such rates are intended to be at least commensurate with the facility's costs and expenditures.

There are many restrictions imposed on a governmental unit in its spending practices. Some of these restrictions are internal to the municipality and may involve political, legal, or statutory constraints. Other restrictions are imposed upon the municipality from outside by the state or federal government, or by legal agreements with some other governmental authority. Because of these internal and external restrictions, a municipality is not able to invest its revenues in each and every project that its financial administrators deem appropriate. The governmental unit must comply with predetermined plans and can only use those funds for the stipulated purposes. Compliance with these requirements is stipulated in the budget, ordinances, and appropriations. Thus the municipality must show legal compliance in its accounting system.

While there is no guarantee that the fund concept will force a municipality to avoid the misuse of funds, it does provide an additional control mechanism because the monies are segregated, as are related expenditures, according to designated purposes.

Funds may be established for a variety of reasons. They may arise because of constitutional requirements or statutes legislated by the state, or they may be established by local charters or ordinances or by the local council. In addition, they are organized to facilitate financial management by the municipality. To determine the extent to which a fund can be utilized, it must be distinguished according to the purpose for which it was created. Funds are also classified according to the sources of revenues and the uses of those monies. Each fund is a separate accounting entity and there are practical and real differences between accounting entities and legal entities. Transactions that occur between funds frequently do so on a creditor-debtor relationship. Thus interfund accounts receivable and payable are usually set up so as to segregate these transactions into the familiar accounting categories of debits and credits in separate columns for each account.

Funds are classified into three basic groups:

1. *Government, or "source and disposition," funds.* These are expendable funds; the revenues allocated are to be spent within a specified period of time and are considered to be current accounts. The difference between the assets and liabilities of the funds in this group is the fund equity, or fund balance. The measurement of these funds is based on changes that occur in the municipality's financial position (i.e.,

sources, uses, and balances of financial resources) rather than on its net income.

2. *Proprietary, or nonexpendable, funds.* This type of fund is similar to a commercial enterprise in that the purpose of the fund is to build on the initial resources allocated to it while meeting current expenses out of current revenues. Thus proprietary funds will last beyond a specified period. The purpose of this group, in that these are "income determination" funds, is to determine the net income, financial position, and changes in financial position.

3. *Fiduciary funds.* With these funds, the municipality acts in a custodial capacity over the assets or resources held in its trust. The governmental unit will act as a fiduciary for a group of individuals, an organization, or another government agency. It is its responsibility to watch over and control the distribution of these funds.

GAAFR recommends eight types of funds to be used within the three classifications of account groups:

Government Funds

1. *General fund.* This accounts for ordinary operations of a governmental unit that are financed from the taxes and other general revenues. All transactions (and unrestricted resources) that are not accounted for in other funds are accounted for in this fund.

2. *Special revenue fund.* This accounts for revenues from specific taxes or other earmarked sources that, by law or administrative action, are designated to finance a particular activity or project. An example would be funds received from a federal grant for a research or training program.

3. *Capital projects fund.* This accounts for resources used for the acquisition of major, long-lived assets other than those financed by special assessment and enterprise funds. This fund includes the collection and disbursement of revenues from a variety of sources, such as bond issues, loans, or grants. A separate capital project fund is usually created for each capital project.

4. *Special assessment fund.* This accounts for the construction of improvements or the provision of services that are financed, totally or in part, by special assessments levied against benefited private property. Examples include sewer, sidewalk, construction, or street improvement.

5. *Debt service fund.* This accounts for the payment of interest and principal on all general obligation debt other than that serviced by enterprise funds or special assessment funds. Primarily, long-term debt is serviced by this fund.

Proprietary Funds

6. *Enterprise fund.* This accounts for funds that resemble a private business in that they are primarily self-supporting from revenues received from user charges for services performed. These include water supply and sewage disposal, public hospitals, public transportation, recreational facilities, and airports.

7. *Intragovernmental service fund.* This accounts for goods and services provided by designated departments on a fee basis for other departments and agencies within a single governmental unit. Examples are a central garage that provides maintenance and repair for all vehicles of the municipality and a centralized purchasing agency for office supplies.

Fiduciary Funds

8. *Trust and agency funds.* This accounts for assets held by a govermental unit in a custodial position or as an agent for individuals, private organizations, or other governmental units and funds. Examples are expendable trust funds, nonexpendable trust funds, and agency funds.

These eight funds are usually reviewed and funded on an annual basis, and in order to ensure budgetary compliance, the fiscal period is used as an accounting period. Yet certain funds are not based on a periodic basis, but rather on a project basis. These funds are capital projects and special assessment funds whose projects will continue beyond the fiscal year. Therefore, the accounting for the eight funds will be for a current period, and an ongoing review of those funds will contain projects of an extended nature. Resources and the use of those funds must be accounted for in order to arrive at the transactions of the fiscal year and to arrive at the financial position of the funds at the end of this period.

The number of funds used should be based on a municipality's size and the complexity of its operations. An inordinate number of funds will prove unwieldy and dysfunctional, whereas maintaining the minimum number of accounts will facilitate financial and administrative management. Each of the eight funds mentioned will be used only if necessary.

Fixed Assets and Long-Term Liabilities

One main objective of governmental accounting is to show the funds available and how those funds are being expended. Assets which belong to the governmental unit as a whole and which are not used in services provided should be recorded in a separate group of accounts called "general fixed assets"; otherwise, their inclusion in the financial statements could be misleading. The general fixed assets are disclosed in the summary of accounting policies, and they should be recorded either at cost (the price of the asset) or at estimated cost, if determinable.

The investor or bond analyst should take note that a municipality's treatment of fixed assets sometimes can be potentially misleading in the balance sheet, but it must be disclosed in the accounting policies note to the financial statements. It is also important for investors to remember that the fixed assets of a municipality are often different in certain crucial respects from corporate assets. This is because, for example, a city's roads or bridges usually cannot simply be sold to improve the city's cash position at any time the city chooses. Likewise, the accounting treatment of fixed assets belonging to municipalities is also somewhat different from the treatment of fixed assets in the private sector, especially with regard to depreciation.

Municipalities usually do not report depreciation for separate government activities, such as the police department, the fire department, or the parks department. However, municipalities have the option of recording the depreciation for all fixed assets of all government activities together, and they are encouraged to exercise this option.

In contrast, each enterprise activity of the municipality *is* expected to record depreciation and is expected to record its fixed assets separately. In the treatment of both fixed assets and depreciation, an enterprise activity of a municipality is quite close to conventional accounting practice in a private enterprise.

It should be noted by investors and bond analysts that since depreciation is a reimbursable item for monies from state and federal governments, municipalities—when they receive external government funding for a specific project—keep records of both the fixed assets and the depreciation for the project.

Depreciation of fixed assets should be included in the fund balance for proprietary and trust funds. *Depreciation* is the allocation, in a consistent and rational manner, of the cost of the asset over the asset's useful life, and it is a major factor in determining income. In governmental accounting, *expenditures*—not expenses—are measured; thus depreciation should be shown in the funds mentioned, but for general fixed assets it is optional. To show depreciation expense would be an incorrect mixture of expenses with expenditures. The general fixed assets that require the use of government funds are shown as expenditures. The sale of these fixed assets provides resources for other uses. Thus depreciation expense is neither a source nor a use of government funds.

As with fixed assets, a distinction must be made for long-term liabilities between those liabilities which are to be accounted for through fund accounts and those which are shown in account groups. Those bonds, notes, and other long-term liabilities (such as for pensions or capital leases) which are directly associated with and will be paid from proprietary funds, special assessment funds, and trust funds should be shown in the fund accounts. Basically, these are liabilities of a specific fund, despite the fact that the full faith and credit of the governmental unit may be backing them.

On the other hand, all other unmatured long-term debt of the municipality is considered long-term debt, and this should be shown in the general long-term debt account group. This includes the unmatured principal of bonds, warrants, or other types of noncurrent long-term indebtedness. Long-term debt is backed by a municipality's authority to raise general credit and revenue rather than being related to specific assets or funds. This type of debt does not require resources available for current appropriation or expenditure of financial resources. As with general fixed assets, it would be misleading to include long-term debt in the current fund balances. Such types of debt would be shown as term bonds, serial bonds, and other general long-term liabilities. The balancing accounts show the funds available in the debt service funds to pay the principal on the debt and show that amount which will be necessary for future payments of principal.

Basis of Accounting

The basis of an entity's accounting should reflect the nature of its transactions in order to provide an accurate and timely matching of revenues with expenditures.

In terms of time period, a municipality's accounts are split according to whether the primary impact or major transactions of the accounts occur in the past, the present, or the future. Prior years' accounts, current accounts, and future years' or deferred accounts thus specifically indicate which period the accounts are meant to cover.

There are three bases of accounting: (1) cash, (2) accrual, and (3) modified accrual. The *cash basis* of accounting recognizes only the cash transactions. Revenues are recognized and recorded when cash is actually received, and disbursements of expenditures are recorded when paid. This method is most susceptible to fraudulent manipulation; moreover, the cash basis is not in compliance with GAAP. Some state or local statutes may require that certain funds be maintained on a cash basis. When this occurs, an auditor cannot give an unqualified opinion on cash-basis financial statements, for GAAP must prevail.

The *accrual basis* is the system whereby revenues and gains are recorded when earned and all expenditures and losses are recorded when incurred. Enterprise funds, intragovernmental service funds, and capital projects funds tend toward the accrual method. Revenues for trust and agency funds and for special assessment funds, however, are not adaptable to the accrual basis; thus revenues for these funds are recorded as received by using the modified accrual basis.

The *modified accrual basis* is a hybrid method of accounting, incorporating characteristics of both the cash method and the accrual method. Revenues are recorded when received or when they are both measurable and available, thereby being susceptible to accrual. Expenditures are recorded when the service is performed, when items (such as prepaid expenses) are incurred, or when interest on long-term debt is due. The general fund, special revenue funds, and debt service funds are required to use the modified accrual basis.

Some municipalities use a combination of the cash and modified accrual bases of accounting in order to avoid deficits at the end of their fiscal years. New York City, for example, was criticized by the SEC, during its investigations of the city's financial and accounting practices in 1976, for its misuse of accounting methodology. The city was recording its revenues on an accrual basis, whereas the cash method was being used to record expenditures; it was halting certain payments, which in actuality were legal obligations, in order to balance the budget; it was recognizing uncertain receivables in order to show that higher revenues were anticipated than were being collected; and it was committing other transgressions.

The cash basis of accounting, although simplistic, is discouraged by AICPA and GAAFR. The accrual basis presents a more realistic and accurate overview of the municipality's ability to maintain accounting records, but using the accrual method alone could cause problems with budgetary and financial accounting requirements.

Another danger of accrual accounting concerns anticipating revenues before they are actually in hand. The municipality can find itself in financial difficulties if, for whatever reason, monies do not arrive on schedule. Thus the convenient rule of thumb used in accrual accounting is to say that amounts should only be counted as having accrued when the sum is definite, its source is definite, and the date is definite. The best examples of accounts that can be accrued are those for property taxes. Property taxes are of a known specified amount, due on a particular date from specific taxpayers. Some enterprise revenues or license fees may also be accrued in this same manner. However, because of the uncertainty about whether, or when, all these sums will come in, each municipality sets aside reserves for losses. Because many funds that are listed as having accrued surpluses can, in fact, have cash deficits, the investor or bond analyst should look not simply at the totals for each fund's assets and liabilities but more particularly at each fund's cash and current liabilities. Recognition of gain and loss under cash, accrual, and modified accrual systems can be quite different.

Municipal Dependence upon External Government Funds

The investor or bond analyst should determine what portion of local revenue is provided by property tax and what portion comes from other internal and external funding sources. In recent years the property tax in many communities has made up a smaller fraction of local revenues, and increasing reliance has been placed upon other types of internal revenues, such as city income taxes, sales taxes, local business taxes, gross receipt taxes, service fees or charges, and license and franchise fees. Increasing reliance has also been placed by many municipalities on external government grants, aid, or revenue sharing.

Since the municipality itself does not have control over transfer payments and revenue sharing from other governments, its main areas of control over its own budget come from setting or raising property taxes, fees, or service charges. Legally, the property tax is a very powerful municipal tool, for if the tax is not paid, the municipality has the legal right to seize and appropriate the property, and later to sell it.

Investors and bond analysts should consider for each bond the specific effect of various intergovernmental funding programs because these funds have become extremely important sources of revenue for some municipalities. Whether such intergovernmental payments to a particular municipality are in the form of revenue sharing, inducements, or equalization grants can make a good deal of difference in evaluating the credit strength of the municipal bonds. This is because external government grants can tend to support or weaken a municipality. Where the federal or state government is in effect forcing a program onto a municipality, it can actually be very expensive and financially disruptive for the municipality to accept a matching grant. Whether the external funding takes the usual form of a matching grant, as for urban renewal or public transit, or is a federal reimbursement for monies the municipality has already spent—either way, the municipality will be called upon to put up its own cash. Where the intergovernmental program is optional and not forced upon the municipality, the local finance officer can carefully determine whether the grant would tend to strengthen the local community or instead make it overly dependent upon continued outside funding. On balance, the effect of most intergovernmental grants has not been to strengthen a local municipal financial administration but to make it more dependent upon external funding than upon its own devices. Investors or bond analysts should thus be wary of interpreting a municipality's budget or books of accounts as necessarily stronger because there are hefty external government funds contributed. The timing of these external grants is of special concern because the grants can be delayed or cut off, and there is little, if anything, that the municipality can do about it. In short, these external funds are outside the local municipality's control; therefore, counting upon them may lead to disappointments.

Equalization grants tend to be more supportive of local municipal finance than do most other forms of external grants or funding. These grants have become quite important in local public school finance because of state supreme court decisions, as, for example, in New Jersey. These court rulings have ordered that a state's funding for education per student be far more equitable than in the past, when the bulk of school funding came from the local property tax, which varied greatly between rich and poor communities. The local property tax has long been argued to be inherently unequal. For example, it produced within one state a disparity regarding the support of school systems: $20 spent per child in one community versus $1 spent per child in another community.

Financial Statements and Reports

Those documents of a municipality which provide information as to the events of the prior fiscal year are the *financial statements and reports.* The nature of these reports and their informational content are determined by the reporting requirements of the municipality and the laws with which it must comply. The overall purpose of financial statements is to provide an accurate, timely, and fair presentation of the financial operations and position of the municipality.

The needs of the users of these statements, whether taxpayers, investors, municipal bond analysts, or financial administrators, must be considered. Consideration of their needs in the light of the financial data, analyses, and adequate disclosure practices will have an effect on the contents of the statements. Audited financial statements are becoming more widespread among both state and local levels. Yet some major municipalities, such as New York City, escaped this requirement for a long time. When audited, financial statements can provide an independent opinion of the financial position of the governmental unit as well as adequate disclosure of its financial and accounting policies and practices.

In addition to audited financial statements, the Municipal Finance Officers Association (MFOA) has for many years awarded a "certificate of conformance," which recognizes a municipality's "sufficient financial control" in financial reporting and conformance with GAAFR. This certificate should be included in the financial statements of a municipality because it not only indicates compliance with GAAFR but also shows that the governmental unit maintains sufficient control over its financial operations.

General-Purpose Financial Statements

In its revision of GAAFR, the National Committee on Governmental Accounting (NCGA) has developed a "financial reporting pyramid" that shows the required as well as the optional reports that make up the annual reports of a municipality. The NCGA recommends that every governmental unit should publish a comprehensive annual financial report (CAFR) that covers all funds and account groups. The general-purpose financial statements (GPFS) by fund type and account group should be included in a CAFR. The GPFS can be issued separately from the CAFR and can be used in official statements for municipal bond issues and for users who require less detailed data than are shown in the CAFR. The GPFS includes only data by fund type and account group, with notes to the financial statements and disclosures of material departures from legal and contractual provisions as well as other necessary material information.

In addition to the comprehensive annual financial report, a GPFS can be published by the municipality and focus on aggregate information as to the fund type and account group information. It is considered to be adequate in presenting an abbreviated picture of the financial operations and position of the municipality.

Notes to the Financial Statements

Integral parts of both financial statements are the notes to these statements. Included in these notes are a summary of the significant accounting policies and a summary of major disclosure items. These items are of a material nature; examples are significant contingent liabilities, pension plan obligations, accumulated unpaid employee benefits, any material violations of finance-related legal and contractual provisions, debt service requirements to maturity, and commitments under noncapitalized leases. These notes and summaries should be read carefully to detect any material events or potential liabilities that could have a major effect on the financial position of the municipality. In addition, such notes indicate the financial and accounting policies utilized by the municipality.

The financial reports presented by municipalities vary, depending on the needs of the users. The types of reports that should be issued, as suggested by the NCGA and the AICPA, are not issued by every governmental unit. Attainment of a standardized governmental accounting system and reporting mechanism for all municipalities is still to be realized. Many times, the problem is that the municipality must comply with the accounting standards as set by the legal and regulatory requirements and environment, which differ from GAAFR and GAAP. Other times, the obstacle is the insufficient resources allocated toward the implementation of an accounting system; other factors are the lack of proper monitoring and the lack of necessary controls that must accompany the accounting and information system.

There are other areas in which adequate disclosure should be investigated. These items are of a "high-dollar" magnitude and could have a major impact on the future financial position of the municipality, but studies have shown that these high-dollar items (which include pension plans, overlapping debt, inventories and receivables, leases, and accrued vacations and sick leave) are not always fully disclosed. Current revisions of accounting practices and reporting methods will effectively deal with this problem. Some of the major areas are discussed below.

Pension Plans

Although the actual funding of the plan is not an accounting question, it is important to be aware of the municipality's financial policy regarding its pension plan and its associated liability. This liability could have major repercussions on the future ability of the municipality to pay its pension plan obligations. Thus disclosure of the nature and degree of obligation of the pension plan provisions to determine their magnitude should be sought.

Overlapping Jurisdictions and Debt

The tax base of a municipal unit is an important determination of the ability of the municipality to finance its obligations, especially in terms of debt incurred. Governmental units, since World War II, have "overlapped" in services and shared the burden of providing the services; school districts, for example, may be supported by two separate governmental entities. Thus the assessable tax base available to both entities must be determined.

The total bonded indebtedness of a municipality also includes *special assessment debt,* which is issued to pay for all or a portion of a specific service or improvement provided by the municipality. (For example, the municipality may issue water and sewer bonds or pollution control bonds.) This type of debt circumvents the legal debt limitation placed on the governmental entity. It is necessary to distinguish the share of debt of another governmental entity that is being carried by the tax base of the governmental unit being reviewed.

Special assessment debt, although not a part of the legal debt limitation, is, in reality, a portion of debt that is charged against the property tax base, which is the main source of revenue for overlapping units of local government. "Piling up" of debt in layers has evolved from the complex structure between state, local, and special districts. Adequate disclosure showing overlapping debt, as well as direct debt, should be reviewed by the analyst or investor. This is essential so that the debt burden taken on by a governmental unit is not understated.

Two other crucial measures are a municipality's success in increasing its tax rates and its history of tax collections. Although these are not strictly accounting issues, they are essential components in the financial analysis of the performance and the revenue base of a municipality. Two tax rates may be indicated: (1) the rate of the governmental unit and (2) the total rate for all the municipalities combined. It is important to separate the tax rates for debt service from the tax rates for operations. If the tax limit has been used up, the means by which the municipality will meet the debt service on additional outstanding debt should be sought. Tax rate information for a 10-year period is useful in the trend analysis of the financial and operational performance of the governmental unit.

The collection history of a municipality indicates its management and financial security. The collection of current and delinquent taxes is a means of measuring the ability to secure revenues for payment of debt service. Default on such payments could cause a substantial loss in revenue and prove to be a critical problem in raising necessary funds to pay debt obligations. Information as to delinquency rates, penalties, rate structure, interest charged, and the tax collection calendar may be found in the annual report and, depending on the nature of the security being issued, in the official statement.

Inventories and Receivables

In governmental accounting, the *inventories* represent the expenditures, and the *receivables* represent the revenues that will be spent when and if collected. The question arises as to whether these are legitimate accounts. A municipal finance officer's foreknowledge regarding the collectibility of taxes and other receivables is essential in planning short-term financing. This planning is based on the estimated, collectible incoming tax revenues. The decline in collectibility of such taxes will severely affect the ability of the municipality to pay off RANs or TANs in the next fiscal year.

In reviewing the accounts and the long-term obligations of a municipality, the overriding concern is whether the municipality is able to carry its debt burden; the information presented must be analyzed to determine this.

Leases

Leasing is used by a municipality to secure the long-term use of facilities without incurring debt service requirements. It is also a means of circumventing the municipality's legal debt limitations and avoiding having to ask the electorate for a vote of approval for a new debt issue.

The theory behind leasing is that instead of purchasing a facility (by issuing notes or bonds), a municipality will rent it. The cost, or indebtedness, of the governmental unit will increase only by the amount of the annual rent and not by the full cost of the facility when the cumulative rents are equal to the full capital costs of constructing it. An alternative method is to create a separate authority that will issue revenue bonds to pay for the construction of the project—which, when completed, will be leased directly to the municipality. The outstanding debt is not the responsibility of the governmental unit, although the lease payments are. In order to analyze the future cash needs of a municipality adequately, such arrangements should be reviewed; however, their disclosure is not always present in annual reports.

Accrued Vacations and Sick Leave

Another major expense area with a potential liability to the governmental unit is accrued vacations and sick leave. Despite the fact that municipal employees will not use their vacations and sick leave all at once, adequate disclosure is necessary in planning the cash needs of the governmental unit. But, once again, most cities neither disclose this financial obligation nor set aside separate funds to handle this expense.

Severe financial repercussions can occur because of the lack of recognition of and provision for these liabilities.

Independent Auditors

If a particular government prepares its own accounting statements, there may be reason for investors and bond analysts to be wary. The accountant, if he or she is part of the state's or municipality's governmental structure, should still in various ways be separate from that government's managers. The accountant should, for example, have a separate office, a separate salary appropriation, and separate powers totally independent of whichever governmental officeholders are in power. Because such independence is rare, and because of the danger of a lack of objectivity on the part of an internal auditor, many governments feel compelled to obtain an external audit from a well-regarded CPA firm.

An investor or bond analyst who does not see an external accountant's opinion should note whether state or local municipal law stipulates that the books of account must be prepared by the state's accountant or by the municipality itself. Legally binding statutory requirements may prevent external accountants from preparing the accounts. However, if no external audit is performed and there is no legal reason why one was not performed, then there may be reason for the investor or bond analyst to be wary of that municipality's bonds.

The investor should also be aware that even when the financial statements have been audited by an external auditor, there may be significant improprieties that go unreported. Other significant problems may be only vaguely alluded to in a note and not spelled out.

Combined versus Consolidated Statements

An important development in municipal accounting is the move toward consolidated financial statements. The NCGA's *Statement 1*, concerning consolidated financial statements, *encourages* municipalities to aggregate all funds statements into one column of account groups but *requires* presentation of the grouping of all eight columns of funds of a homogeneous nature (e.g., the fixed asset group and the long-term debt group of accounts). Thus even if a municipality has 100 funds, it is expected to group them into eight groups of funds.

Many authorities have differed as to whether municipal accounting should introduce one single consolidated statement instead of listing only separate funds or groups of funds. In terms of municipal accounting, combined statements are recommended over consolidated statements, whereas the reverse is true for a commercial enterprise. Consolidation in terms of a municipality would encompass the merging of all eight funds and two account groups into one overall economic unit. The problem encountered with this is the necessary segregation of funds for reporting purposes. Each fund is a distinct entity, and to consolidate all of them into one unit would, again, obscure the legal and other requirements which, by nature, must be separated.

Consolidation for a corporation is also based on ownership: A corporation that owns 50 percent or more of a subsidiary represents that subsidiary as part of itself in its financial statements. Ownership considerations for a municipality differ: There are no "equity" interests as with a corporation. Legal requirements also distinguish certain authorities or agencies within the jurisdiction of a governmental unit as not being part of it. Thus ownership must be determined, and this is, indeed, a difficult task—one that would hinder the realistic reporting of the financial operation and position of a municipality.

The Basis of Accounting

The question has arisen as to whether the use of funds as the basis for accounting municipalities is valid. Some contend that municipalities should be accounted for just as private commercial enterprises are. Yet there are reasons for the use of the fund as the basis for municipal accounting: Governmental units receive funds through grants; through local, state, and federal allocations; and by other means. They are not profit-motivated. The monies received must be spent as specified. Thus the accounting system must fulfill two objectives: (1) to show compliance with legal requirements and (2) to show compliance with GAAP. Furthermore, the segregation of funds is necessary to show that the municipality has been properly using its allocated resources. The fund basis of accounting accomplishes these objectives. To treat municipalities as commercial enterprises would obscure the characteristics that distinguish the two types of entities. Moreover, the necessary accounting information and controls of a private enterprise would not be instituted over a governmental unit.

Fixed Assets and Depreciation

The general fixed assets of a municipality are not recorded in the funds but are segregated. Depreciation of these fixed assets is optional, at the discretion of the governmental unit. The decision not to record fixed assets is made by the municipality, which, basically, does not feel the need to expend resources to maintain such information. Yet with the increasing cost of maintenance as well as inflation, this attitude is changing.

While municipalities tend not to record depreciation, commercial enterprises do record such expenses. Depreciation is a means of allocating the cost of the asset over its useful life. It is not an actual expense but is maintained for tax purposes. For a municipality, once resources have been expended for a fixed asset, it is considered to be a sunk cost. The fact that no depreciation is taken on an asset in no way affects its cost to the municipality.

Encumbrances

Encumbrances are defined as obligations in the form of a purchase order, contract, or salary commitment. These obligations are chargeable to an appropriations item for which a part of the appropriation is reserved. Once the actual liability is established or the encumbrance is paid, it ceases to exist. The problem with encumbrances is that they are not actual liabilities of the municipality. Those who favor their use believe that encumbrances are in line with the "flow of funds" that underlies the basis of measurement of resources for a governmental unit. In essence, encumbrances are part of the allocation process and segregate those resources which are no longer available for expenditure. An encumbrance represents a contractual liability; therefore, although it is not an actual liability, it must be represented as one. Confusion does arise as to the differences between an actual liability and an encumbrance, and care is needed when distinguishing between them on financial statements.

Conclusion

Municipal accounting theory is complex. It is undergoing changes and refinements to provide a sound framework that municipalities can implement in their accounting practices. Many obstacles are blocking the path for the incorporation of a standard set of accounting principles. Legal and statutory requirements of the individual states and localities do not accommodate the institution of a standardized municipal accounting practice; however, the need to concentrate on the development and refinement of their accounting systems and reporting practices must be satisfied.

Since reporting practices are not standardized, major organizations, such as the NCGA and the AICPA, are working jointly to promote the use of suggested reporting formats. Yet, due to the various needs of the different users of these reports, the design and content are not uniformly presented from municipality to municipality. The trend is toward presenting meaningful statements that conform to a general standard and toward increased disclosure not only of financial information but also of economic, demographic, and statistical data.

The overall objective is to develop a reporting system that will provide relevant information for managers and enhance financial decisions by internal and external readers. A reader of the reports must be aware of the underlying accounting theory and the practical limitations involved. Since complete disclosure of every major area is not evidenced by recent studies, a reader must be careful in assessing the reports.

Many times it is not the amount of information furnished that matters, but the quality of the data presented. The municipal analyst or investor must recognize this fact and be able not only to pinpoint the potential trouble spots but also to have a basic understanding both of the reports and of the accounting theory behind the reports.

18

Legal Protection, Disclosure, and Liability

Introduction

Why is the question of full disclosure so crucial today in the area of municipal bonds? Municipal securities have been considered second to federal securities in terms of safety in timely payment of interest and principal, and the dollar figures for defaulting municipal issues are minimal in comparison with the actual dollar volume of municipal debt outstanding.

Federal Legislation

Municipal securities were considered relatively sound investments in the 1930s when federal legislation for them was being enacted. Apparently, it was the legislator's attitude at the time that "misrepresentation" by municipal issuers was unlikely. In addition, the municipal securities marketplace was not a primary source of revenue for governmental units. Moreover, in light of the stock market crash of 1929, private corporate securities were in dire need of regulation. Thus the Securities Act of 1933 (1933 act) and the Securities Exchange Act of 1934 (1934 act) exempted municipal securities from stringent regulatory and registration requirements and from the general reviewing scope of the newly formed Securities and Exchange Commission which was imposed on private corporate securities. These securities were perceived as posing a greater risk to the investor because of the greater probability of fraud.

In the 1933 act, municipal securities were categorized as one type of security and enumerated as "exempt" from the regulations contained in the act. *Exempt*, according to the 1933 and 1934 acts, did not mean exempt from federal income taxation (according to Section 103 of the 1954 Internal Revenue Code), but exempt from the provisions of the acts unless otherwise stated. In the 1933 act, this exemption excluded municipal securities from registering prospectuses and disclosures. In addition, the exemption excluded these securities from the "extensive civil liabilities" of sections 11 and 12, which relate to the sales of securities made prior to the registration of prospectuses. Section 17 [and Section 17(a) in particular], which covers general antifraud regulation, does apply to municipal securities. This section deals with the omission of facts and/or the material misstatement of facts in an official document given to a potential investor. The liability associated with this act is very broad in nature, and it needs definitions through the courts as to the degree of negligence attached to the participants in the offering. This section is the only restraint on municipal bonds in the 1933 act.

The 1934 act does not contain a broad definition of exempted securities, and each section must be reviewed to determine if municipal securities are exempted from it. The "comprehensive" reporting rules contained in Section 12 of the act do not apply to municipal securities. Section 10 prohibits the use of any deceptive device in connection with the purchase or sale of any security. Rule 10(b)(5) of this section, in particular, covers antifraud but does not specifically state that municipal securities are included in its stipulations.

The two antifraud provisions—sections 17(a) and 10(b)—in the 1933 act are relied upon for recourse in cases of alleged fraud, and power is given to the SEC to investigate such cases. The distinction between fraudulent intent and error of omission is not clearly defined in these acts. The definitions must be provided by the courts in their interpretations of the laws as cases are adjudicated. In court cases, Section 17(a) is usually referred to, whereas Rule 10(b)(5) of Section 10(b) is the major law ruled upon in the decisions set forth.

Court cases have arisen over the topic of reasonable care in performing "due diligence" investigations of issuers of municipal securities and their actual financial positions and in defining the responsibilities of the participants who bring municipal securities to market. These cases, generally on the level of the federal circuit courts, have defined the actual legal responsibility under Rule 10(b)(5): Initially, the issuer is responsible for all the facts it presents in the official statement. Yet the circuit courts have had little difficulty in widening the scope of responsibility—and thus the scope allowed for negligence in cases of alleged fraud. With the decision from *Ernst & Ernst v. Hochfelder* (1976), the Supreme Court narrowed the definition of liability of the parties and allowed for a good-faith defense on their party, thereby reducing the scope of negligence liability.

The two provisions—sections 17 and 10—were the only federal limitations relating to the issuance of municipal securities until amendments to the 1934 act were legislated in 1975. Further federal regulation of the municipal marketplace was felt unnecessary, as the risks of default and potential fraud were considered minimal. Extensive disclosure requirements that were applied to private corporate securities were not applicable to municipal bonds. Disclosure requirements are evolving as standards and guidelines set by the securities industry, establishing the degree of acceptable practice, yet there exist no disclosure guidelines (those which should be used in every municipal offering) that are uniform, legal, and federally required.

The 1934 act empowered the SEC to regulate broker-dealer activities through the antifraud provisions. In addition to Section 10b and Rule 10(b)(5), rules 15(c)(1) and 15(c)(2) also relate to any fraudulent means of purchasing or selling any security (these sections do not relate to issuers). It should be noted that the substance of the two securities acts is basically the same. The main concern of the 1933 act was the issuance and sale of securities by underwriters, whereas the 1934 act was directed toward the stock exchanges and broker-dealers in terms of purchasing, selling, and trading. In the 1934 act, the SEC was also granted the power to regulate and supervise any registered broker. Self-regulatory bodies primarily regulate the securities markets, and all national securities exchanges must register with the SEC. The over-the-counter market is accounted for in Section 15(a), which requires national securities associations to register with the SEC, although membership in these associations is not required. The National Association of Securities Dealers (NASD) has established a set of comprehensive rules designed to protect the investor and govern its members' practices. The SEC supervises the NASD, and if any action is taken against a member, both the NASD and the SEC will do it. Yet before this can be initiated, the rules require a very high burden of proof for enforcement.

Even before the 1974–1975 fiscal crisis in New York, the indifference of the federal government to the self-regulatory ability of the municipal securities market was shaken.

Amendments in 1975 to the 1934 act in effect removed the exemption of brokers and dealers who were trading municipal securities from registering with the SEC. Anyone involved in this activity is required by law to register with the SEC. Applications must be filed with the SEC, and the SEC may deny an applicant acceptance according to its guidelines. Thus any "nonbank" dealer who is not a member of NASD will be regulated directly by the SEC.

The amendments also created the Municipal Securities Rulemaking Board (MSRB), which requires every broker or dealer of municipal securities to comply with its rules. The MSRB is a product of a joint effort of Congress, the SEC, and the securities industry. The purpose of the MSRB is to oversee practices within the municipal securities industry. It was established as an independent, self-regulatory organization that would be the primary rule-making authority for the industry. The MSRB is composed of 15 members coming from three groups: securities firm representatives, bank dealer representatives, and public members. Each group has equal representation on the board. The MSRB is mainly concerned with the standards of professional practice, including qualifications of broker-dealers, rules of fair practice, record keeping, and so forth.

The MSRB does not deal directly with the problem of disclosure, for it is in a precarious legal position. Due to the fact that municipal securities are authorized and issued by states and their political subdivisions, federal regulation of that activity may be contested on the age-old battlefield of states' rights. Thus the MSRB does not directly regulate the disclosure practices of municipal issuers; more important, these issuers are still exempt from federal securities laws. The "Tower Amendments," which were two sections tacked onto the 1975 amendments, codified the exemption of municipal issuers. This only resulted in greater confusion among underwriters, issuers, and dealers as to who is responsible for adequate disclosure.

The MSRB requires dealers to provide certain information, and this must be obtained from the issuers, who are not subject to MSRB rulings. This, then, further complicates the issue of disclosure and adequate investigation of the issuer by the underwriter. The end result is still the lack of clearly defined disclosure requirements for the municipal securities marketplace.

A major participant who does not fall within the 1934 act's definition of a broker-dealer is the commercial bank. In order to limit commercial bank involvement in the securities marketplace, Congress passed the Glass-Stegall Banking Reform Act of 1933, a product of the environment of great depression. This arguably limits the underwriting capabilities of national commercial banks to only GO bonds and prohibits their involvement with most revenue bonds. The congressional intent was to limit the risks of bank-financing activities and further regulate the commercial banks and ensure their solvency, in the aftermath of the bank collapses of the late 1920s and early 1930s. Regulatory authority was granted to the traditional bodies, such as the Comptroller of the

Currency and the Federal Reserve. A consequence of this limitation is that commercial banks underwrite over 50 percent of the new GO bonds; however, they have become involved with revenue issues, particularly with those for housing, universities, and dormitories. When questions arise as to whether a commercial bank is allowed to underwrite certain types of municipal issues, the Comptroller of the Currency determines the solution.

On the whole, since 1938, federal legislation and regulation in the municipal securities arena have remained comparatively minimal. The Internal Revenue Code does provide restrictions that must be complied with in determining a tax-exempt security. Furthermore, the rules and regulations of the IRS are being revised, rewritten, and ruled on in the courts. It is the responsibility of bond counsel in drafting the bond opinion to carefully review the tax laws as they apply to the specific issue. If there is any uncertainty as to the tax-exempt nature of the offering, a ruling may be requested from the IRS. If a ruling is necessary, counsel's opinion will not be released absent a favorable ruling, but the underwriter will not begin to sell the issue until the bond counsel has rendered its opinion.

Other federal regulations have been enacted over the years. Arbitrage regulations came into being in 1969, when Congress amended the Internal Revenue Code of 1954. The intent of the amendment was to ensure that the issuer of tax-exempt bonds did not take an "improper" advantage of the difference in the interest rates of tax-exempt issuances as opposed to the rates available to taxable securities. The statute was initially fairly simple in purpose, yet with subsequent temporary and proposed regulations of sinking funds and refundings, the area has become extremely complex. Bond counsels must deal specifically with the tax consequences of differing financing methods and must render advice on structuring financings and drafting arbitrage certificates. Regulations in other areas, such as pollution control, must be complied with. The traditional roles and practices of bond counsels, underwriters, and their counsels were under attack. The question of what is reasonable care in investigating and presenting the nature of the issuer within the confines of cost and time considerations was argued.

After the financial emergency of 1974–1975, action was taken at federal, state, and local levels to remedy the fiscal situation facing New York City; this action dealt with the accounting system and disclosure practices of the city's financial operations and issuance of securities. In early 1979, New York City issued and successfully marketed $125 million in short-term notes, the first public issuance in almost 5 years. The 200-page official statement that accompanied the notes was described by local officials as the most comprehensive disclosure statement ever carried out by a local government.

In 1976 an attempt to protect the continuing functioning of local governments was implemented by the amendment of the Bankruptcy Act of 1938. The amendment was due to the fact that the original act was not designated to provide a plan of relief for creditors and securities investors of major municipalities, such as New York City. The purpose of the amendment was to relieve the burden the municipality had in obtaining approvals from difficult-to-identify creditors. Under the original act an identification was essential. Basically, the act, as now amended, provides the municipality with easier access to judicial relief in case of default and subsequent bankruptcy.

Self-Regulation by the Municipal Securities Industry

Regulation of municipal securities has also come from within the industry on a voluntary basis; it has responded to the evident need for improved reporting mechanisms and disclosure practices. State constitutional limitations and statutory requirements, such as blue-sky laws, vary from state to state. The state regulations and sometimes even the constitutional limitations are amended from time to time, in the process of implementing changing public policies and redefining *public purpose*. This redefinition allows for a wider range of municipal financings. Debt limitations by state constitution or statute are often placed on municipalities as to the amount of general obligation debt and (sometimes) revenue debt they may issue. Few states, however, set disclosure requirements for the types of debt instruments used, and the guidelines have usually emanated from the industry itself.

The active response has come from major organizations within the industry, such as the MFOA and the NCGA, as well as from those outside the industry, such as the AICPA. These changes are a result of the desire of the participants to determine their legal exposure and liability by delineating their responsibilities and to enhance the degree of professionalism practiced throughout the industry.

In general, there has been greater disclosure in official statements and offering circulars for revenue issues and industrial development bonds than for GO bonds. A major reason for this is that investment bank managers of negotiated revenue bond issues have for many years voluntarily and customarily retained underwriter's counsel with securities act experience to assist them in the preparation of official statements that would meet high full-disclosure standards. This practice, which began in the 1940s and 1950s with the large toll road issues, continues unabated in all types of revenue bonds. In 1976 the MFOA published *Disclosure Guidelines for Offerings of Securities by State and Local Governments*. These guidelines resulted from a concerted effort by the industry to provide an outline for the format and information that should be contained in the official statement of GO issues.

The MFOA guidelines are fast becoming the "bible." They are followed by participants in providing timely and sufficient material information for the ultimate investor. Underwriters, bond counsels, and issuers have become increasingly aware of their potential legal liabilities in their roles in drafting the official statements. Therefore, these parties are attempting to include material data that will help the investor gain an overall picture of the issuer as well as of the issue. The guidelines are not legally binding, and compliance is on a voluntary basis, but since their inception there has been a positive response to them. This is but one effort by the industry to standardize within flexible constraints the structure of official statements.

In conforming to these guidelines, official statements for municipal bonds have become more comprehensive than in the past. Each issue is unique in type of issuer, structure of the issue, and financing agreements securing the issue. Thus compliance with the guidelines is based on their applicability to the offering.

An ongoing review is made of the MFOA guidelines by representatives of bond counsels, underwriters, and other participants. The MFOA has issued further exposure drafts which refine the guidelines and which are commented on by the industry. It has also issued position statements that recommend changes in disclosure practices, such as that releases should be made by an "issuer or enterprise" that bring the investor up to date as to current, material changes that may affect the issue.

The accounting profession has also responded to the need for standardized accounting methodology and reporting disclosure for governmental units. The NCGA and the AICPA are working together in revising GAAFR so as to refine the financial statements that independent auditors generate and to standardize the accounting practices used by municipalities. Auditors, in refining these accounting techniques, are lessening their exposure as reporting systems are improved. Timely and accurate information will thus be presented to investors, taxpayers, public officials, underwriters, bond analysts, and other users of the statements.

Although self-regulation of the municipal securities market has appeared successful in increasing disclosure so far, there has been an adverse reaction to federal regulation and SEC supervision of the industry. This type of potential regulation is generally felt to be restrictive in terms of cost versus benefit, in view of the associated investment risk. Burdensome registration requirements will increase the costs to the issuer and also the price to the investor. It is also possible that they could hinder the timing in bringing the municipal issues to market.

With increasing evidence of voluntary compliance with disclosure guidelines, reporting mechanisms will be improved and material information provided. Information, as outlined by the guidelines, consists not only of financial detail but also of data as to the environment and the constraints under which the issuer must function. The overall picture presented is extensive and informative. In the past the rating agencies were relied upon for evaluating the financial solvency of the issuer, but with the advent of more comprehensive disclosure practices, the external users of these documents will be given more information on which to base their investment decisions. In sum, with the success evidenced by the industry in controlling, updating, revising, and concertedly moving toward establishing its own regulation, the need for or threat of federal intervention will lessen. The end result will be beneficial for internal participants as well as for investors, analysts, and taxpayers.

Documents Found in a Municipal Offering

Before continuing with the discussion of disclosure and the roles of the participants in a municipal offering, it is important to become familiar with some of the major documents found in a municipal offering. The following are descriptions of those major documents and agreements.

The Official Statement

Similar to a corporate security prospectus, the *official statement* is the major tool used to market municipal securities. Basically, the official statement is a legal document that summarizes all the salient features of the underlying documents and agreements that support the offering. It is considered to be the disclosure document that presents information "material" to the offering. Unlike a corporate prospectus, the municipality's official statement is neither registered nor reviewed by the SEC. The content and format of the official statement depend on the type of security (GO bond versus revenue bond versus industrial development bond) and on the complexity of the issuance itself.

Initially, a preliminary statement is drafted that is known as the "red herring" because of the words in red ink on the front, which state that it is preliminary in nature and subject to change. The red herring is used to market the proposed issue prior to the date of sale. The official statement is then circulated, and the exact terms of the sale, such as the redemption provisions and interest rates, are summarized. In competitive bid financing agreements, the red herring is used to premarket the issue and arouse interest among various underwriters and institutional investors. The recipients will analyze the proposed offering and decide whether or not to submit a bid. If submitted, the bid will contain the interest rate at which the bond will be sold. Once a bid is accepted by the issuer, the terms outlined in it will be incorporated into the final, official statement. It should be noted that the final statement usually varies slightly from the preliminary statement. In a negotiated sale, the red herring is used to solicit interest in the marketplace. The underwriter will, during an initial sales period, determine the price at which the issue will be sold in the secondary marketplace.

The official statement should contain what a reasonable investor would need to know in making a decision about the issue. Thus this document will usually include a description of the issuer, a description of the purpose of the project being financed, a description of the security of the bond, a summary of the principal financing documents, any feasibility studies relating to the security, and any other key information, such as major contracts or obligations of the municipality in general which are specifically related to the issue and/or which might affect the issue. Contained in the description of the security of the bond is the lien, which describes the protection of the bondholder by outlining what is pledged and what is not in terms of remedies in the event of default. The types of funds provided are discussed; e.g., if there is a debt service fund, how it is to be funded might be discussed. Other security protection afforded is described: redemption of funds; the flow of funds in the trust indenture; the existence of a building, equipment, and a reserve fund; and so on. In essence, this description contains any facts relevant to the security of the bonds, the nature of the issuer, and any problems the issuer may be having or did have in the past with other bonds issued. Full disclosure about the security provisions is essential.

The Bond Opinion

In the front of the official statement, there is usually a reference to the bond counsel; the opinion of the bond counsel is rendered within the statement. The role of the bond counsel is not to opine as to the creditworthiness of the issue or the issuer, but to state whether the interest on the issue is tax-exempt according to federal income tax laws, state laws, and local laws. In addition, the opinion verifies that the issue is a legal, valid, and binding obligation of the issuer. The bond opinion is often a requisite component in any official statement. This opinion may be the only legal opinion contained in the official statement.

The specific topics that the bond opinion refers to are as follows:

- The organization and legal existence of the issuer, including its power and authority to issue and sell bonds
- Whether the ordinance has been duly adopted (thus making the issue legal) and is valid, binding, and enforceable
- Whether the bonds are duly authorized, executed, and delivered and are valid, binding, and enforceable
- Whether the lien on revenues is valid, and whether there is a perfected first lien and security interest
- Whether the bonds are tax-exempt under state and federal laws

No underwriter will release an offering until the bond counsel has provided a "clean" opinion. This opinion may be quite complex since the financing agreements have to comply with the Internal Revenue Code and other regulations. The official statement may say that the counsels of the underwriter and the issuer may opine on certain outstanding items, but their opinions will not appear in the official statement. They may have relevance to the issue but are not of a material nature to be mentioned in the official statement, whereas the bond opinion is generally an essential component.

Indenture of Trust

One of the fundamental documents included in the official statement is the *indenture of trust*, or the contract, that is made between the borrower (the issuer) and the lender (the trustee representing the interests of the bondholder). The trust indenture establishes the exact nature of the security of the bonds and the trust provisions. It is frequently a two-party agreement. Different names are used for it, such as "bond resolution," but essentially its purpose is to satisfy the legal formality of a "trust" type of relationship whereby the issuer enters into a trust with the trustee.

The nature of the document varies, depending on the type and financial complexity of an issue. For a general obligation issue, a bond ordinance is adopted. A state statute usually provides for the provisions of the issue, such as the revenue and security terms. In a general obligation issue, a trust indenture is not normally necessary. In a revenue bond issue, the trust indenture is the primary document. It defines the terms of the security and financing structure of the issue, outlines the type of revenue utilized to pay the principal and interest, includes the flow of funds, and sets forth the security terms. A summary of these terms is provided in the official statement.

With the move toward fuller disclosure, the full text of the trust indenture is often appended to the official statement. Provisions in a revenue bond indenture define the degree of protection for the bondholder in use of the pledged revenues and detail the management of the project. Sections commonly included in a revenue bond trust indenture are as follows:

- Definition of terms
- Description of the project to be built
- Definition of pledged revenue and its segregation, if necessary
- Definition of the way in which revenue is to be applied in meeting various claims against it
- Provision for advance retirement of bonds by either a refunding call or a sinking fund, if any
- Permitted investment for idle funds
- Conditions under which additional bonds may be issued
- A commitment as to the maintenance of rates so that income covers debt service
- Remedies on default
- Conditions under which an amendment to the contract will be permitted
- Covenants concerning faithful observance of agreements and general good management of the project in the bondholder's interest

The sections concerning revenues, their definitions and rate coverage, and the bondholder's claim on them are of major concern to the investor.

It is to this contract that the bondholder will look for satisfaction in case of default. For this reason, the terms of the financing agreements must be carefully and completely outlined and defined.

The Rate Covenant

The *rate covenant*, in most issues, is the promise by the issuer that the rate structure of the facility (e.g., water rates or electricity rates) will be increased in line with rising costs and expenses each year to provide the necessary revenues for the maintenance of the facility or project and the debt service. In the early 1970s, 125 percent rate coverage of net revenues was adequate. Today, 125 to 150 percent rate coverage is considered more than necessary and allows room for error by the management of the facility. Usually, rate coverage is 100 to 110 percent, which gives the management greater leeway. Contained in the rate covenant, the rate coverage is unique to each issue and is dependent on various factors, such as the type of facility, its ability to change its rate structure, the jurisdiction or area it serves, and the financing structure.

Additional Bond Clause

In order to be able to finance future expansions to serve the needs of the community, the issuers of revenue bonds need the alternative of issuing additional bonds. The *additional bond clause*, created for the purpose of financing future needs, is contained in a lien that, in general, determines the position and status of the bondholder, especially in the case of default. The additional bond clause provides terms for the issuance of further *parity bonds*, which protect the original investors against the dilution of the debt service coverage. One of its major terms, which protects the original bondholders, is the *earnings test*; this test sets a minimum level of coverage of debt service, interest, and principal for all outstanding bonds and for future debt. Included in the terms is the allowance for an increase in the debt service fund to handle new debt. The most conservative method of determining the earnings test is to use current financial performance, such as net revenues of the last 1 or 2 fiscal years, against estimated future maximum annual debt service.

Financial Statements and the Annual Report

The official statement contains the financial statements of the issuer. Accompanying these statements, if they are audited, is the *cold comfort letter* written by the independent accounting firm that audits the statements. The cold comfort letter provides an opinion that attests to the financial performance of the issuer over the past fiscal year and reassures the bondholder of the accuracy of the financial figures presented. Yet this letter does not attest to the eventual solvency of the issue at the maturity date of the bond. This letter does verify the accuracy and full presentation of material information in the financial statements. Depending on the scope of the audit, the accountant will specify those funds it did not review and thus cannot provide an opinion on.

The number of municipalities issuing annual reports is increasing. In the past, revenue bond issuers who came to market frequently would usually issue annual reports, whereas fewer GO issuers did so. The *annual report* is used by the issuer as a summary of its operations for the prior fiscal year, but its information content varies from issuer to issuer. Major organizations involved in municipal accounting are working together to provide a more comprehensive and meaningful annual report format. Alternative reporting methods are being suggested by the AICPA, the NCGA, and other accounting organizations.

As evidenced by all these documents and agreements, the municipal securities industry is moving toward providing the investor and the taxpayer with increasing disclosure of material information. The documents are structured so as to protect not only the bondholder but also the participants within the municipal industry who bring these issues to the marketplace.

Participants in a Municipal Security Offering

The expansion of the municipal securities market can be largely attributed to the creative energies of the investment banking community. By designing innovative financing mechanisms and structuring new forms of offerings, the investment community has greatly assisted the municipal sector in the ever-expanding concepts of and projects for "public purpose" programs. Concomitant with this market growth, the participants in municipal bond offerings have assumed greater responsibilities and have also increased their legal exposure and liability. The traditional roles of the bond counsel, underwriter and its counsel, issuer, financial advisers, and other participants have changed over the years. In light of the "consumer beware" environment, the participants in this industry are under greater scrutiny by the SEC and the courts in their practices and in their disclosure of material information.

The role each assumes is not clearly defined because it depends on the complexity of the issue and the sophistication of the participants. Each issue is unique and has its own history. Smaller offerings are generally simple in structure, and the roles of the participants are relatively clear. As an issue grows in complexity owing to factors such as financing agreements, structure, and underlying security, the distinction between individual functions becomes less clear, and as the functions become more interwoven, the delineation of legal responsibility becomes more difficult. The investor or analyst should therefore be familiar with the general duties performed by the usual participants in a municipal offering as well as their expanded roles.

Depending on the nature, size, and type of issuance, the number of legal counsels involved varies. Usually, the number of participants, including legal counsels, is three to five sets: There is the bond counsel, the issuer, the underwriter, the issuing authority, and, in the case of an industrial development bond, the corporation (and its counsels—both internal and external). The issuer may not have its own legal counsel and thus may depend on bond counsel for guidance. The underwriter may also be without legal counsel and may thus utilize the experience of bond counsel.

With a revenue bond, for instance, the nonactive market issuers usually remain in the background during the drafting of the official statement. This process is left to the underwriter and bond counsel. The more active issuer has gained experience in bringing the security to market and is invaluable in this process. Yet even this becomes qualified, for it depends on whether the issue is a negotiated sale or a competitive bid situation.

In a negotiated sale, the underwriter is involved in the early stages of the development of the issue. Usually, if the issuer has come to market frequently, the underwriter has an ongoing relationship with it. On the other hand, if it is a competitive bid situation, the underwriter's involvement is limited to the final stages of bringing the bonds to market. The issuer and, at times, its financial adviser will take a more active role. In this instance, the issue is open to public bids. The underwriter submits a bid based on a preliminary official statement. If its bid is accepted, the underwriter is awarded the bonds and sells them on the market. The underwriter has little involvement, if any, in drafting the official statement, other than finalizing the statement according to terms agreed upon in the bid.

It should be noted that in most states an issuer is required to sell GO bonds through competitive bidding. On the other hand, revenue bonds are often free from this requirement, and depending on the price the issuer can receive, revenue bonds are sold through a financing arrangement that is negotiated. After a bid is accepted in a competitive bid situation, the liabilities of the underwriting syndicate are determined by contract. The issuer and underwriter enter into the bond purchase agreement, whereby the underwriter protects its liabilities and sets forth certain stipulations. The underwriter also includes in the bid a "good-faith check" (usually 1 to 5 percent), which is lost if the bidder breaches the contract by failing to pay for bonds upon delivery.

Since there are no clear-cut definitions of the functions of the participants, the issue of responsibility for disclosing types of information is further complicated. At the same time that the participants are developing their own definitions of what constitutes necessary disclosure practices in conjunction with various legislation, they are also attempting to define their individual duties more clearly. Standardization of these definitions within the industry has not yet been achieved, but the overall direction is toward greater disclosure and increased protection of the ultimate investor.

The Bond Counsel

The traditional role of bond counsel is to act as an independent "legal auditor" serving two purposes. The first is to render an opinion as to the unqualified, legal validity of the bond issue as a binding obligation of the issuer in accordance with state and local laws. Second, bond counsel opines as to the tax-exempt nature of the interest on the issue in compliance with federal, state, and local tax laws. The analysis of bond counsel's duties follows this traditional definition that bond opinion is narrow in both "scope and reach," which delineates the bond counsel's function and the reliance on the opinion by the investor.

According to the traditional definition of responsibility, counsel will jeopardize its independent status if it becomes involved in the drafting of the official statement. By complying with the defined duties, bond counsel limits its legal liability to only the investor's reliance on the bond opinion. Although bond counsel is retained by the issuer and is paid from the proceeds of the bond issue, it does not usually act as a regular counsel to any of the participants in the issuance. Bond counsel may suggest financial alternatives that are open to the issuer, but such advice should originate from the legal requirements that bond counsel must fulfill when drafting its opinion. The course of action undertaken by the issuer will be determined by the final advice provided by its own counsel and financial advisers.

In drafting the bond opinion, bond counsel determines and requests the material information it needs from the issuer. The documentation requested from the issuer is similar for most issues, but there are some exceptions, particularly in the case of revenue issues, where it is more complex. Listed below are the types of documents that bond counsel requests from New York City, for example, prior to writing its opinion.

- A copy of the charter of the municipality
- A certified copy of delegation of authority by the mayor to the comptroller to issue the securities
- The certificates authorizing the issuance of the securities

- A confirmation of sale
- A certificate of the chief of the Division of Municipal Securities concerning compliance with certain notice requirements
- A copy of the bids by managing syndicates received by the city
- A certificate of award to the winning syndicates
- Certificates as to the genuineness of signatures on various documents and as to the absence of litigation
- A certificate of delivery and payment
- A specimen of a security
- An arbitrage certificate

Once the documents are received, bond counsel relies on the certificates for the validity and accuracy of the facts presented. Counsel then opines on the issuance. It performs a "formal review" of the facts presented but usually does not delve into the material in an investigative capacity. The opinion states that bond counsel has examined the certified copy of the transcript of the bond proceedings of the authorized bonds as well as one of the executed bonds.

On the basis of these representations, bond counsel states whether the securities are actually legal and binding obligations of the issuer. In addition, counsel specifies any specific funds pledged and any obligations of the issuer that are exempt from federal income tax. In the case of an industrial development bond, the legal opinion varies from the norm. The security's underlying credit is that of a private corporation, and so the bond opinion is more extensive due to the risk associated with the issue. Bond counsel may attest to the incorporation of the company, the accuracy of those portions of the offering circular which describe the bonds, and the primary documents that are directly related to securing the bond.

In general, the scope of the bond opinion does not include the creditworthiness of the issuer or the associated interest and market risks of the security. Reliance on the documents presented by the issuer is made by bond counsel. Investor reliance on the bond opinion has brought the expanded role of bond counsel and its responsibilities into the limelight; therefore, bond counsel may extend its duties beyond those traditionally defined. It may provide a negative assurance as to the fact that neither material omissions nor a misstatement of material facts exists in the official statement. The negative assurance is based on the documents presented to bond counsel by the issuer, and counsel may perform a limited review of this information. A traditional bond counsel may be retained by the underwriter, and if so, it is not paid from the proceeds of the bond issue; it will act as the underwriter's counsel and provide legal advice as to the issue and its structure.

Bond counsel may play a crucial role in implementing an innovative financing concept. Furthermore, it may act in a lobbyist capacity or be retained by state legislative or executive branches to draft the legislation and try test cases. Such a trial is done to see if the concept withstands statutory and constitutional limitations. The state, in implementing public policy and social programs, may need revenues to finance these projects. Bond counsel may be retained to provide the legislative ability to seek this financing. Counsel may also opine whether such legislation will meet a constitutional test, whether it satisfies the definition of public purpose, whether state monies could be appropriated for the project, and so forth. This legislation will either create an agency or authority to issue the securities to finance the program or empower a jurisdiction to do so.

Once this is accomplished, bond counsel may work closely with the in-house counsel of the authority or municipality and with other special counsels to establish guidelines that will comply with statutory and constitutional requirements.

With the increasing complexity of financing structures, more sophisticated legal advice is required. Bond counsel is able, with its expertise, to provide this advice, which consequently increases its direct involvement with the various parties to the transaction. Yet the nature and degree of the involvement of bond counsel depends on the history of the issue, its complexity, and the interests of the parties involved. The following list summarizes some of the duties of bond counsel:

- Preparation of the ordinance under which the bonds are issued.

- Preparation of the bonds.

- Representation of the issuer in connection with the negotiation of the bond purchase agreement with the underwriters.

- Direct involvement with those parts of the official statement relating to the ordinance and the bonds. (Since many new issuers lack sufficient staff to develop an official statement, bond counsel frequently drafts the entire statement.)

- In financings that involve power sales contracts, installment purchase agreements, leases, mortgages, or back-to-back loans, the preparation of those documents.

Bond counsel has departed from the traditional role of the "legal auditor" to become an active participant in the drafting and developing of legal standards that are applied to municipal financings.

Although the duties and responsibilities of bond counsel have become complex, there is no straightforward answer to the issue: To whom is counsel responsible, the investor or the issuer? Opinions as to the ultimate nature of bond counsel's responsibility vary from counsel to counsel. A definite fact is that the legal liability and exposure of bond counsel have increased as bond counsel's duties have expanded. Its role can be both "broad and narrow." Yet bond counsel is trying to help a municipality achieve a social purpose while at the same time attempting to present a security worthwhile for investment. In fulfilling its responsibility, bond counsel also tries to protect the investor as well as the issuer within the confines of its duties.

The Underwriter and Underwriter's Counsel

The underwriter is in a tenuous position in that it must represent the interests of both its clients: the issuer and the investor. The underwriter's relationship with the issuer is determined by whether the financing agreement of the issue is to be a competitive bid or a negotiated sale. Like bond counsel, the underwriter may be involved in promoting an innovative financing structure for a municipal securities issue and may act as a lobbyist in state legislatures and executive branches. Its relationship with the issuer may be a historical one, and it may also recommend to the issuer which bond counsel it should retain.

In its responsibility toward the investor, the underwriter negotiates contractual agreements with the issuer and reviews the financing and security agreements set forth in the underlying documents supporting the offering. By doing so, it attempts to give the investor as much security as possible in terms of payment of interest and principal and adequate debt service provisions.

An underwriter should not release an offering unless adequate disclosure and legal verification are provided. The rating agencies may perform a review of the issue, but a thorough analysis of the issue, the issuer, and the financing supporting the issue should also be performed by the underwriter. Depending on the degree of involvement with the municipal issuance, the underwriter's duties can range from those of a lobbyist (which sees the implementation of the financing concept, the creation of an agency, or the empowering of a jurisdiction to issue the security) to those of a participant in the drafting of the official statement. During this process, the underwriter works closely with bond counsel and the issuer.

There is a concerted effort in the municipal industry to improve disclosure requirements, and underwriters have been involved with this movement. With the increasing complexity of the issues, underwriters may retain separate counsel in negotiated sale offerings. The need for this counsel is due to the underwriter's awareness of potential liability under federal and state securities laws and the need to lessen its legal exposure. Also, underwriters are regulated in the secondary market by the MSRB. To assure compliance with MSRB regulations, the underwriter's counsel will provide advice. The underwriter will take on those roles which bond counsel does not. This does depend, though, on the issue and the relationships between the parties. By retaining a separate counsel, the underwriter provides the investor with an added assurance that its interests are being protected.

The underwriter's counsel reviews the exempt status of the security. Relying on the opinion of the issuer's counsel, this counsel determines whether the bond purchase agreement between the issuer and underwriter is "legal, valid, and binding"; it provides a negative assurance as to information contained in the official statement, other than the financial statements and consultant's reports, that there is neither omission nor misstatement of material facts. In addition, counsel drafts the memorandum on the blue-sky laws applicable in the state where the issuer is located. The underwriter's counsel must advise the underwriter on any of the potential legal liabilities associated with the issue.

The Issuer and Issuer's Counsel

The issuer of a municipal security may be a municipality, an agency, an authority, or a combination of a municipality and a corporation (as in the case of an industrial development bond). The interrelationships the issuer has with federal, state, and local governments should be clarified and understood. In a revenue bond issue, for example, the issuer may be a public authority created for a distinct purpose. Such authorities were sometimes created to circumvent the bureaucracy encountered within a jurisdiction or by a constitutional restriction. In essence, the powers granted to this agency are specific in nature, and the authority cannot assume powers beyond those stated in either the state legislation or the state constitutional amendment that created the authority. Issuers such as municipal hospitals may have special relationships with federal agencies; the issuer must be in compliance with the regulations stipulated by the agency.

The issuer may be inexperienced in the municipal marketplace and lack the staff and/or financial sophistication to draft the necessary financing agreements. During the negotiation of the bond purchase agreement and the drafting of financial agreements, the issuer will rely on bond counsel's advice so that the provisions of the covenants in the bond resolution (in a revenue issue, for instance) will not prove too restrictive. It will also rely on the expertise of the underwriter and its counsel.

Counsel separate from bond counsel may be retained by the issuer. In other cases, in-house counsel may be present. The issuer's counsel will take on the role played by bond counsel in drafting the underlying financing documents and official statement if it has the necessary expertise. The nature of the issuer, the size and complexity of the issue, and the expertise of this counsel will determine the degree of involvement that the issuer and its counsel will have in the offering.

The Trustee

The trustee is purportedly the representative of the bondholders in a third-party beneficiary relationship with the issuer. The trustee enters into an agreement with the issuer with the intent of protecting the interests of the bondholders. Once chosen, the trustee will also assist in the marketing and placing of the bonds.

A trustee, such as a local bank, can be in a locality other than a major money market center. In this case, and if the bonds are expected to be widely held, a cotrustee (or paying agent) located in a major financial center is chosen in order to ensure that the funds will be available for payment of interest and principal on the bonds. This results in the trustee acting also as the paying agent on the bonds.

The responsibilities of the trustee include a surveillance function; it ensures that the covenants are adhered to, thus protecting the bondholders' interests. To protect these interests further, the trustee generally takes a conservative interpretation of the provisions in the trust indenture. If problems arise with the issue, the trustee must follow certain courses of action set forth in the bond covenants. If the issuer desires to alter certain provisions in the indenture agreement (for a refunding plan, for example), the trustee must be consulted. Before any changes can be made, the trustee must approve the proposed alterations—to safeguard the legal standing and interests of the original bondholders.

The participants in a municipal security offering have overlapping functions; nevertheless, they work closely together in bringing the municipal issue to the marketplace. On the other hand, the complexity of the relationships and the intricacy of the roles these participants undertake further complicate the issue of disclosure and the responsibility as well as exposure of the individual participants.

PART 6

Future Perspectives on Municipal Bond Analysis

19

The Art of Municipal Analysis and Attendant Issues

The analysis of municipal bonds has come a very long way over a short time. It was not long ago that most municipal bond issues were sold without detailed official statements and without any in-depth evaluation completed by financial actors involved in the underwriting, distribution, sales, and purchasing processes. Today, municipal bond analysis has become a very important part of the securities industry, and this trend has been contemporaneous with the tremendous outflow of information prepared by general obligation and revenue bond issuers alike. Much of the attention given to municipal bond research was fueled largely by the financial difficulties of New York City in the mid-1970s and has been refueled, in a sense, by the financial morass of the Washington Public Power Supply System. As a result, over recent years there has been the development of relatively sophisticated techniques for analyzing municipal bonds. Municipal analysis, however, still remains more of an art than a science, and this is just one issue that must be addressed here.

In addition, other important aspects of the municipal market should not be left undiscussed. For instance, attention should be paid to the nature and kinds of financial problems that major issuers have encountered over the years and to the financial ameliorative efforts that have been used to solve such difficulties. Also, some perspective should be provided on past and potential taxpayer revolts and on the impending tax legislation. A final discussion should be presented on how the municipal bond industry, working together with state and local governments, could better provide for government services to American citizens nationwide and, at the same time, serve up to investors municipal bonds of sound security.

The Art of Municipal Analysis

The foregoing chapters have painted a somewhat accurate picture of municipal analysis on Wall Street today. The picture is only somewhat accurate because, as any good painter knows, the finishing touches are as important as the basic painting itself. What has not been explained thus far is that municipal analysis is in no way a science. To carry the metaphor one step farther, after analyzing a municipal bond—with the basic ratios and economic, financial, and legal considerations taken into account—municipal credit determinations require painstaking finishing touches. To be sure, the analysis of municipal bonds, especially in the critical areas of potential upgradings and downgradings, is clearly less a science than an art. Ratio analysis notwithstanding, there is really no cookbook way to analyze municipal bonds. Because every revenue bond category is evaluated a little differently and because every type of general obligation bond must be analyzed on a case-by-case basis, the fine-tuning of municipal credit analysis really involves a different weighting of analytical factors for each and every evaluation of every municipal bond. As a result, it seems clear that although certain financial ratios, economic norms, and debt ratios seem to apply to the different rating categories of all kinds of municipal bonds, those semiscientific tools, taken alone, are not nearly sufficient to make accurate credit evaluations.

Indeed, ratio analysis of municipal bonds does have inherent limitations on the general obligation side; economic data must be treated differently for each state, for each city, and, as shown earlier, for each region. For different revenue bond categories, such as public power, housing, water and sewer, and transportation, ratios only provide a general indication as to what quality category these bonds may fit. Very strong ratios on a certain given series of characteristics may not really be a true determinant of municipal quality and thus of a given rating. More often than not, other factors exist that are pivotal in making the bond worth more or less in a quality sense than would normally be the case if ratios and other tools were strictly used as determinants of relative quality. The results of these evaluative tools serve only as guideposts for analysis. As a consequence, in securities analysis on Wall Street today, municipal analysis truly stands apart in terms not only of how evaluations are made but also of the kinds of individuals who must make those evaluations. Corporate securities provide many more useful, precise, timely, and well-publicized analytical tools, ratios, and other information with which to make quality determinations. In most cases, municipal bonds just do not serve up this kind of information from the municipal menu.

Philosophic Problems

Even more important are certain quasi-philosophic issues relating to the qualitative evaluations of municipal bonds. One has to do with the time factor involved in a bond rating. Investors buy a bond of a particular maturity assuming that the rating on that bond holds for that particular maturity. Yet is it likely that a double-A–rated credit is as secure a double A at the last maturity of a 30-year bond as it is during the very first year the serial bond will mature? Or is it more likely to be the case, from a logician's standpoint, that the first year's maturity of the bond is more apt to carry the true rating than is the 30-year maturity of the bond? Moreover, is the bondholder more likely to get paid during the first year the bond is held than during the last year, when over a 30-year period any number of economic or financial events could possibly occur?

In a similar vein, municipal analysis, as in the analysis of most investment vehicles, provides a quality determination (or rating) for all types and kinds of municipal bonds. However, is a double-A–rated hospital bond truly as secure as a double-A–rated general obligation bond, and are all revenue bonds less secure or more secure than general obligation bonds? For instance, analysts really compare public power bonds against similarly rated public power bonds specifically, and against all public power bonds in general, based on a long list of definable qualitative characteristics. The analyst does not usually compare an A-rated public power bond to an A-rated city general obligation bond to make sure that they are of the same quality, even though the A rating is supposed to apply across the board. As a matter of fact, most rating agencies, securities firms, and banks themselves, have analysts who specialize in certain types of bonds. There is also an interesting companion problem to this issue.

What most individuals assume is that a comparison of states or cities or other issuing entities across a wide array of ratios and economic and financial variables will break down these credits into a variety of discernible quality categories. This assumption, however, may or may not be so. For instance, if an analyst were to compare all the triple-A states across a certain number of important economic and financial characteristics, the analyst would find that certain states truly do not belong in that group. Similarly, if the analyst were to do the same with the double-A–rated states, it would be found that certain of such states would appear to be better in credit quality than certain triple-A–rated states. Similarly, other double-A states would seem to be worse in credit quality than states rated double-A. This points up the twin problem of ratio analysis and comparative evaluations.

Another problem in municipal analysis is that once a rating is assigned, one would think that it represents a semipermanent imprimatur or evaluation of that particular credit. Municipal evaluations today usually do not include a trend analysis for every credit, and it is exceedingly difficult to monitor credits continually because of the sheer number coming to market and remaining outstanding. This is so for three important reasons. One is that accurate financial information is usually not available on an ongoing basis covering short periods of time. Another is that certain credit situations, be they problematic or positive, may occur and come to light too quickly for analysts to have discerned this particular quality trend. The third is that certain financial characteristics of the credit may become particularly important over a short period of time, while other characteristics remain constant. An example would be a large increase in the contingent liabilities of a municipality or a state because of the issuance of debt by another related entity, or the increasing importance of unfunded pension liabilities because the program to fund those liabilities has not been effective.

These problems make it difficult for the analyst or investor to predict the trend of credits from a quality standpoint. At best, discerning future trends and predicting upgrades and downgrades in ratings can be a hazardous occupation. This situation is made more problematic when the analyst's opinion about what credit should be upgraded or downgraded does not coincide with the opinion of the rating agencies. Analysts may predict what should happen in their view, but whether or not it will occur remains an open question.

The Human Element

A difficulty facing investors when trying to understand the opinions of municipal bond analysts is that the human dimension very often comes into play when analysts opine on a particular credit. Analysts, like most individuals, may have stereotypical feelings and beliefs about certain regions of the country, and certain states and cities, and these feelings may affect their evaluations. Very often people have biased beliefs about the ability of less populated and less urbanized areas to weather economic downturns, and on the other hand, they may feel more comfortable with urbanized areas. Other analysts, however, may view urbanization as a source of decay, or as an indication of portending financial difficulties, and may see stability in less populated and less urbanized areas. There is certainly something to be said for these opinions, but to argue that they do not come into play in the evaluation of municipal credits, an activity that is so qualitative and complex in nature, may not be truly realistic.

Analyzing the politics of a particular jurisdiction and the extent to which the voters and/or the elected officials are willing to make good on financial commitments presents other problems to analysts and investors. Proposition 13–type reactions to increased taxes can come swiftly in certain political jurisdictions and, in a certain percentage of those, may need only a short time for approval. In other situations in which issuers have entered into contracts for payments on bonds, the contractual agreements may receive such full-blown negative publicity that when they come center stage in a potential default scenario, elected or judicial officials may turn their backs on them. On the other hand, certain impending financial catastrophies have shown that political pressure within a confined geographic area and strong financial need can turn a potentially mammoth disaster into a relatively stable situation over a short period of time.

Another problem facing municipal analysts is the evaluation of feasibility studies, which have often been the last word on the financial viability of a very large percentage of municipal revenue bond projects (from public power to water and sewer to hospitals to resource recovery, and so forth). While the credentials of the firms writing these reports are in almost all cases above reproach, even the best analysts today may have little background or expertise in understanding the development of these reports and may not have the tools, such as sophisticated computer modeling apparatus, to adequately critique them and question their financial projections. Additionally, feasibility studies are only projections and often do not, and realistically cannot, run for the term of a bond issue, thus leaving room for problems years ahead.

Municipal Defaults

Municipal bonds are by no means the pristine debt securities of the American securities market, but they do have a relatively good record of safety. As have most debt instruments over the years, municipal bonds have weathered cyclic periods in which numerous defaults occurred. The largest percentage of these defaults, as might be expected, has paralleled the series of American depressions dating back to the mid-nineteenth century. The largest number of municipal defaults (approximately 75 percent of the total number of all municipal defaults) occurred during the depression years of the 1930s and had problems similar to those associated with other marketable securities. Interestingly, it should be noted that most municipal defaults during those years were actually industrial development revenue bonds whose corporate guarantors defaulted on the payment of principal and interest of their tax-exempt securities. These were not municipal bond defaults in the classical sense of the term.

The record of municipal bonds stands in contrast to that of corporate securities in one important way: The repayment record of municipal bonds appears to be much better than that of their corporate counterparts. During the depression years, corporate defaults outstripped municipal defaults by about 2 to 1. In the wake of the depression, however, approximately $3 billion of corporate debt remained unpaid and only approximately $200 million worth of municipal debt remained outstanding. One hypothetical reason for the fact that the municipal bond repayment record appears to be relatively good is that, in default scenarios, tax-exempt issuers are more easily able to find ways to work out their debt repayment problems than are other issuers of securities. It would be difficult to prove this hypothesis, but some examples are worth noting. Among them are the seemingly recurring problems of New York City and the bailout of the city in 1975 by the investment vehicle called the Municipal Assistance Corporation for the City of New York.

The Case of New York City

A century ago, James Bryce, government scholar of international renown, concluded in his 3-volume treatise *The American Commonwealth* that the one conspicuous failure of the United States was the government of cities, and he argued further that the vices of extravagance and mismanagement revealed themselves on the largest scale in New York City. In the wake of the New York City fiscal crisis of the 1970s, many financial analysts rendered the same remarkable verdict. Lost to many observers of the New York debacle was the city's problem in 1871: European bankers refused to extend it loans in light of its debt growth, and subsequently the trading of the city's bonds on the Berlin Stock Exchange was suspended. As a condition for additional loans to the city, New York bankers required that financial reforms be instituted and that audits of the city books be conducted. The city relented, and during the electoral year the Tweed Ring fell from power.

About 60 years later, in 1933, a similar fiscal crisis beset New York City, and on September 28 of that year *The New York Times* ran this headline: "Banks Agree to City Finance Plan." After a year of negotiations with Wall Street financiers in an effort to stave off default, the city concluded what was known as the 1933 Bankers Agreement with the nation's major banks, led by Thomas W. Lamont of J. P. Morgan & Company. The city agreed to institute a seven-point austerity program in return for the refunding by the banks of its outstanding revenue bonds issued against uncollected taxes. It was against this backdrop that New York City skidded toward default again in the 1970s.

Two default scenarios were almost played out in the mid-1970s that give some support to the earlier hypothesis about municipal repayments in financial emergencies. When New York City was on the brink of bankruptcy in 1975, the newly created municipal financing vehicle that rescued the city from its fiscal crisis was the Municipal Assistance Corporation for the City of New York (aptly dubbed "Big MAC"). MAC was a financing vehicle authorized to refinance the city's outstanding debt obligations and issue additional debt, which totaled well into the billions, in the name of New York City, but without the backing of the city. The security behind MAC's municipal obligations consisted of earmarked revenues for the city and certain taxes levied within the city, which more than adequately covered MAC's debt service requirements. The lesson here is not that MAC may have been an undervalued municipal bond issuer because of the high coverage of its debt service, and it is not the simple fact that New York City was rescued from bankruptcy by the creation of MAC. Rather, the lesson lies in the proposition that even in a potential and likely default scenario, the untapped and largely disguised resources inherent in the confined structure of a municipal finance system have the resiliency to turn a potentially mammoth fiscal disaster into a much more stable financial situation within a relatively short time. Similarly, and at about the same time, the New York State Urban Development Corporation defaulted on $104.5 million in notes. To avoid further financial difficulties and to rectify the agency's financial problems, the state created the New York State Project Finance Agency to help the Urban Development Corporation continue financing its program and making payments under its obligations.

The Aftermath

It is interesting, for a number of reasons, that during the late 1970s and early 1980s there were some notable municipal problems in New York City and elsewhere. The difference between these problems and the ones of earlier years is that they attacked large, important issuers and did not come during the severe economic dislocations of American depressions. More notable, in the case of WPPSS, is that the Supply System's financial difficulties and ultimate default occurred almost 10 years after New York City weathered its financial difficulties, which had the effect of spurring a burgeoning municipal research effort in securities firms and other financial institutions around the country.

The Washington Public Power Supply System

The Washington Public Power Supply System weathered the largest municipal default in American history when it defaulted on payment of $2.25 billion worth of bonds outstanding in January 1984. As discussed in Chaps. 1 and 7, the following are some noteworthy facts of the case. WPPSS, a joint operating agency of the state of Washington, was authorized to construct five nuclear fuel electric generating units with a total capacity of 6,080,000 kW. The total cost for the five projects was originally estimated in 1975 to be about $7 billion. By 1982 the estimated cost of the project had risen dramatically to over $20 billion. Project Nos. 1, 2, and 3 were in effect obligations of the Bonneville Power Administration, a seller of wholesale power in the northwest, and their bonds were secured by payments from certain participants. Project Nos. 4 and 5 were secured by payments from 88 public utility districts, which had signed take-or-pay contracts under which the participants were obligated to make payments on their obligations to WPPSS whether or not the projects were operating or electricity was provided. Later, the Washington State Supreme Court ruled that the public utility districts did not have the authority to enter into those contracts and therefore did not have to make payments under them. At the time of the default, about $6.12 billion was outstanding for Project Nos. 1, 2, and 3, together with the $2.25 billion outstanding for Project Nos. 4 and 5. Project Nos. 1 and 3 were mothballed until further notice. This is the broad framework of the the Washington Public Power Supply System's financial debacle.

In the wake of the default, certain concepts of events surrounding the Supply System's financial difficulties emerged. It is now generally believed that the Supply System's construction delays led to construction cost problems, which called into question the viability of the project. It is also known that the cost of power for those who expected to receive it would rise because of the project's increased costs. Moreover, the original projected demand for the electricity did not materialize. Finally, later there was a question as to whether the participants in the projects had the authority to enter into their contractual agreements. There was also substantial public outcry by certain customers (who would be required to pay higher rates for electricity) against making payments under those contractual obligations because of the ongoing problems associated with the Supply System's construction of the projects over the years.

In any event, there are a number of aspects of the analysis of power bonds specifically, and of revenue bonds in general, that will be undertaken in the future in light of the WPPSS situation. These include a more in-depth study of the ability of governmental entities to enter into contractual arrangements, a greater scrutiny of projected costs, a closer monitoring of construction costs and construction delays, and a general surveillance of the building of nuclear plants and the government regulation of that type of construction. What seems to separate the WPPSS problem from other impending financial disasters is the fact that it stretched across a large geographic area, notably two different states and many municipalities, where there was a substantial public sentiment against problems associated with the project. This led to a situation of many people holding divergent views as to how the problem should be solved. In the cases of New York City, the New York State Urban Development Corporation, and other impending financial problems, these default situations were generally confined within a single political domain in which there was a political as well as a financial need to right the problem. These characteristics were not really representative of the situation with the Washington Public Power Supply System.

Tax Revolts and Tax Reform

The precursor to the federal movement toward tax reform was a taxpayers' revolt that spread throughout many states in the late 1970s. This event was spearheaded by Proposition 13 in California, which was a major initiative to decrease measurably real property taxes within the state. It appeared on the ballot on June 6, 1978, as the Jarvis Initiative, was passed later by a 2 to 1 majority, and became an amendment to the California State Constitution, Article XIII A. The following November, similar spending limitations and taxing limitations appeared on the election year ballot in many states nationwide. Although most were not as stringent as that enacted by California, many states passed limited editions of that general concept.

The consequences of these taxing and spending initiatives did not have the tragic effects that some believed they would, such as crippling state and local governments in providing public services and impacting the credit of municipalities and states. The effect has been more subtle, and perhaps more far-reaching. It is generally held to have moved states toward issuing revenue bonds and away from general obligation bonds, although this is an idea that is extremely difficult to prove quantitatively. Another subtle, though more far-reaching, consequence of the taxpayers' revolt is the simple fact that legislation has been passed and put in place at the insistence of citizens to curtail tax increases and limit government spending. To suggest that this will not be repeated again at the state and local levels of government is to deny a very real possibility.

Over the years, and most recently in 1985 and 1986, the federal government and Congress have embarked on a number of plans to revamp the tax structure of the United States, most of which have included restrictions on the issuance of tax-exempt municipal bonds. Many of these limitations are contained in the Tax Reform Act of 1986, which will be discussed in Chap. 21 and the Appendix.

Whatever additional costs local governments must bear in the future to provide the kinds of services that the public expects, desires, and needs, the higher interest costs resulting from the proposed tax measures may ultimately be paid for by the public itself. Moreover, the extent to which the bond issues will no longer be feasible because interest rates are too high (for any number of reasons) is the extent to which those kinds of services will probably not be provided to citizens in the foreseeable future. However, whether interest rates on municipal issues will actually move higher is also a function of the interest rates of all securities in general and of the desire of institutions and individuals to buy municipal bonds, whether they be tax-exempt or taxable. Securities are not to be issued in a tax vacuum, but rather within a system that has yield relationships among all the different kinds of securities. It is those relationships which may be changed by the Tax Reform Act's structure and which will determine the relative attractiveness of municipal yields.

Taxable Municipal Bonds

In light of the enactment of the Tax Reform Act of 1986, there arises the possibility that some municipal bonds will have to be issued as taxable securities. Such an event is not brand new to the municipal bond market. For instance, the Alaska Housing Finance Corporation has issued taxable housing bonds over recent years, and a number of industrial development revenue bonds have been issued in taxable form.

In 1986 Los Angeles County issued taxable municipal debt in the form of lease revenue refunding notes. This was one of the first instances in which a traditional general obligation bond–issuing entity that previously issued tax-exempt bonds has issued securities in taxable form. By the end of 1986, taxable municipal bonds had been issued nationwide in a volume totaling into the billions for a wide variety of purposes. In any case, it is important to note that municipal bonds have come into the market in taxable form, and the door should not be closed on the possibility that this may be an important part of the market in years to come, largely as a result of the Tax Reform Act of 1986.*

* See Official Statement of $50,000,000 Medium Term Notes in the form of Certificates of Participation, Los Angeles County Public Properties Refunding Project of 1985, dated November 15, 1985.

NOTE: Part 6 (Chaps. 19 and 20) was written by Stephen P. Rappaport in a paper entitled "Political, Financial, and Philosophic Concerns of Municipal Bond Analysis: The 1990s and Beyond" at Prudential-Bache Securities Inc., 1986. Reprinted by permission.

20
Implications for Governments and Investors

The Historical Perspective

Many political and financial writers have long since documented the events anticipated as an outgrowth of the skeletal framework of government set up by the Founding Fathers of the federal system. Major volumes of scholarly study have been devoted to the changing nature of the federal system of government and its relationships to the state governments and local communities. Much of this work has described the metamorphosis in the way that the federal government has provided for state and local governments through the intermingling of financial resources. Additionally, later literature has been devoted to the changing nature of state and local relations. The material alluded to here has encompassed governmental revenue and expenditive patterns and intergovernmental financial aid of all types.

Compared to the voluminous amount of material available on federal, state, and local financial relations, very little has been produced in the way of describing some of the unanticipated structural changes which developed over recent years and which radically altered the nature and structure of state and local financial systems. Indeed, most of the changes that have resulted have been so totally unanticipated that their structural elements were never even mentioned in the U.S. Constitution and early state constitutions. The framework and parameters for these changes have come through major amendments to state constitutions, most of which were accomplished during the twentieth century. Even more remarkable is the fact that the major underpinnings of state and local governmental systems and the true mechanisms that allow governments to function have rarely, if ever, been assessed in academic literature and have not been studied in depth in most academic institutions. This whole area is the growth and analysis of state and local government debt, with particular emphasis on public services provided by the extragovernmental creatures commonly known as public revenue authorities.

It has been well established that the volume of debt issued by state and local governments and revenue authorities is enormous. In 1985 alone, approximately $160 billion of municipal bonds was brought to market, an amount that seems staggering by any standard. It is this issuance of government debt, together with the growth of revenue authorities, that has played a key role in America's governmental operations. Many observers have argued that without this ability of governments to issue debt—with the concomitant growth of revenue authorities as major debt issuers and as wholesale providers for such basic services as water and sewers, public power, and transportation—America would cease to function and exist as we know it today. Yet there has been little detailed analysis of municipal bonds and revenue authorities by government and financial writers over the years. Without an in-depth understanding (1) of government debt, (2) of the purpose and the impact of providing public services through revenue authorities, and (3) of the effect that these entities and the issuance of their debt have on taxpayers, on the political system, and on the status and quality of public services, very little can be known about the American system of government and its relationship to its taxpaying citizens.

Over the years, and beginning largely in the twentieth century, the nature and growth of public debt at the state and local levels has not been as regular as it might have seemed. In earlier years, certain states and municipalities felt financially constrained in providing government services through their own revenue sources and sought relief by entering the debt market. A contemporaneous trend developed in which the revenue authority came center stage as a new financing vehicle to provide government services and to issue debt in order to build the necessary facilities; such debt was backed by fees from users and therefore stood outside the purview of most local governments of general jurisdiction and of most states. During most of the twentieth century, however, the rate, growth, and volume of general obligation debt far outstripped those of revenue bonds, and this held constant for a long period of time—until the 1970s, when the volume of revenue debt issued became twice that of general obligation debt issued. By the mid-1980s, there was a discernible movement back to general obligation debt, but that was less important than it seemed, given the total volume of debt issued. The irregular trend in how municipal debt is issued and the wide variety of public services that this debt provides, coupled with the extraordinary increase in the volume of municipal bonds, give evidence of a much larger trend in the changing nature of American government finance. Indeed, the changes in the kinds of municipal debt issued and which entities sell them have little to do with the ability of states and cities to issue general obligation bonds or to embark on projects largely of their own making.

The early trend away from general obligation bonds and toward revenue bonds was the result of a variety of converging forces. Among them was the desire to move certain enterprises away from the competitive processes of politics and place them in a more corporate-oriented structure, such as the revenue authority. An underlying reason, however, was the desire to skirt the constitutional debt limits of local governments of general jurisdiction, which would potentially prohibit the issuance of debt for much-needed services through bond issue referendums. The more basic underlying reason for the movement to revenue authorities could be found in the simple structural inadequacies present in the skeletal structure of American state and local financial systems. Indeed, both the political process and the structure of state and local governments seemed to prohibit the provision of much-needed government services to the American populace to the extend needed. The revenue authority was never really conceived of by the Founding Fathers of the American republic, but was a structural governmental solution to an apparent need. Viewed from this angle, the movement back and forth from general obligation bond issuance to revenue bonds, against a backdrop of burgeoning increases in municipal bond issuance, tells the story of a vastly increasing need by Americans for certain governmental services and of the provision of those services through any viable financial means that appeared to be politically palatable and financially justifiable.

Present trends have begun to feed rapidly on what has previously happened in the municipal market and, coupled with a rapid growth in the volume of municipal debt issued, are presenting new problems as well as important possibilities for state and local governments nationwide. For instance, the federal government has begun a process of retrenching from its involvement in state and local financial affairs by curtailing grant monies and excising programs, thereby encouraging (if not mandating) governments to finance public services on their own. Additionally, the federal government is seeking limitations on the issuance of tax-exempt municipal bonds; this would have the effect of putting additional pressure on state and local financial systems by making services more expensive through higher interest rates or by forcing the curtailment of programs altogether. Not surprisingly, capital improvements completed years ago are beginning to far outrun their useful lives. This fact, together with the public's need for new and improved services (such as more efficient transportation networks, larger water and sewer programs, more housing, larger power resources, better solid waste treatment facilities, improved school systems, and funds to support the historically high cost of running government itself), has fueled the fire of state and local government needs in ways that were previously unanticipated and unforeseen. In many ways, therefore, the dilemmas and needs of the early issuers of state and local debt (both of general obligation debt and revenue bond debt) are simply being replicated on a much larger scale in the 1980s and will continue to become magnified in the 1990s and probably beyond.

Many state and local governments are beginning to meet these problems with a variety of new financing mechanisms and market-related debt vehicles. These concepts include bond banks, development authorities, pooled financing facilities, and all types of credit enhancement techniques, such as insurance and bank credit supports. Also, a whole new wave of market-oriented investment alternatives—such as variable rate securities, demand bonds, and other inventive short-term instruments—have created markets in themselves. All these financing vehicles and market mechanisms are being employed to ease the entry into the debt market of major programs on a scale that has, in many cases, not only never before been attempted but also never before been conceived. The wholesale redoing of transportation networks (including turnpikes, bridges, tunnels, and airports), the pooling of revenues (among other financial arrangements) to provide multiple cities with water and sewer services or garbage collection, or the combining of hospitals and the joining of municipal electric districts to provide lower-cost services are just some of the ways in which the municipal bond community is attempting to meet the demands of state and local governments for new services and for the improvement of old ones. As a result, whether these services are provided by general obligation bond issuers, revenue bond issuers, or combinations of these, ultimately the ways that government services are delivered will be much different than the ways originally conceived and anticipated.

What Does This Mean for Investors?

Investors now have a wealth of opportunities in the new types of municipal bonds with different forms of security, and they have more market-related alternatives to choose from as personal investment vehicles. Nevertheless, a number of credit concerns largely overlooked in the past must be examined when buying these new debt instruments.

Massively large financings, such as the ones now being attempted for infrastructure purposes, carry with them certain characteristics that must be examined more carefully than if these bond issues had been brought to market in much smaller size. Of primary importance is the fact that the need for the project, or its projected demand, must be well scrutinized. In large projects or programs in which the construction is projected to go on for a number of years and in which the size of the debt can begin to run into the billions of dollars, the projections of the demand for the project in terms of the services it provides must be highly accurate. Minor miscalculations of demand can lead to major miscalculations in potential revenue generation and to important mis-judgments about the public appeal of the project, which can ultimately lead to market resistance in the selling of such securities. In a similar way, the construction costs must be closely evaluated—as must manage-ment's ability to contain those costs and bring the project on-line in time. If construction is constantly delayed, the cost of the project may rise dramatically, far outstripping the potential available revenues for pay-ment of the project's debt. Competing sources of services that are comparable and compatible to the public's needs must also be carefully assessed. What is critical to note here is that these kinds of assessments are ongoing processes. They just cannot be completed at the time of the first bond issue of a large program, but must be done throughout the bond issue's life and when subsequent issues are brought to market.

Another potential credit problem of large future financings for infrastructure-type purposes and other major public programs is the effect that the additional debt would have on the credit rating of the surrounding state or municipality, which must often divert revenues from its own revenue streams to the payment of principal and interest on the new bonds. In most cases, states bear this kind of responsibility, because many of these programs (such as bond banks, lease financings, or other state-related projects) are considered contingent liabilities of the state. Often these entail the use of a revenue authority, but they use diverted state monies from other sources for a collective pool to pay debt for an ongoing program. In certain other instances a similar prototype is involved, but it is overlayed on a municipality's debt structure so that monies coming to the municipality (from such sources as state funds or revenue generated by local revenue authorities from user charges) are slated to pay the costs of a project. Over time, these large financings could have an impact on the credit of the surrounding jurisdiction, either a municipality or a regional group of local governments, or even a state. It is especially important that a substantial amount of fore-thought had gone into placing these new financing vehicles with their major debt requirements within the debt structure of any government. Adequate safeguards must be employed to prevent downgrades in their ratings or in the ratings of other surrounding entities whose revenue would have to be diverted if the large project were not capable of paying debt service through its own generated revenues.

In brief, the rush to the market of issuers in large start-up programs in the mid-1980s has begun to harness as security for bonds other previously available revenue sources that were seen to be cushions for states and municipalities for their own potential financial difficulties. These pockets of revenue were long viewed either explicitly or implicitly by analysts as one of the great hallmarks of municipal bond security. As the federal government began a process of retrenching from providing monies for state and local services, and as the need for such services and the improvement of present capital projects loomed large, states and localities began a seemingly proper procedure of joining together in efforts to provide government services through the effective intermin-gling of revenue sources and also by securing bond issues with the series of governmental revenue sources that were previously either unused for bond security or had legal prohibitions against their use as such. With the creation of new authorities or the refunding of outstanding debt, state and local governments were able to circumvent these restrictions and develop a truly remarkable partnership to gain access to the American debt markets. Access, however, does not imply successful projects or mean that there will be no effect on governmental financial stability years hence; consequently, a careful examination of the way in which a large financing's revenue sources are derived from surrounding governmental jurisdictions and of the effect that this revenue diversion would have on surrounding governmental entities takes on much greater importance in the 1980s and the 1990s than it has in the past.

Another area of investor concern that must be evaluated more in future years is the increasing corporate involvement in the municipal bond arena that has come about with the rising number of emerging municipal bond insurance companies, which insure a large proportion of municipal debt, and with the rapidly growing involvement of banks, which provide such credit enhancements as lines and letters of credit for municipal debt obligations. The immediate trade-off has been a higher-rated bond with an additional layer of security and a slightly lower yield to the buyers, and lower interest rate costs to the issuers or guarantors. Aside from the sporadic financial problems of banks and insurance companies over very recent years, the real issue, from a credit perspec-tive, is the fact that the investor is in effect buying a corporate credit that has all the necessary requirements for a corporate-type analysis. A purchaser must therefore be prepared not only to make these kinds of corporate evaluations but also to make some decision as to whether it is better to purchase a corporate-backed obligation that has a lesser quality underlying municipal credit or to buy a higher-rated municipal bond that is rated the same as the bond with the corporate backing, but without the corporate credit as additional security.

Very often, over recent years, these kinds of corporate credit enhancements have been used for short-term municipal bond instruments, notably variable rate demand notes and other kinds of short-term obligations. This situation has given rise to three analytical complications for investors interested in buying tax-exempt bonds and notes. The first has to do with the corporate nature of the short-term instrument, for which the security consists of a put to a bank, to an insurance company, or to another corporate-type financial entity. A second and larger concern is that regarding the issuer's long-term debt. If a buyer is interested in purchasing an issuer's long-term debt that is not secured by any type of credit enhancement vehicle, then a careful analysis must be made of the issuer's entire short-term loan obligations when the issuer has a large amount of short-term debt outstanding that must be repaid either to the bondholders or to the corporate guarantor. A third, somewhat related issue simply concerns the entity's amount of short-term debt outstanding, which normally could not be issued without bank and insurance company guarantees or insurance. All these analyses become not only complicated but also very subjective. To be sure, given the large amounts of short-term municipal obligations outstanding, coupled with the tremendous increase in the volume of municipal bonds that carry insurance or other credit enhancements, a much closer look at the corporate security behind these debt obligations, as well as at the underlying security itself, would be a logical and necessary result.

Another concern of municipal bond investors in future years might be that a large project within a given taxing district or within an area where individuals would have to pay user fees for the project's services might result in tax levies or fee charges that would become so burdensome that it would be financially worthwhile for individuals to relocate from that area. In areas where there is a great need for water and sewer services, where the mass transportation system has fallen into disrepair, or where power supplies are inadequate, individuals might be forced to move from that area which has become unlivable. These large movements of population would have more than a moderate effect on the credit rating of a governmental entity. As a result, a careful analysis should be made of the surrounding governmental jurisdiction in which bonds for large projects are being contemplated or have been issued, the objective being to ascertain the possibilities of growth and/or projected population inflow, the chances of population stabilization and a moderation in industrial growth, and the potential for economic dislocation. These are examples of the kinds of potential scenarios that could possibly occur in governmental systems in need of large amounts of money to finance the rehabilitation of capital infrastructures or the creation of new services required by a municipality.

All these possible credit concerns have potential upsides. For instance, large financings which are completed on schedule, which achieve their projected demand, which have no cost overruns, and which charge competitive rates that provide sufficient revenues to pay their facilities' debts will go a long way toward improving the status of life in a local government of general jurisdiction, in a group of municipalities, or even in a state. After all, this was what the financing was designed to do. Moreover, if projects involving the coordination of state and local financing structures, the use of surplus monies, or the diversion of revenues are successful, these would probably have very little impact on the credit ratings of the surrounding governmental jurisdictions. Furthermore, if credit enhancements provided by banks and insurance companies are effectively employed by state and local governments, the bonds may achieve a wider distribution in the marketplace, resulting in much lower costs, higher ratings, and better security than would otherwise have been the case. Also, the judicious use of short-term investment vehicles may provide significant savings for issuers nationwide. Finally, where major projects are successful, this may lead to an influx of people, an increasing tax base, and a flourishing community, city, or region. All of these are examples of what might be called notable successes in the municipal finance arena.

It seems clear that the future of America hinges in large part on the ability of states and localities to provide adequate government services. What is also obvious is that state and local debt issuance and the use of the public revenue authority play a vital role in keeping the American system of government moving forward on a steady course. Even more interesting is the way that the municipal bond industry's issuers, investment bankers, and buyers have adapted to the changing needs of state and local governments over the years. The continuation of the municipal bond market will thus do much to keep these governments growing and vibrant in the years ahead.

NOTE: Part 6 (Chaps. 19 and 20) was written by Stephen P. Rappaport in a paper entitled "Political, Financial, and Philosophic Concerns of Municipal Bond Analysis: The 1990s and Beyond" at Prudential-Bache Securities Inc., 1986. Reprinted by permission.

21
The Tax Reform Act of 1986

Many keen observers of the American political scene believed that tax reform would never actually happen, largely because it had to overcome substantial hurdles along the way to passage. Nevertheless, in late 1986 the Tax Reform Act of 1986 finally received both congressional and presidential approval. To be sure, this act will change the financial situations of every American and every company, small or large, as long as the act is law. It should therefore come as no surprise that the Tax Reform Act of 1986 will affect the entire municipal bond industry—its buyers, its sellers, its underwriters, and most importantly its issuers. Indeed, the act represents the skeletal framework upon which the municipal industry will structure its business in future years. Many aspects of the Tax Reform Act of 1986 as they relate to municipal bonds are discussed in detail in the Appendix of this volume.

Structural Elements

In general, the act divides municipal bonds into two types: those bonds considered to be essential *governmental bonds* and those which are in a category termed *private activity bonds*. The interest on governmental bonds is exempt from federal taxation, while the interest on private activity bonds is not, unless the bonds are "qualified." A private activity bond is one that passes either a private loan test or a private business use and security interest test. Qualified private activity bonds generally include exempt facilities, qualified small-issue bonds, qualified mortgage bonds, qualified veterans' mortgage bonds, qualified student loan bonds, qualified redevelopment bonds, and qualified 501(c)(3) bonds. Eligible exempt facility bonds, the interest on which remains tax-exempt, include bonds issued for: airports, docks and wharves, mass commuting facilities, sewage disposal facilities, solid waste disposal facilities, facilities for the local furnishing of electric energy or gas, facilities for the furnishing of water, and local district heating or cooling facilities.

In addition, the act establishes a volume limitation based on a state's population for certain categories of bonds. Bonds designated as "governmental" are not subject to volume caps; however, the nongovernmental proportion of governmental bonds above $50 million is subject to the volume limitation. This limitation is applied to most private activity bonds, except those private activity bonds issued for airports, docks and wharves, and government-owned solid waste disposal facilities. Most 501(c)(3) organizations are limited to issuing $150 million for each institution, with the exception of hospitals, for which the volume is unlimited.

There are other structural elements of the act which deserve attention and which will affect the market for municipal bonds. The interest earned on municipal bonds that were issued prior to August 8, 1986, remains tax-exempt and is not considered a preference item and is thus not subject to calculations for the alternative minimum tax (AMT). Additionally, the interest earned on essential-function governmental bonds and bonds of 501(c)(3) corporations, which is tax-exempt, is not to be treated as a preference item for AMT calculation purposes. However, the interest earned on private activity bonds [except those of 501(c)(3) corporations] issued after August 7, 1986, is a preference item for AMT calculations. It should be remembered that individuals and corporate purchasers may or may not be subject to the AMT.

The act will also affect corporate buyers of municipal bonds. In general, the act disallows the interest deduction for borrowing by banks and other financial institutions when it is used to buy or hold most tax-exempt obligations. Furthermore, the act reduces the deduction taken from losses by property and casualty insurance companies when they calculate their income; the reduction is equal to 15 percent of the tax-exempt interest received or accrued during the taxable year. Finally, the corporate alternative minimum tax is adjusted by the act so that it may potentially account for a certain percentage of tax-exempt interest.

Market Effects

It is obvious that the behavior of municipal bond buyers will be affected by the above structural changes wrought by the Tax Reform Act of 1986 on the municipal market. Indeed, the needs of both individual and corporate purchasers may be reflected in yield levels resulting from the purchasers' need to compensate for revisions in the tax law. For instance, certain private activity bonds may have to bear somewhat higher yields to attract certain buyers.

On the individual investor side, even with the lower marginal tax rates projected, many will find that tax-exempt bonds are one of the only investment alternatives available that provide interest which is exempt from federal taxation and which in certain instances is also exempt from state and local taxes. The levels of such yields may make the bonds rather attractive when compared to their taxable counterparts. Individual marginal tax rates under the Tax Reform Act will range generally from 28 to 33 percent and beyond, and many people may have combined marginal tax rates of over 40 percent when state and local taxes are taken into account.

It should be noted that the alternative minimum tax for individuals is levied when it is larger than regular tax calculations. Investors should be aware that the calculation of the AMT is complicated and is a function of an individual's income, deductions, and tax preference items; as a result, AMT calculations usually require the professional expertise of an investor's tax advisor or the like. Those individuals whose incomes will not be subject to the AMT may be wise to purchase those nongovernmental or private activity bonds which may bear higher yields than comparable essential or governmental purpose bonds; this may compensate buyers for the possibility of the interest on such bonds being subject to the AMT. Individuals who fall under the AMT may want to purchase bonds not subject to AMT calculations but it must be kept in mind, however, that each individual's financial situation may be quite different.

On the corporate side of the ledger, it seems clear that banks and casualty and property insurance companies may require that yields be higher, on a relatively proportionate basis, than they previously were in order to offset the loss of the deduction for purchasing tax-exempt bonds through borrowings by banks and the reduction in loss reserves of the property and casualty companies. For corporations, however, the new alternative minimum tax may also be important in their buying decisions regarding tax-exempt obligations. To be sure, complicated calculations are needed in order to arrive at a company's regular tax and alternative minimum tax, taking tax-exempt interest into account in a number of ways.

Appendix

Analysis of Provisions of the Tax Reform Act of 1986 Affecting Tax-Exempt Obligations

by Hawkins, Delafield & Wood*

Hawkins, Delafield & Wood wishes to call attention to the fact that the provisions of the Tax Reform Act of 1986, to the extent that they relate to the exclusion from Federal gross income of interest on obligations issued by state and local governmental units, in many ways merely modify or supplement slightly or, in effect, reenact in a slightly different form pertinent provisions of the Federal income tax law as it existed prior to passage of such act. Thus, in his or her consideration of "new" law, the reader must not loose sight of "prior" law and all relevant interpretations thereof.

The analysis that follows does not necessarily reflect the ongoing opinion of Hawkins, Delafield & Wood or any of its members. It can be expected that interpretations of the various provisions of the Tax Reform Act of 1986, as with any major piece of legislation, will become more refined and perhaps vary with the experience that can only be obtained by applying such provisions to specific sets of circumstances and as a result of the issuance of regulations and revenue rulings and the passage of additional income tax laws (which seem almost inevitable, given Congress's proclivity toward blockbuster tax legislation in recent years).

TABLE OF CONTENTS

I. INTRODUCTION.

After nearly two years of legislative activity that began with the United States Treasury Department's report to President Reagan on Tax Reform for Fairness, Simplicity and Economic Growth in November, 1984, Congress has produced H.R. 3838, The Tax Reform Act of 1986. H.R. 3838 was passed by the United States House of Representatives on September 25, 1986 and by the United States Senate on September 27, 1986. H.R. 3838 was signed by the President on October 22, 1986. While many commentators will differ over whether this tax reform legislation is indeed fair or will produce economic growth, it certainly does not achieve simplicity, especially in the context of the changes affecting the issuance of tax-exempt bonds by state and local governments.

H.R. 3838 alters and reorganizes many of the provisions of the Internal Revenue Code of 1954, as amended (the "1954 Code"), and establishes a new Internal Revenue Code of 1986 (the "1986 Code"). As part of this reorganization, H.R. 3838 substantially changes the rules currently contained in Section 103 of the 1954 Code relating to the tax exemption of interest on bonds of state and local governments, and distributes these rules among Section 103 and Sections 141 through 150 of the 1986 Code.

H.R. 3838 establishes a new test for tax-exemption of interest on bonds of state and local governments by replacing the present law concept of industrial development bonds ("IDBs") with a broader, and thus more restrictive, concept of "private activity bonds." Interest on private activity bonds will be taxable unless the obligations are characterized as "qualified bonds," as defined in H.R. 3838. Tax-exempt financing for many exempt facility projects currently permitted by Section 103(b)(4) of the 1954 Code is eliminated. In addition, H.R. 3838 establishes a new unified volume limitation on the issuance of certain qualified private activity bonds and the nongovernmental portion (in excess of $15,000,000) of "governmental bonds" (*i.e.*, bonds that are not private activity bonds). H.R. 3838 also imposes new arbitrage rules and a number of new restrictions applicable to all obligations including governmental bonds and qualified private activity bonds.

In addition to imposing direct restrictions on the issuance of tax-exempt obligations, H.R. 3838 makes several changes that will directly affect the marketability of bonds of state and local governments. H.R. 3838 includes interest on private activity bonds as a preference item in the calculation of the alternative minimum tax on both individuals and corporations, and adjusts the alternative minimum tax on corporations by reference to adjusted net book income. In addition, H.R. 3838 eliminates the interest deduction for borrowings of banks and other financial institutions to the extent such borrowings are deemed to be incurred to purchase or carry tax-exempt obligations.

This Memorandum will begin with a discussion of the new restrictive test for tax-exemption found in the definition of a private activity bond. It will discuss the new restrictions on qualified private activity bonds, including the unified volume limitation, and will discuss the new arbitrage restrictions. It will conclude with a brief discussion of the other proposed changes that will affect marketability of bonds of state and local governments. References are made in this Memorandum to the "House Report," "Senate Report" and "Conference Report." These refer to the reports of the House Committee on Ways and Means (H. Rept. No. 99-426), the Senate Finance Committee (R. 99-313), and the Conference Committee (H. Rept. No. 99-841), which accompanied the legislative proposals advanced by such committees. References made to current, existing or present law are to the 1954 Code.

Except as otherwise provided below, the changes made by H.R. 3838 are effective with respect to obligations issued after August 15, 1986. With respect to obligations that would not have been IDBs, mortgage subsidy bonds or consumer loan bonds as described in the joint statement of The Honorable Dan Rostenkowski, Chairman of the Committee on Ways and Means, The Honorable Bob Packwood, Chairman of the Committee on Finance, The Honorable John J. Duncan, Ranking Member of the Committee on Ways and Means, The Honorable Russell Long, Ranking Member of the Committee on Finance and The Honorable James A. Baker, III, Secretary of the Treasury, on the Effective Dates of Pending Tax Reform Legislation, dated March 14, 1986 (the "Joint Statement"), the changes will generally apply to obligations issued after August 31, 1986.

II. GOVERNMENTAL BONDS AND PRIVATE ACTIVITY BONDS.

Section 103 and Section 141 of the 1986 Code will establish new tests for the tax-exemption of interest on bonds of state and local governments that distinguish between governmental bonds, the interest on which is exempt from Federal taxation, and private activity bonds, which must be "qualified" to be tax-exempt. Section 141 of the 1986 Code will define a private activity bond as any bond that satisfies either a private business use and private security interest test or a private loan test.

A. PRIVATE BUSINESS USE AND SECURITY INTEREST TESTS.

The first alternative definition of private activity bond includes any bond issued as part of an issue if:

(i) more than 10 percent of the proceeds of the issue are used for any private business use, *i.e.*, a use (directly or indirectly) in a trade or business of a person other than a governmental unit, and

(ii) the payment of the principal of, or interest on, more than 10 percent of the issue is directly or indirectly (a) secured by any interest in property used or to be used in such a trade or business or by payments in respect of such property or (b) to be derived from payments (whether or not to the issuer) in respect of property, or borrowed money, used in such a trade or business.

A special rule, applicable only to power financings, caps at $15,000,000 the aggregate amount of proceeds that may be used by nongovernmental persons on a basis other than as members of the general public.

At first glance this private activity bond definition appears to be primarily a restatement of the IDB definition, substituting 10 percent for 25 percent. There are, however, several key differences (in addition to the significant limitation on power financings). First, under H.R. 3838, the trade or business test would be satisfied if the trade or business is that of a Section 501(c)(3) organization whereas under the 1954 Code, Section 501(c)(3) organizations were considered exempt persons and obligations issued for the benefit of such exempt persons were not IDBs. The new definition refines the universe of exempt persons to include only governmental units. Second, trade or business use is changed to provide that use includes any activity by any person other than a natural person, but use as a member of the general public will not be taken into account. (See discussion below.)

The 25 percent security interest test of current law is to be replaced with a test that is met if direct or indirect payments exceeding 10 percent of the debt service on the bonds are made with respect to such trade or business use. There is no requirement that the payments be used to pay debt service, or even that they be received by the issuer. Revenues from generally applicable taxes are not treated as payments. Special charges imposed on persons who satisfy the use test but are not members of the general public, however, would be considered direct or indirect security if such charges constitute fees paid for the use of bond-financed property. The Conference Report provides that amounts paid by private persons for the purchase of land will be payments within the meaning of the security interest test even though incremental tax revenues are the stated security for repayment of the bonds issued to finance such land.

1. *Special Rules on Use.*

   a. *General Public Use.*

   Whether a facility is being used by the general public is determined by the facts and circumstances. The House and Senate Reports provide examples in the context of convention centers, schools and electric generating facilities. These facilities will be considered used by the general public if no one organization or limited group of organizations has an extended right to use the facilities. Thus, a school building used at night by community groups must be available for use on an equal basis by all such groups. Bonds for a governmentally owned and operated electric utility that serves the general public will be considered governmental bonds as opposed to private activity bonds, even though some customers may purchase more power than others or purchase at a different rate reflecting a volume discount for bulk sales of power, so long as the arrangement under which such purchases are made is an arrangement available to other members of the general public and is not in substance a take-or-pay or output arrangement. Although not specifically addressed, this same analysis would appear to extend to governmentally owned and operated sewer and water facilities.

   b. *Management Contracts.*

   Management or operations contracts with nongovernmental persons may cause governmentally owned projects to be considered used in a trade or business. H.R. 3838 directs the Treasury Department to liberalize its current ruling position with respect to management contracts and provides that a nongovernmental person's use of bond-financed property pursuant to a management contract generally will not be treated as private trade or business use if (1) the term of the contract, including renewal options, does not exceed five years, (2) at least 50 percent of the payments to be made pursuant to the contract are on a fixed-fee basis and no portion of the payment is to be made on a net revenue basis, and (3) the governmental unit owning the facility may terminate the contract without cause at the end of any three-year period.

c. *Power Financings.*

In determining whether the $15,000,000 limitation on private use with respect to power projects (gas or electric, but not water) is exceeded, the Conference Report provides that all outstanding obligations issued with respect to a project are taken into account, including obligations issued before enactment of H.R. 3838. Certain pooling and exchange agreements and certain spot sales of output capacity are not to be taken into account in determining use. On the other hand, the Treasury Department is directed to amend the output regulations under Section 103 of the 1954 Code to delete the exception for users of 3 percent or less of output.

d. *University Cooperative Research Agreements.*

H.R. 3838 adopts the Senate version of a special rule dealing with basic research at state universities. The Senate Report provides that use of bond-financed property by nongovernmental persons such as private industry pursuant to cooperative agreements with state universities may be disregarded in determining the degree of nongovernmental use so long as the research performed is general (as opposed to product development) research. Moreover, the research will not be considered direct or indirect use of the bond proceeds provided that use by a nongovernmental person of resulting technology is permitted only on the same terms by which the university permits such use by any other nonsponsoring unrelated party. Thus, a cooperative research agreement which provides for a license of any resulting technology at a royalty rate fixed in advance of the performance of the research could constitute such a trade or business use; however, an agreement with only a right of first refusal (at a competitive price) for the sponsoring person would not constitute such a use. The Conference Report provides that the amount charged the private businesses for use of patents or technology must be determined when such patents or technology is available for use.

2. *Related Use Requirement-Overlay.*

To complicate matters further, H.R. 3838 imposes as an overlay on this first private activity bond definition, a "related use" requirement. This test is essentially a parallel calculation that must be made even when the 10 percent limit described above is met. Obligations will nevertheless be considered private activity bonds if the two tests described above would be met by substituting 5 percent for 10 percent and by taking into account in those 5 percent calculations only unrelated business uses and disproportionate related business uses. Two new concepts are introduced, a business use that is unrelated to a governmental use financed with the bonds and a business use that is related, but is disproportionate to the governmental use. The latter concept is the easier one to apply, because it is basically a one-for-one test: for every dollar of related private use, there must be a dollar of governmental use related to it. Any excess of related private use is the disproportionate amount required to be taken into account in the 5 percent limit.

The determination of whether a business use is related to a governmental use appears from the Conference Report to be a question of "operational relationship." The examples provided, *e.g.*, a newsstand in a courthouse, do not provide much guidance in the analysis of other real life problems. For example, consider a bond issue the proceeds of which are to be used to finance sewer projects located throughout a state. If one project serves primarily one private user under a special payment arrangement, would that use be related in function to the governmental use if they are all discrete projects?

B. PRIVATE LOAN FINANCING TEST.

As its second definition of private activity bond, H.R. 3838 incorporates and modifies the 1954 Code consumer loan bond test. H.R. 3838 provides that a bond will be considered a private activity bond if an amount exceeding the lesser of 5 percent or $5,000,000 of bond proceeds is used to make or finance loans to nongovernmental persons. In determining whether the proceeds of obligations are being used to make or finance loans to nongovernmental persons, the Conference Report provides that loans are present in transactions involving indirect transfers (or deemed transfers) that are in substance loans. The Conference Report describes an exception to the general rule for the financing of sewers, water facilities or street paving through the issuance of tax assessment bonds which are considered "in substance loans." In these cases, the loan deemed to arise from mandatory taxes or other assessments of general application that the governmental unit permits its residents to pay over a number of years is not taken into account as a loan for purposes of the private activity bond definition. Other examples of transactions that may constitute "in substance loans" include installment payment arrangements, leases and take-or-pay or output contracts.

III. QUALIFIED PRIVATE ACTIVITY BONDS.

The term "qualified private activity bond" includes the following classes of obligations:

- exempt-facility bonds,
- qualified small issue bonds,
- qualified mortgage bonds,
- qualified veterans' mortgage bonds,
- qualified student loan bonds,
- qualified redevelopment bonds, and
- qualified 501(c)(3) bonds.

Each of these classes is discussed in more detail below. Certain new restrictions are applicable to all private activity bonds and are set forth in Section V below.

A. EXEMPT-FACILITY BONDS.

Since the provisions of H.R. 3838 parallel many of the provisions under current law relating to exempt-facility bonds, present law requirements not specifically discussed herein should be considered to be unchanged.

1. *Ineligible Facilities.*

Current law allows a tax exemption for interest on industrial development bonds used to finance the following specified categories of exempt activities: multi-family residential rental projects, sports facilities, convention or trade show facilities, airports, docks and wharves, mass commuting facilities, parking facilities, sewage disposal facilities, solid waste disposal facilities, facilities for the local furnishing of electric energy or gas, facilities for the furnishing of water, local district heating or cooling facilities, and air or water pollution control facilities.

Subject to the requirements described in this Memorandum, H.R. 3838 retains the tax-exemption for interest on bonds issued to finance the above activities, with the exception of bonds issued to finance pollution control, parking, sports, convention and trade show facilities, the exemptions for which are repealed for bonds issued after August 15, 1986, subject to the transition relief described in Section VIII below. Consideration regarding the tax-exempt financing of these ineligible facilities should be given to the applicable transitional rules, as well as to the possibilities of financing such facilities with the use of governmental (non-private activity) bonds; qualified 501(c)(3) bonds; and exempt small issue bonds.

The authority for bonds issued to finance qualified hydroelectric facilities expired after 1985, except for a provision extending such authority through 1988 for property with respect to which an application was docketed by the Federal Energy Regulatory Commission (FERC) before January 1, 1986. The Conference Report provides that in order for the present-law transitional exception to apply, an application for a license (rather than for a preliminary permit) must have been docketed with FERC by December 31, 1985.

H.R. 3838 repeals the present-law exemption for bonds issued to finance the acquisition or development of land as an industrial park. This provision is effective for bonds (including refunding bonds) issued after August 15, 1986, subject to the transitional exceptions discussed in Section VIII below.

2. *Eligible Exempt Facilities.*

a. *Airports.*

As under present law, exempt-facility bonds may be issued to finance airports, and related storage and training facilities. However, all such facilities financed with tax-exempt bond proceeds must be owned by or "on behalf of" a governmental unit. Ownership by a public authority operating on behalf of a governmental unit will satisfy this requirement. Under present law, the term "airport" includes runways, terminals, and other public facilities, as well as functionally related and subordinate airport hotels and commercial facilities; hangars for one or more airlines; and certain other property not for use directly by the general public. The Conference Report limits this definition by providing that the term "airport" does not include any of the following facilities if they are used in a private business use:

(i) Airport hotels (or other lodging facilities).

(ii) Retail facilities (including food and beverage facilities) located in a terminal in excess of a size necessary to serve "passengers" (which term for these purposes includes persons meeting or accompanying persons arriving and departing on flights to and from the airport) and employees at the airport.

(iii) Retail facilities for passengers or the general public (including but not limited to rental-car lots) located outside the airport terminal (this provision does not limit public airport parking so long as it is no more than a size necessary to serve passengers and employees at the airport).

(iv) Office buildings for individuals who are not employees of a governmental unit or of the public airport operating authority.

(v) Industrial parks or manufacturing facilities.

For purposes of the above exclusions, property is considered to be used in a private trade or business if it is leased to or managed by any person other than a qualified governmental unit or an airport authority acting on behalf of a qualified governmental unit.

b. *Docks and Wharves.*

Exempt-facility bonds may be issued to finance docks and wharves and related storage and training facilities (including long-term storage where permitted under present law, *e.g.*, a grain elevator, silo, warehouse, or oil and gas storage tank used in connection with a dock or wharf and located adjacent thereto). All such property financed with tax-exempt bond proceeds must be governmentally owned (*i.e.*, owned by a governmental unit or public authority acting on behalf thereof). The term "dock and wharf" excludes the same types of facilities which are excluded from the term "airport" when such facilities are used in a private business use (see paragraph a. above). Private business use includes for these purposes leases and management contracts of persons who are neither governmental units nor "on behalf of" entities.

c. *Mass Commuting Facilities.*

Exempt-facility bonds may be issued to finance governmentally owned mass commuting facilities, defined generally as under present law (*e.g.*, excluding mass commuting vehicles) but excluding those types of facilities proscribed with respect to airport and dock and wharf financings (see above). The Conference Report indicates that the retention of the present-law definition of mass commuting facilities as modified does not prejudge the possible need in the future to allow tax-exempt financing for high-speed rail systems in a manner similar to that allowed under H.R. 3838 for mass commuting facilities.

d. *Sewage Disposal Facilities.*

The present-law exemption for bonds issued to finance sewage disposal facilities, defined as under present law (including property used for the collection, storage, treatment, utilization, processing or final disposal of sewage), is continued.

e. *Solid Waste Disposal Facilities.*

The present-law exemption for bonds issued to finance solid waste disposal facilities, defined generally as under present law, is continued. Under this provision, tax-exempt financing may be provided for the processing of solid waste or heat into usable form, but not for further processing that converts the resulting materials or heat into other products (*e.g.*, turbines or electric generators). The special rule in Section 103(g) of the 1954 Code for certain qualified steam-generating or alcohol-producing facilities is repealed. Further, the Conference Report clarifies that the term solid waste does not include most hazardous waste (including radioactive waste).

f. *Facilities for the Furnishing of Electric Energy or Gas.*

The present-law exemption for bonds issued to finance facilities for the local furnishing of electric energy or gas, in areas not exceeding two contiguous counties, or a city and one contiguous county, is continued.

g. *Facilities for the Furnishing of Water.*

H.R. 3838 continues the present-law exemption for bonds issued to finance facilities for the furnishing of water, defined generally as under present law, including artesian wells, reservoirs, dams, related equipment and pipelines, and other facilities used to furnish water for domestic, industrial, irrigation, or other purposes.

h. *Local District Heating or Cooling Facilities.*

H.R. 3838 continues the present-law exemption for bonds issued to finance local district heating or cooling facilities, defined as under present law (including equipment and other property used as an integral part of a local heating or cooling system).

i. *Qualified Hazardous Waste Facilities.*

There is no provision under the 1954 Code allowing tax-exempt financing of hazardous waste treatment or disposal facilities (solid waste as presently defined by regulations does not include liquid or gaseous wastes, including most hazardous waste). H.R. 3838 permits exempt-facility bonds to be issued to finance hazardous waste treatment facilities, which term is defined to mean any facility for the disposal of hazardous waste by incineration or entombment, but only if the facility is subject to final permit requirements under subtitle C of title II of the Solid Waste Disposal Act (as in effect on the date of the enactment of the Tax Reform Act of 1986). H.R. 3838 provides that the portion of the facility which is to be provided by the issue may not exceed the portion of the facility which is to be used by persons other than the owner or operator of such facility or any "related person" (defined as under present law). The Conference Report clarifies this somewhat ambiguous provision, indicating that its intent was to provide that tax-exempt financing be available only for facilities (or the portion of a facility) to be used by the public as opposed to the generator of the waste. This requirement is considered to be satisfied under the Conference Report if 95 percent or more of the net proceeds are to be used with respect to that portion of the facility used by persons other than the owner or operator of the facility (or any "related person"). The Conference

Report further indicates that the term hazardous waste does not include radioactive waste, and that rules similar to the present-law rules regarding solid waste disposal bonds will apply, including rules limiting hazardous waste to materials having no market or other value at the place at which they are located and rules limiting tax-exempt financing to the portion of a facility which is actually engaged in the incineration or entombment of hazardous waste. The authorization to issue bonds for qualified hazardous waste facilities applies after August 15, 1986.

3. *Miscellaneous Restrictions on Exempt-Facility Bonds.*

a. *Functionally Related and Subordinate Test: Office Space.*

The present-law rule that exempt-facility bond proceeds may be used to finance property that is "functionally related and subordinate" to the exempt activity of such facility is retained. However, office space is not to be treated as functionally related and subordinate to an exempt facility unless the office space is located on the premises of the facility, and not more than a *de minimis* amount of the functions to be performed in such space is not directly related to the day-to-day operations at such facility. Thus, as the Conference Report indicates, a separate office building, or an office wing of a mixed-use facility, is not treated as functionally related and subordinate to an exempt facility. The Conference Report sheds no light on what amount might be considered *de minimis*. A 5 percent limit on office space was proposed by the Joint Tax Committee in 1984 in reference to the definition of "manufacturing facilities" for purposes of the small issue sunset provision. *See*, General Explanation of the Revenue Provisions of the Deficit Reduction Act of 1984, JCS-41-84, at 942.

b. *Governmental Ownership—Safe Harbor for Leases and Management Contracts.*

H.R. 3838 provides a "safe harbor" for leases and management contracts under which property leased by a governmental unit shall be treated as owned by such governmental unit if (i) the lessee makes an irrevocable election (binding on the lessee and all successors in interest under the lease) not to claim depreciation or an investment credit with respect to the property; (ii) the lease term is not more than 80 percent of the reasonably expected economic life of the property (determined as of the later of the date on which the bonds are issued, or the date on which the facility is placed, or expected to be placed, in service); and (iii) the lessee has no option to purchase the property other than at fair market value (as of the time such option is exercised).

B. SMALL ISSUE BONDS.

1. *Sunset Dates for Small Issue Bonds.*

Under current law, the small-issue bond exception is scheduled to expire generally for bonds issued after December 31, 1986. In the case of small-issue bonds used to finance manufacturing facilities only, the exception expires after December 31, 1988.

H.R. 3838 retains the present-law sunset date for non-manufacturing small issue bonds, but extends the date for manufacturing small issue bonds for one additional year, through December 31, 1989. The extension also applies to certain farm property described in more detail in Section V. F. 2. below.

2. Transitional Rule.

A transitional exception applies to certain current refunding bonds that may be issued under current law but that may not be issued under H.R. 3838, and for current refundings of small issue bonds (*e.g.*, non-manufacturing facility issues) issued after the prescribed termination dates. Current refundings qualifying under this exception are issues that do not extend the maturity of the refunded issue; that have a lower interest rate than the rate on the refunded issue; and the amount of which does not exceed the outstanding amount of the refunded bonds.

C. MULTI-FAMILY HOUSING BONDS.

1. Use of Proceeds of Tax-Exempt Financing.

H.R. 3838 retains the current-law rules relating to the physical characteristics of multi-family housing property. The substitution of a 95 percent rule for the current rule requiring 90 percent of the proceeds to be spent on qualified costs (discussed in Section V, below) means that less bond proceeds will be available for typical unqualified costs in a multi-family housing project, such as commercial space and costs of land incurred before official action.

2. Continuing Requirements.

a. Low or Moderate Income Occupancy Requirement.

While Section 103 of the 1954 Code requires that at least 20 percent (15 percent in targeted areas) of residential rental units in a bond-financed project be set aside during the qualified project period for tenants whose incomes represent 80 percent or less of the area median income, the low income set-aside requirements are modified by H.R. 3838 to conform to the requirements applicable to the new low income housing credit. Issuers of tax-exempt multi-family housing bonds must elect (on or before the date bonds are issued) to set aside either 20 percent or more of the units for occupancy by tenants having incomes of 50 percent or less of the area median gross income, or 40 percent or more (25 percent in New York City) for tenants with incomes of 60 percent or less of the area median gross income. The more limited set-aside for targeted area projects is eliminated.

b. Determination of Income Limit.

H.R. 3838 provides, as does present law, that the determination of low or moderate income status is to be made in a manner consistent with Section 8 of the United States Housing Act of 1937 ("Section 8"). H.R. 3838 also incorporates the requirements set forth in Prop. Treas. Reg. Section 1.103-8(b), 50 Fed. Reg. 216 at 46303 (Nov. 7, 1985), concerning adjustments for family size which require that such adjustments be made for bonds issued after December 31, 1985.

Applying the Section 8 rules to a project in which 20 percent of the units has been set aside, a family of four will be treated as a low or moderate income family if its income is 50 percent or less of the area median income; a family of three's income must be 45 percent or less; a family of two, 40 percent or less; and an individual, 35 percent or less. For a project setting aside 40 percent (or 25 percent in the case of New York City), a family of four will be treated as a low or moderate income family if its income is 60 percent or less of the area median income, the income of a family of three must be 54 percent or less; a family of two, 48 percent or less; and an individual, 42 percent or less. Similar adjustments are to be made for larger families.

c. *Continuous Rental Requirement.*

H.R. 3838 requires, in addition to the low-income set-aside during the qualified project period, that bond-financed units remain rental property throughout the term of the qualified project period.

d. *Qualified Project Period.*

H.R. 3838 redefines the qualified project period as the period beginning on the date on which at least 10 percent of the units in the project is first occupied (or, if later, the date on which the bonds are issued) and ending on the latest of (i) the date that is at least 15 years (as compared to the currently mandated 10 years) after the date on which at least 50 percent of the units is first occupied, (ii) the first day on which no tax-exempt private activity bond issued with respect to the project is outstanding (as compared to the date which represents the number of days after the date on which any units are occupied equal to 50 percent of the number of days comprising the term of the bonds having the longest maturity), or (iii) the date on which any assistance provided with respect to the project under Section 8 terminates. H.R. 3838, in effect, extends the period during which the set-aside requirement must be continuously satisfied and the project maintained as a rental project.

e. *Annual Current Income Determinations.*

H.R. 3838 provides that the determination of whether a tenant qualifies as a low or moderate income tenant must be made on a continuing basis (at least annually) rather than only upon such tenant's initial occupancy as under current law. An increase in a tenant's income or a decrease in a tenant's family size may disqualify such tenant as a person of low or moderate income if it has the effect of increasing the tenant's family income to more than 40 percent in excess of the maximum income for the tenant's family size under the standard applicable to the project. Because the continuing compliance requirement of H.R. 3838 is not intended to promote the eviction of initial low income tenants who no longer qualify as low income tenants, any post-issuance noncompliance with the set-aside requirement must be cured by renting the first available residential unit of comparable or smaller size to a tenant meeting the applicable low or moderate income standard.

f. *Annual Current Income Determinations for Deep Rent Skewed Projects.*

With respect to the annual current income determination requirement, H.R. 3838 provides a special rule for projects that charge significantly lower than market rents to low-or-moderate income tenants and elect to satisfy a stricter low income set-aside requirement ("deep rent skewed projects"). A project is a deep rent skewed project if the owner elects to meet and, at all times during the qualified project period, the project meets the following requirements:

(i) 15 percent or more of the low income units in the project are occupied by individuals whose income is 40 percent or less of area median income;

(ii) the gross rent with respect to each low income unit in the project does not exceed 30 percent of the applicable income limit which applies to individuals occupying the unit; and

(iii) the gross rent with respect to each low income unit in the project does not exceed one-third of the average rent with respect to units of comparable size which are not occupied by individuals who meet the applicable income limit.

The applicable income limits referred to in (ii) and (iii) above are the 20/50, 40/60, 25/60 (in New York City only) or 15/40 limits described in Subsections (a) and (f)(i) of this part.

A low-or-moderate income tenant of a deep rent skewed project will continue to qualify as such as long as the income of such tenant does not exceed 170 percent of the applicable income ceiling. If the project ceases to comply with the set-aside requirements because of an increase in an existing tenant's income or a decrease in family size, no penalty is imposed if the next available comparable or smaller low-or-moderate income unit is rented to a tenant having an income of 40 percent or less of area median income.

g. *Low Income Certification to the Secretary.*

H.R. 3838 requires that the operator of a project with respect to which an election as to income limitations has been made submit to the Secretary an annual certification evidencing the project's compliance with the low or moderate income set-aside requirement. The failure of the operator to make timely reports will not affect the tax-exempt status of any bond or the deductibility of interest on the bond-financed loans, but will subject the operator failing to comply to a fine of $100 per occurrence.

h. *Rebate Requirement.*

H.R. 3838 extends to multi-family housing bonds the current law industrial development bond requirement that the excess of the amount earned on all nonpurpose obligations over the amount that would have been earned if the gross proceeds of the issue were invested at a rate equal to the yield on the issue (without regard to the recovery of a costs of issuance) be rebated to the United States. See Section VII below for specific restrictions and exceptions to the rebate requirement.

i. *Change in Use of Facilities Financed with Tax-Exempt Multi-Family Housing Bonds.*

Failure to comply with the requirements of a. through g. above will subject the interest on obligations issued to finance the noncomplying projects to federal income taxation, retroactive to the date of issuance, and will result in all interest on bond-financed loans being nondeductible during the period beginning on the first day of the taxable year in which the project fails to meet such requirements and ending on the date the project meets such requirements. While tax deductions may be restored by subsequent compliance, the tax exemption of interest on the bonds will not. This change in use rule applies to any change in use after August 15, 1986 with respect to financings (and refinancings) provided after such date.

D. SINGLE-FAMILY HOUSING BONDS.

1. *Mortgage Eligibility Requirements.*

a. *The Residence Requirement.*

Under H.R. 3838, the residence requirement continues to limit the availability of bond-financed mortgages to those mortgagors who can reasonably expect to make the residences for which the financing will be provided their principal residences within a reasonable time (*i.e.*, 60 days after such financing has been provided). As a parallel to the other change in use sanctions, H.R. 3838 will deny a deduction for interest paid with respect to a bond-financed mortgage loan on a residence if such residence should cease to be the principal residence of at least one of the mortgagors for a continuous period of one year or more. The Treasury Department is authorized to waive the penalty in certain instances where the application of the penalty would result in undue hardship and the failure to meet the residence requirement resulted from circumstances beyond the mortgagor's control.

b. *The Prior Ownership Limitation.*

The prior ownership limitation set forth in H.R. 3838 increases the amount of net bond proceeds (determined without reduction for costs of issuance) which must be used to finance residences for mortgagors who had no present ownership interest in their principal residences during the three-year period before the mortgage is executed (*i.e.*, to first-time homebuyers) from the 90 percent required under pre-H.R. 3838 law to 95 percent. H.R. 3838 reverses the prior rule of the 1954 Code that proceeds used to provide qualified home improvement, qualified rehabilitation, or targeted area loans are not taken into account for purposes of the former 90 percent rule, and provides instead that proceeds applied to provide qualified home improvement, qualified rehabilitation, or targeted area loans will be counted toward the satisfaction of the 95 percent requirement. [With respect to the definition of qualified rehabilitation, H.R. 3838 changes the requirement that at least 75 percent of the existing external walls remains intact through the rehabilitation process to a requirement that (i) at least 50 percent of the existing external walls remains in place as external walls, (ii) at least 75 percent of the existing external walls remains in place as internal or external walls, and (iii) at least 75 percent of the existing internal structural framework remains intact.] As under present law, there is no requirement that a minimum percentage of financing in targeted areas be provided to first-time homebuyers.

c. *Acquisition Cost Limitations.*

Under H.R. 3838, the current-law acquisition cost limitations on a residence financed with single-family housing bonds of 110 percent of the average area purchase price applicable to such residence or 120 percent in the case of residences located in targeted areas will be reduced to the 1981 levels of 90 percent and 110 percent, respectively.

d. *Income Limitations.*

The most significant change in the mortgage eligibility requirements is H.R. 3838's imposition of income limitations on mortgagors. Pursuant to these limitations, loans made with the proceeds of qualified mortgage bonds are restricted to mortgagors whose family incomes (without adjustment for family size) do not exceed 115 percent of the greater of (i) the median family income for the area in which the residence is located or (ii) the statewide median income. In the case of targeted area financing, in lieu of the 115 percent ceiling, two-thirds of the amount of mortgage financing provided to mortgagors in targeted areas must be provided to those whose family incomes do not exceed 140 percent of the greater of the median income for the area or the state. The remaining one-third to be used in targeted areas may be used to make mortgage loans in such areas without regard to income limitations.

For purposes of this rule, family income is to be determined by the Secretary after "taking into account" the regulations prescribed under Section 8 of the United States Housing Act of 1937. (Contrast this language with the language relating to multi-family housing which directs the Secretary to determine income in a manner "consistent with" the Section 8 determination.)

2. *Nonmortgage Eligibility Requirements.*

a. *Sunset.*

The sunset provision of December 31, 1987 relating to the issuance of qualified mortgage bonds under Section 103A of the 1954 Code is extended one year to December 31, 1988.

b. *Use of Proceeds and Cost of Issuance Limitations.*

As does present law, H.R. 3838 defines a qualified mortgage bond as an obligation issued as part of a qualified mortgage issue in which all of the net proceeds of the issue (proceeds less proceeds used to pay costs of issuance and to fund a reasonably required reserve fund) are to be used to finance owner-occupied residences. H.R. 3838, however, limits the costs of issuance financed with bond proceeds to (i) 2 percent of the average aggregate face amount of the issue for issues in excess of $20,000,000 and (ii) 3.5 percent of the aggregate face amount of the issue for issues of $20,000,000 or less.

c. *Use of Proceeds Prohibitions.*

H.R. 3838 extends to mortgage subsidy bonds the current-law industrial development bond prohibition on the expenditure of any portion of the proceeds of an issue to provide any airplane, skybox, other private luxury box, health club facility, facility primarily used for gambling, or store, the principal business of which is the sale of alcoholic beverages for consumption off premises. While it may be unlikely that any financing would ever be provided for these facilities under a typical single-family program, Congress has determined that such a limitation is necessary.

d. *Unified Volume Limitations.*

The current law qualified mortgage bond state ceiling rules are incorporated into the H.R. 3838–reduced unified volume limitation, described in Section IV below.

e. *Arbitrage Rules.*

H.R. 3838 makes no changes to the special arbitrage rules applicable to single-family housing. As discussed in Section VII below, costs of credit enhancement will be an adjustment to bond yield.

f. *Public Hearing and Approval Requirement.*

H.R. 3838 will extend to all single-family housing financings the public hearing and approval requirement made applicable to current law industrial development bonds by the Tax Equity and Fiscal Responsibility Act of 1982. Pursuant to this requirement, the issuer will be required to conduct a public hearing and obtain approval of the bonds by the elected representative or the legislature before each issue of bonds. This provision is effective with respect to single-family housing bonds issued after December 31, 1986.

g. *Repeal of Annual Policy Statement.*

H.R. 3838 repeals the current law requirement that, for bonds issued after 1984, the applicable elected representative of the governmental unit which is the issuer or on whose behalf the bonds are issued file a report outlining the issuer's housing policies with the Secretary of the Treasury.

3. *Qualified Veterans' Mortgage Bonds.*

a. *Use of Proceeds.*

H.R. 3838 changes to 95 percent the existing law requirement that 90 percent or more of the net proceeds of qualified veterans' mortgage bonds be used to finance loans to qualified veterans for the purchase of single-family, owner-occupied residences. H.R. 3838 redefines net proceeds as proceeds less the amount of proceeds deposited into a reasonably required reserve or replacement fund, and eliminates the deduction of costs of issuance in the determination of net proceeds.

b. *Qualified Veterans.*

As under present law, mortgage loans financed with qualified veterans' mortgage bonds may be made only to veterans who served on active duty before 1977, and who apply for a loan before 30 years after their termination of active service.

c. *Volume Limitation.*

Qualified veterans' mortgage bonds remain subject to their present-law state volume limitations. Tax-exempt qualified veterans' mortgage bonds may be issued only by the five states that issued such bonds before June 22, 1984.

d. *Current Refunding Exception.*

H.R. 3838 provides that in order not to be counted against the state volume limitation, the amount of current refunding bonds may not exceed the outstanding amount of the refunded bonds, and the maturity date of such refunding bonds may not exceed the later of the maturity date of the refunded bonds or the date that is 32 years after the date of issuance of the refunded bonds (original bonds in the case of a series of refundings).

4. *Mortgage Credit Certificates.*

a. *Exchange of Qualified Mortgage Bond Authority for Mortgage Credit Certificates.*

H.R. 3838 permits issuers of qualified mortgage bonds to elect to exchange part or all of their bond authority for authority to issue mortgage credit certificates, but increases the exchange rate from 20 to 25 percent.

b. *Targeting Requirements.*

The targeting requirements for mortgage credit certificates are revised by H.R. 3838 to conform to those applicable to qualified mortgage bonds.

c. *Sunset.*

The December 31, 1987 deadline for the issuance of mortgage credit certificates is extended one year to December 31, 1988.

5. *Certain Cooperative Housing Corporations.*

a. *Single-Family or Multi-Family Restrictions.*

While housing units owned by general or limited cooperative housing corporations are financeable under current law with single-family housing bonds and subject to all targeting rules applicable to such bonds, H.R. 3838 permits limited equity cooperative housing corporations to elect to be subject to and eligible for tax-exempt financing under the rules applicable to multi-family residential rental property.

b. *Effect of Election.*

If financing is provided to a cooperative housing corporation pursuant to the qualified mortgage rules, tenant-shareholders of cooperative housing corporations are allowed a deduction for rents paid to the cooperative equal to their allocable share of interest and taxes paid by the cooperative. If a cooperative elects to be a limited equity cooperative and treated as a multi-family project, tenant-shareholders forego such deductions. The election to forego such deductions and to satisfy the multi-family targeting rules will apply throughout the qualified project period described above in Section III. C.

c. *Sunset.*

H.R. 3838 provides that the authority to issue tax-exempt bonds for certain cooperative housing corporations will expire on December 31, 1988.

E. Qualified 501(c)(3) Bonds.

1. *General.*

An obligation is a qualified 501(c)(3) bond if (a) all of the property provided by the net proceeds of the issue (face amount of issue less reasonably required reserves) is owned by a Section 501(c)(3) organization or a governmental unit, and (b) no more than 5 percent of the net proceeds of the issue is used in a trade or business carried on by any person other than a governmental unit or Section 501(c)(3) organization and no more than 5 percent of the debt service is secured by or derived from payments in respect of an unrelated trade or business. Note that costs of issuance are not treated as spent for the exempt purpose of the borrowing and must fit within the 5 percent "bad money" portion.

2. *$150,000,000 Limitation on Nonhospital Bonds.*

H. R. 3838 restricts the amount of nonhospital qualified 501(c)(3) bonds that may be issued for a beneficiary where that person already benefits from a significant amount of such bonds. Under this provision, interest on an issue of nonhospital qualified 501(c)(3) bonds is not tax-exempt if the aggregate face amount of all nonhospital qualified 501(c)(3) bonds (including the bonds to be issued and the outstanding amount of any prior bonds that have been advance refunded, but no bonds that are being currently refunded) that would be allocated to any beneficiary after issuance of the bonds exceeds $150,000,000. A qualified hospital bond is an obligation 95 percent or more of the net proceeds of which is used to provide a hospital facility that is accredited; is primarily used to provide inpatients, under the supervision of physicians, with diagnostic and therapeutic services for medical diagnosis, treatment and care; and provides 24-hour nursing services. The term hospital does not include rest or nursing homes, daycare centers, medical school facilities, research laboratories or ambulatory care facilities. In making the $150,000,000 computation, the following guidelines are to be taken into account:

(i) A "test-period beneficiary" means any person who was an owner or principal user of the facilities financed with the proceeds of the issue in question during the three-year period beginning on the later of the date of issue or the date the property was placed in service.

(ii) Test-period beneficiaries who are owners are allocated an amount of bonds based on the amount of the project they own. Test-period beneficiaries who are principal users are allocated an amount of bonds based on their percentage share of use. A "principal user" is generally anyone who uses 10 percent or more of a facility measured by fair rental value or square footage of occupancy.

(iii) The allocation rule will require each test-period beneficiary of an issue to determine whether it or its related persons are or were test-period beneficiaries of other outstanding bonds to which the limitation applies by reason of either ownership or use of a bond-financed facility during the relevant time period.

(iv) The $150,000,000 rule applies only to (a) qualified 501(c)(3) bonds other than qualified hospital bonds and (b) bonds issued before August 16, 1986 more than 25 percent of the proceeds of which were used by a Section 501(c)(3) organization, but only to the extent that the proceeds of such issue were not used with respect to a hospital. In addition, if 90 percent or more of the net proceeds of a pre-August 16, 1986 issue was used with respect to a hospital, the issue is disregarded for purposes of the $150,000,000 limitation. Notwithstanding the above, bonds issued for Section 501(c)(3) organizations for exempt facilities, industrial parks or as exempt small issues pursuant to paragraphs (4), (5) or (6) of Section 103(b) of the 1954 Code are excluded from (b), above.

(v) Two or more Section 501(c)(3) organizations under common management or control are treated as one organization for purposes of the $150,000,000 limitation.

(vi) Where a qualified 501(c)(3) bond is used in part for a hospital facility and in part for a nonhospital facility, only the bonds allocable to the nonhospital facility are counted against the $150,000,000 limitation.

3. Bond Maturity Limitation.

The weighted average maturity of qualified 501(c)(3) bonds may not exceed 120 percent of the reasonably expected economic life of the bond-financed property. This provision calls into question the ability to continue the common practice of financing operating expenses with longer-term bonds. The provision focuses on "property" and does not address the issue of how operating expenses are to be treated for purposes of the economic life test.

F. QUALIFIED REDEVELOPMENT BONDS.

1. Introduction.

Qualified redevelopment bonds represent a new category of bonds subject to the requirements of H.R. 3838. While new to the list of bonds specifically exempted from tax by the 1954 Code, these bonds represent a long-standing financing technique in certain areas of the country, referred to as tax increment financing, and are now issued in over 30 states.

In a tax increment financing, property acquired or improved in the course of a redevelopment project is generally transferred to private individuals. It is not pledged as security for repayment of the redevelopment bonds because they are typically repaid from property tax increments. Because the bond-financed property never stands as security for the bonds, it was consistently the ruling position of the Internal Revenue Service under the 1954 Code that tax increment financing bonds were not industrial development bonds within the meaning of Section 103(b)(2) of the 1954 Code. *See, e.g.,* Rev. Rul. 73-481, 1973-2 C.B. 23; Let. Rul. 8105079.

Doubt was cast on the status of tax increment financing bonds with the passage of the consumer loan bond provisions of the Tax Reform Act of 1984. These provisions subject interest on a bond to Federal income tax if a significant portion of its proceeds is used "directly or indirectly" to finance loans to non-exempt persons. The possibility of construing the term "indirect loan" to encompass any use by a non-exempt person raised the possibility that the interest on tax increment financing bonds would be taxable under Section 103(o) of the 1954 Code while still failing to fall within the definition of "industrial development bond" set forth in Section 103(b)(2). H.R. 3838 settles the question for tax increment financing bonds issued before August 16, 1986, expressly excluding them from the provisions of Section 103(o).

Tax increment financing bonds issued after August 16, 1986 will, however, fall within the definition of private activity bonds. H.R. 3838 classifies these bonds as "qualified redevelopment bonds" that now must meet the requirements imposed on private activity bonds to qualify as exempt from Federal income tax.

2. *Prerequisites for Issuance of Qualified Redevelopment Bonds.*

   a. *Legal Authority and Plan.*

   The redevelopment bonds must be issued pursuant to a state law that authorizes redevelopment of blighted areas by local governmental units. Prior to issuance of the bonds, a general purpose local governmental unit with jurisdiction over the area to be redeveloped must adopt a redevelopment plan for a designated blighted area that includes affirmative findings with respect to the definitional criteria of a blighted area. General purpose local governmental units are the smallest governmental units having general purpose sovereign powers over a particular area. Neither the state nor any special authority is treated as a local governmental unit.

   b. *Criteria for Designation of Blighted Areas.*

   Mandatory criteria for designating an area as blighted must be specified by state law and must include:

   (i) excessively vacant land on which structures were previously located,

   (ii) abandoned or vacated buildings, and

   (iii) substandard structures and delinquencies in real property taxes.

   c. *Value Limitation for Redeveloped Areas.*

   A governmental unit may designate as blighted areas no more than 20 percent of all the real property located within its jurisdiction. The percentage is to be determined according to assessed property values calculated for each designated area at the time it is so designated. Thus, increases in property values that result from successful redevelopment projects will not have the effect of forestalling further redevelopment.

   d. *Minimum Size Requirement for Designation of Blighted Areas.*

   A designated blighted area must have an area greater than one hundred contiguous acres unless, alternatively, no one person or group of related persons owns more than 25 percent of the bond-financed land in the area and the area itself occupies at least ten contiguous acres.

3. *Use of Bond Proceeds.*

   a. *Allocation to Redevelopment Purposes.*

      Ninety-five percent of the net proceeds of a qualified redevelopment bond must be used for redevelopment purposes in a designated blighted area. New construction or enlargment is not a redevelopment purpose although rehabilitation qualifies as such. Redevelopment purposes include the acquisition of real property by the power or threat of eminent domain; the clearing and preparation of land and the sale of real property at fair market value to nongovernmental persons; the rehabilitation of real property; and the relocation of occupants of the redeveloped area.

   b. *No Restriction on Use of Proceeds to Acquire Land.*

      The limitation on the use of bond proceeds to acquire land found elsewhere in H.R. 3838 does not apply to qualified redevelopment bonds with the exception that no bond proceeds may be used to acquire agricultural land.

   c. *Use of Bond Proceeds to Acquire Existing Property.*

      Qualified redevelopment bonds are subject to the rule restricting the acquisition of existing property unless rehabilitation is undertaken. See Section V below.

   d. *Transfer of Property Acquired for Redevelopment Purposes.*

      A governmental unit that transfers to a nongovernmental entity property it has acquired pursuant to its redevelopment plan must do so at the property's fair market value taking into account any covenants or restrictions on use imposed on the property.

4. *Repayment of the Bonds.*

   a. *Repayment with Tax Revenues.*

      Redevelopment bonds are to be repaid or secured with incremental property tax revenues, general tax revenues of the issuing governmental unit, or any combination of the two. The increase in property tax revenues attributable to enhanced value resulting from redevelopment of the area must, to the extent necessary, be reserved exclusively for debt service on the bonds. The method or rate of assessing real property taxes for property within the redevelopment area must be the same method or rate that is used for property located elsewhere.

   b. *No Special User Fees to Be Imposed.*

      No user fees or charges may be imposed within the redevelopment area unless similar user fees are imposed for use or ownership of property located elsewhere. This provision applies whether or not the user fees are earmarked to repay the bonds. It will prevent taxing entities from recouping through such fees any forgone property tax revenues.

5. *Other Limitations on the Bonds.*

   a. *Prohibition on Use of Bond Proceeds to Finance Certain Facilities.*

      No redevelopment bond can qualify as tax-exempt if any bond proceeds are used to finance any of the following facilities or land on which they are located: a private or commercial golf course, country club, massage parlor, hot tub facility, suntan facility, racetrack or other gambling facility, or any facility for the sale of alcoholic beverages for off-premises consumption.

  b. *Twenty-Five Percent Limitation on Use of Bond Proceeds to Finance Certain Other Facilities.*

No more than 25 percent of bond proceeds may be used to finance any of the following facilities or land on which they are located: facilities that have the primary purpose of providing food and beverage services, automobile sales or service or recreation and entertainment: tennis clubs, skating facilities (roller skating, skateboarding, and ice skating), racquet facilities (including handball and racquetball courts), health clubs, sky boxes or other luxury boxes, and airplanes.

  c. *No Special Requirements for Housing Located in Redevelopment Area.*

In some cases, the redevelopment area may be an inner-city neighborhood of houses or apartment buildings that will be rehabilitated under the redevelopment plan. In contrast to requirements contemplated in earlier versions of the legislation, H.R. 3838 does not require such housing that is located in a redevelopment area to meet the requirements otherwise imposed on housing financed by tax-exempt multifamily or mortgage revenue bonds.

6. *Volume Limitation.*

In addition to the foregoing requirements concerning the use of bond proceeds and provisions for repayment of the bonds, the unified volume limitation, discussed below, will also apply. Before now, qualified redevelopment bonds were issued under Section 103(a) of the 1954 Code without the necessity of meeting any of the restrictions, including the volume limitation, on industrial development bonds.

G. QUALIFIED STUDENT LOAN BONDS.

1. *New Rules Added to the 1954 Code by the Tax Reform Act of 1984.*

  a. *Prohibition on Consumer Loan Bonds.*

The Tax Reform Act of 1984 added to Section 103 a prohibition against use of any significant portion of bond proceeds to finance loans to nonexempt persons. Bonds to finance student loans were specifically exempted from this prohibition on consumer loan bonds but only if the loans financed by the bonds were part of a program which met certain specified requirements. One basic requirement was that the loan program be one to which the Higher Education Act of 1965 applied. The consumer loan bond prohibitions thus introduced substantive requirements to be applied to student loans financed by tax-exempt program bonds.

  b. *Mandate for the Secretary of Treasury to Promulgate Arbitrage Regulations.*

Student loan bonds remained free of the statutory arbitrage restrictions imposed on industrial development bonds. Congress, however, mandated the Secretary of the Treasury to promulgate arbitrage rules including similar restrictions for student loan bonds, which might include similar restrictions. The Secretary has not yet complied with this legislative directive.

2. *Treatment Under H.R. 3838.*

a. *Classification as Private Activity Bonds.*

Under H.R. 3838, student loan bonds are classified as private activity bonds and as such will be subject to all the restrictions generally imposed thereon, but with some special provisions, as discussed below.

b. *Substantive Requirements to Be Imposed on Student Loans.*

Loans financed by qualified student loan bonds must be made in conjunction with a qualified program established under the federal Higher Education Act, or, alternatively, as a part of an eligible state supplemental student loan program. The student scholarship recipient must reside in the issuing state unless (s)he is enrolled in an educational institution located in that state.

c. *Allocation of Bond Proceeds.*

In the case of bonds issued to finance federal program loans, 90 percent of bond proceeds must be used to finance student loans. In the case of bonds issued to finance state supplemental loan program loans, 95 percent of bond proceeds must be use to finance student loans.

d. *Limitation on Private Business Use of Bond Proceeds.*

An issue of student loan bonds will not be treated as tax-exempt if the bonds meet the private business tests for private activity bonds either by virtue of use of more than 10 percent of bond proceeds in a private trade or business or by virtue of the extension of security by a private trade or business for repayment of more than 10 percent of principal or interest on the bonds. For purposes of applying these tests, Section 501(c)(3) organizations will be treated as governmental units with respect to their activities which do not constitute trades or businesses.

e. *Arbitrage Requirements.*

Arbitrage restrictions that are now extended to student loan bonds include (i) the rebate rule for excess investment earnings from investments in assets other than student loans, and (ii) the 150 percent of debt service limitation on the investment of bond proceeds in assets other than student loans.

The arbitrage limitation on permissible yield will not be imposed with respect to qualified student loan bonds funding federal program loans during an initial temporary period of 18 months immediately following issuance of the bonds for obligations issued prior to January 1, 1989. For obligations issued after such date the general six-month rule applicable to pool financings will apply. See Section VII below. Note, however, that excess earnings are nevertheless subject to rebate if all bond proceeds have not been expended after an initial six-month period except to the extent the special exception described below is applicable. Obligations issued to finance a state supplemental student loan program are subject to the general arbitrage restrictions described in Section VII.

For purposes of calculating excess investment earnings that would otherwise be subject to rebate, the issuer of qualified student loan bonds funding federal program loans may disregard such earnings to the extent that they are used to finance (i) administrative and carrying costs of the bond-financed program and (ii) costs of issuing the bonds. This special exception will terminate after December 31, 1988.

Three conditions attach to the availability of the special exception:

(i) It is available only during the temporary period specified above.

(ii) It is available only to the extent the issuer has actually expended bond proceeds for permissible costs for which it has not been reimbursed.

(iii) It is available only to the extent the issuer is not reimbursed for such costs from loan payments.

f. *Extension of Treasury Department Authority to Promulgate Additional Arbitrage Regulations.*

The Technical Corrections Act of 1986, included as part of H.R. 3838, continues the authority conferred on the Secretary of the Treasury by the Tax Reform Act of 1984 to promulgate additional arbitrage regulations specifically for student loan bonds to the extent not inconsistent with the provisions of H.R. 3838.

IV. UNIFIED VOLUME LIMITATION.

A. Consolidation of Separate Limitations into a Single Unified Volume Limitation.

Under current law, separately enacted volume limitations for private activity bonds, mortgage revenue bonds, and qualified veterans mortgage bonds operate on three parallel tracks with separate ceilings and separate, though similar, rules governing the allocation of available amounts among prospective bond issues. H.R. 3838 consolidates the private activity bond and the single-family housing bond limitations into a single unified volume limitation that will be applied to all private activity bonds including multi-family housing bonds and single-family housing bonds. Qualified veterans' mortgage bonds will retain their own separate volume limitation.

B. Obligations Subject to the Volume Limitation.

1. *General Application to Private Activity Bonds.*

The volume limitation is generally imposed on all private activity bonds including the newly authorized category of qualified redevelopment bonds. Except as provided below, governmental obligations and qualified 501(c)(3) bonds are not subject to volume limitations. However, the nongovernmental portion in excess of $15,000,000 of any governmental bond is subject to the limitation.

2. *Specially Excepted Private Activity Bonds.*

Private activity bonds issued to finance any of the following facilities will not be subject to the volume limitation:

a. airports,

b. docks and wharves, or

c. governmentally owned solid waste disposal facilities.

The safe harbor for governmental ownership described with respect to airports, docks and wharves in Section III. A. 3. b., above, is to be applied here, and for this purpose is extended to cover solid waste disposal facilities. In the context of solid waste facilities, the second requirement of the safe harbor relating to the term of the contract being limited to 80 percent of the economic life of the property is deemed to be satisfied if the contract term is not longer than 20 years.

3. *Exception for Current Refunding Issues.*

Private activity bonds issued to refund outstanding private activity bonds will not be includible in the volume limitation except to the extent the principal amount of the refunding bond exceeds the outstanding amount of the prior bond. Student loan bonds and single-family housing bonds must satisfy specific requirements as to the maturity date of the refunding bond to take advantage of this exception. The maturity date of the refunding bond must not be later than the later of the maturity date of the refunded bond or 17 years from date of issue of the original bond in the case of student loan bonds, 32 years from date of issue in the case of single-family housing. The exception does not apply in the case of advance refundings.

C. DETERMINATION OF STATE VOLUME CEILING.

1. *Determination of Amount.*

For the balance of 1986 and for 1987, the annual volume ceiling for any state will be the product of $75 and the state's population based on the most recent census estimate preceding the calendar year or, if greater, $250,000,000. After 1987, the annual volume ceiling for any state will be the product of $50 and the state's population based on the most recent census estimate or, if greater, $150,000,000.

2. *Special Rule for United States Possessions.*

For possessions with a population less than that of the least populous state, the volume for any year will be the product of the population of the possession based on the most recent census estimate and a fraction the denominator of which is the population of the least populous state based on the most recent census estimate and the numerator of which is $250,000,000 in 1987 or $150,000,000 for years after 1987.

3. *Availability of Ceiling for Facilities within the State.*

State volume ceiling as determined under these rules is available only for facilities located within the state. The only exception to this requirement exists for sewage, solid waste, hazardous waste, and water facilities that a state is entitled to use on a basis that is proportionate to its contribution of bond proceeds to the project.

D. ALLOCATION OF VOLUME LIMITATION AMOUNT AMONG ISSUERS WITHIN A STATE.

1. *Federal Statutory Allocation.*

Under H.R. 3838, 50 percent of the volume limitation available for the calendar year shall be allocated to state agencies. The remaining 50 percent of the state's ceiling shall be allocated to local issuers in proportion to population. Under this rule, an issuer with jurisdiction over a population that represents 10 percent of the population of the state should receive 10 percent of the ceiling that is allocated to local issuers. In the case of overlapping jurisdictions, however, if an area is within the jurisdiction of two or more governmental units, the area will be considered within the unit having jurisdiction over the smallest area. Thus, for example, if an area is in both a county and a city, it is considered within the city. The county's population is thus determined by excluding the city.

2. *Power of States to Vary the Federal Allocation Scheme.*

States are authorized to adopt their own allocation provisions by statute. No substantive limitations or set-asides are imposed on this authority. The Conference Report makes clear that state legislation enacted before the enactment of H.R. 3838 will be effective to vary the federal allocation scheme as long as the legislation refers to the new volume limitation on private activity bonds. Any obligations issued in reliance upon an allocation made by a state or local issuer pursuant to the statutory format may not be withdrawn by any subsequent allocation by the legislature or the governor.

3. *Interim Power of Governor before Enactment of State Legislation.*

If the state legislature has not yet enacted legislation to vary the federal allocation scheme, the governor is authorized to do so by proclamation. The governor's authority will expire when the legislature enacts a reallocation statute or, if it does not do so, on the last day of the first calendar year after 1986 in which the legislature meets in regular session.

E. ELECTIVE CARRYFORWARD OF UNUSED VOLUME LIMITATION.

1. Calculations of statewide ceiling and allocations among issuers are effective only for the calendar year when they are made. Any issuer failing to issue bonds up to its volume ceiling for the year will lose the allocation without an affirmative carryforward election that, once made, is irrevocable.

2. *Requirements for Valid Election.*

a. *Identification of Carryforward Purpose.*

The electing issuer must identify the purpose for which the ceiling carried forward will be used and the amount of ceiling that will be allocated to that purpose. In contrast to the prior procedure for carryforward, it is sufficient in the case of exempt-facility bonds to identify the carryforward purpose by the type of facility rather than by the name of beneficiary and location of project.

b. *Bonds Eligible for Carryforward Allocations.*

The only bonds eligible for carryforward elections are bonds to be issued for exempt facilities, qualified mortgage bonds or mortgage credit certificates, student loan bonds, and qualified redevelopment bonds. Thus, unused volume limitation allocated for a small issue bond would be lost at the end of the year unless it reverted to the state by some specified date for reallocation or carryforward at the state level.

3. *Expiration of Carryforward.*

The carryforward election survives for three years. The amount carried forward will be lost after that time if still unused. A FIFO method will be applied to determine the order of use.

F. TRANSITIONAL RULES.

Transitional rules are provided in H.R. 3838 that explain the effect that will be given carryforwards of volume limitation that were made in 1984 and 1985. As a general rule, except as provided in the two exceptions described below, no carryforward elections made under the 1954 Code shall be recognized for purposes of the unified volume ceiling. Under the first exception, if a carryforward with respect to a specific project was made before November 1, 1985 and if the project meets the general transitional rule described in Section VIII B below, the carryforward will be recognized. Under the second exception, if the project was included in a list of specifically enumerated projects, which list refers to solid waste disposal facilities that meet the transitional rule for depreciation (see Section IX below), and either no state ceiling amount would have been required if the bonds had been issued before August 15, 1986 or a carryforward election was made for the project before January 1, 1986, then the carryforward will be recognized.

V. RESTRICTIONS APPLICABLE TO ALL PRIVATE ACTIVITY BONDS.

A. NINETY-FIVE PERCENT USE OF PROCEEDS REQUIREMENT.

At least 95 percent of the "net proceeds" of all issues of private activity bonds must be used for the exempt purpose of the borrowing. (Under current law, at least 90 percent of net proceeds must be so used.) This percentage is reduced to 90 percent in the case of qualified student loan bonds issued in connection with the Federal GSL and PLUS programs. Net proceeds is defined as the proceeds of the issue minus amounts invested in a reasonable required reserve or replacement fund. This modifies current law, under which the term "net proceeds" also reflects a deduction for amounts paid for costs of issuance.

B. COSTS OF ISSUANCE.

Under the new definition of "net proceeds" bond proceeds are not reduced by the costs of issuing the bonds, and hence the issuer must pay costs of issuance from the 5 percent of the issue which need not be spent on the exempt purpose of the borrowing (the so-called "bad money" portion of an issue).

The issuance costs financed by the issue may not exceed 2 percent of the face amount of the issue. Any use of bond proceeds in excess of 2 percent of the aggregate face amount of the issue to pay costs of issuance will cause the bonds to be taxable. This amount is increased to 3.5 percent in the case of issues of qualified mortgage bond or qualified veterans' mortgage bonds the face amount of which does not exceed $20,000,000.

Costs of issuance subject to the 2 percent limitation include all costs incurred in connection with the borrowing—in general, all costs that are treated as costs of issuance under the present Treasury Department regulations and rulings. Examples of costs of issuance that are subject to the 2 percent limitation include (but are not limited to):

(i) underwriters' spread (whether realized directly or derived through purchase of the bonds at a discount below the price at which they are expected to be sold to the public);

(ii) counsel fees (including bond counsel, underwriters' counsel, issuer's counsel, company counsel in the case of borrowings such as those for exempt facilities, as well as any other specialized counsel fees incurred in connection with the borrowing);

(iii) financial advisor fees incurred in connection with the borrowing;

(iv) rating agency fees;

(v) trustee fees incurred in connection with the borrowing;

(vi) paying agent and certifying and authenticating agent fees related to issuance of the bonds;

(vii) accountant fees (*e.g.*, accountant verifications in the case of advance refundings) related to issuance of the bonds;

(viii) printing costs (for the bonds and for preliminary and final offering materials);

(ix) costs incurred in connection with the required public approval process (*e.g.*, publication costs for public notices generally and costs of the public hearing or voter referendum); and

(x) costs of engineering and feasibility studies necessary to the issuance of the bonds (as opposed to such studies related to completion of the project, but not to the financing).

Bond insurance premiums and certain letter of credit fees may be treated as interest on the bonds under the arbitrage restrictions (see discussion in Section VII below). To the extent of their treatment as interest, the initial cost of these types of costs of issuance may be financed in addition to the 2 percent limit on financing other costs of issuance. It is not clear whether these costs are also included in the "bad money" portion or whether they will be included in the 95 percent qualified portion of an issue.

C. Change in Use of Bond-Financed Property.

A change in use of property financed with private activity bonds to a use not qualified for tax-exempt financing will generally result in loss of income tax deductions for rent, interest, or equivalent amounts paid by the person making the nonqualified use of the property. Section 501(c)(3) organizations realize unrelated business income with respect to any such use. These consequences apply in addition to the loss of tax exemption on bond interest provided under present low.

This provision applies to changes in use of bond-financed property occurring after August 15, 1986, with respect to financing provided after that date.

D. SUBSTANTIAL USER RESTRICTION.

H.R. 3838 retains the present-law substantial user restriction. Under this provision, a private activity bond shall not be a qualified bond (*i.e.*, shall be taxable) for any period during which the bonds are held by a substantial user (or any "related person") of the bond-financed facilities. This provision does not apply to mortgage revenue bonds, qualified student loan bonds, and qualified 501(c)(3) bonds.

E. BOND MATURITY LIMITATION.

H.R. 3838 retains the present-law limitation on bond maturity. Under this provision, the weighted average maturity of private activity bonds included within an issue (taking into account the respective issue prices of the bonds) may not exceed 120 percent of the average reasonably expected economic life of the facilities financed with bond proceeds (taking into account respective costs of such facilities), determined as of the later of the date of issue or the date the facility is placed in service.

1. *Economic Life for Land Acquisitions.*

Under current law the economic life of property is a factual determination, but the Asset Depreciation Ranger (ADR) midpoint life may be as a safe-harbor. Generally, land is not taken into account in determining average economic life, except where land cost entails use of more than 25 percent of the net proceeds of an issue, in which case land is taken into account in determining economic life. H.R. 3838 reduces the present-law safe-harbor maturity to be used for bond-financed land from 50 years to 30 years.

2. *Limitation Applicable to Private Activity and Qualified 501(c)(3) Bonds.*

H.R. 3838 extends the bond maturity limitation to qualified 501(c)(3) bonds. As under present law, the limitation does not apply to mortgage revenue or qualified student loan bonds.

F. LAND ACQUISITION LIMITATION

1. *General Rules.*

H.R. 3838 retains the present-law limitation on bond-financed land acquisitions. Under this provision, a private activity bond will not be considered a qualified bond (*i.e.*, will be taxable) if it is issued as part of an issue more than 25 percent of the proceeds of which are used (directly or indirectly) for the acquisition of land. This provision also applies if *any* portion of bond proceeds is used (directly or indirectly) for the acquisition of land to be used for farming purposes, subject to an exception for acquisitions by first-time farmers. As under present law, an exception is provided for land acquired by a public agency in connection with an airport, mass commuting, or dock or wharf facility if such land is acquired for a noise abatement, wetland preservation or future use as one of such facilities, and there is no other significant use of the land. This provision does not apply to any qualified mortgage bond, qualified veterans' mortgage bond, qualified student loan bond, or any qualified 501(c)(3) bond.

2. *Exception for First-Time Farmers.*

The present-law exception for bonds to finance farmland for first-time farmers is expanded to include financing for individuals who previously owned land which they disposed of while insolvent. The amount of used equipment that may be financed for first-time farmers is also increased to 25 percent of the financing provided, regardless of whether such equipment is financed in conjunction with financing for the purchase of farmland. A $250,000 lifetime limit is imposed on the amount of depreciable farm property (including both new and used property) that may be financed for any principal user or related persons. Bonds issued prior to the effective date of this provision (August 15, 1986) are not affected, but count in determining the amount of financing allowed to be provided to any person by subsequent issues.

G. EXISTING PROPERTY LIMITATION.

H.R. 3838 retains the present-law prohibition on the acquisition of existing property as well as the present-law exception for existing real property which is rehabilitated with expenditures amounting to 15 percent or more of the portion of the cost of acquiring the property that is financed with the net proceeds of the issue (100 percent or more in the case of existing structures). The provision does not apply to any qualified mortgage bond, qualified veterans' mortgage bond, qualified student loan bond, or any qualified 501(c)(3) bond.

H. PROSCRIBED FACILITIES.

H.R. 3838 extends to all private activity bonds the present-law restriction on bond-financing for certain specified facilities. Under this provision a private activity bond will not be treated as a qualified bond (*i.e.*, will be taxable) if any portion of bond proceeds is to be used to provide any airplane, skybox or other luxury box, any health club facility, any facility primarily used for gambling, or any store, the principal business of which is the sale of alcoholic beverages for consumption off premises. HR 3838 provides that the restriction on health club facilities does not apply to qualified 501(c)(3) bonds. The Conference Report indicates that for these purposes the health club facility must be directly used for the purpose qualifying the Section 501(c)(3) organization for tax exemption. Qualified redevelopment bonds are subject to a specific list of facilities for which financing is restricted or may not be provided in lieu of this general restriction. See Section III. F., above.

I. PUBLIC HEARING AND APPROVAL.

The Act extends to all private activity bonds the present-law requirement that bonds may be issued only after the issuer holds a public hearing and the issuance of the bonds is approved by a designated elected official. Alternatively, issuance of the bonds may be approved by a voter referendum of the applicable governmental unit. This provision applies to bonds (including refunding bonds) issued after December 31, 1986. (IDBs presently subject to the requirement are not affected by this prospective effective date.)

VI. RESTRICTIONS APPLICABLE TO ALL TAX-EXEMPT BONDS.

A. CONTINUED RESTRICTIONS.

H.R. 3838 continues a number of requirements of current law applicable to all tax-exempt obligations and would add several new restrictions. In particular it continues the requirement that all bonds (with limited exceptions) be issued in registered form, that obligations not be federally guaranteed and that the tax exemption of obligations be derived from the income tax title. In addition, it extends to all tax-exempt obligations issued after December 31, 1986 which are not currently subject to such requirement, the information reporting requirement now applicable to IDBs and exempt organization issues.

B. ADVANCE REFUNDINGS.

H.R. 3838 restricts advance refundings of governmental obligations and Section 501(c)(3) obligations. First, it would treat an issue as an advance refunding if it is issued more than 90 days in advance of the redemption of the prior issue, in contrast to the 180-day period of current law. Refunding obligations issued before January 1, 1986, however, will be treated as advance refundings only if the refunded bonds were not redeemed within 180 days of the issuance of the refunding bonds. Second, subject to the transition rule discussed below, advance refundings of governmental and Section 501(c)(3) obligations will be permitted only under certain restrictive conditions discussed below. Advance refundings of other private activity bonds are prohibited.

1. *New Conditions.*

Advance refunding obligations will be subject to the following restrictive conditions:

(i) for bonds originally issued before January 1, 1986, the refunding bonds must be only the first or second advance refunding of the original bond unless the bonds were advance refunded two or more times before March 14, 1986, in which case a transition rule will permit one additional advance refunding; for bonds originally issued after December 31, 1985, the refunding bond must be the first advance refunding of the original bond;

(ii) for bonds originally issued before January 1, 1986, the refunded bond is required to be redeemed not later than the earliest date on which such bond could be redeemed at par or a premium of 3 percent or less if the advance refunding is expected to produce a debt service savings; for bonds originally issued after December 31, 1985, the refunded bond is required to be redeemed not later than the first date on which its call is not prohibited in the case of a refunding producing debt service savings;

(iii) the arbitrage temporary period ends with respect to the refunding bond, 30 days after date of issue, and with respect to the refunded bond, on the date of issue of the refunding bonds;

(iv) advance refunding escrow accounts are not subject to the 150 percent limitation on nonpurpose investments discussed in Section VII below;

(v) if the refunded bonds were not subject to the new minor portion amount limit, described in Section VII. E., below, the amount of proceeds of the refunded bond invested in higher yielding nonpurpose investments may not exceed the amount invested as a reasonably required reserve fund or during an allowable temporary period plus the new minor portion amount;

(vi) interest on advance refunding bonds will be taxable if a "device," described below, is used to obtain a material financial advantage other than savings arising from lower interest rates.

Note that unexpended proceeds of a refunded bond become subject to the arbitrage rebate rules described in Section VII, below, as these amounts become transferred proceeds of the refunding bonds.

2. *Devices.*

The use of a "device" in connection with an advance refunding is prohibited. A device is a transaction used to obtain a financial advantage other than from lower interest rates. The Senate Report provides detail on what will be considered a device through examples of four transactions, including:

(i) a debt service fund flip-flop—a transaction in which moneys in a debt service fund, which otherwise would be used to pay current debt service, are invested in the escrow in long-term higher-yielding obligations, and refunding bonds are issued to pay the current debt service coming due;

(ii) construction fund flip-flop—a transaction in which moneys in a construction fund, which otherwise would be used for project costs, are invested in an escrow to defease outstanding bonds and new bonds (characterized in the Senate Report as refunding bonds) are issued for project costs;

(iii) a direct monetary benefit received and not taken into account in yield—for example, an advance refunding that enables the issuer to obtain a rebate of insurance premiums which are not taken into account in calculating yield (as an increase in issue price of the refunding bond);

(iv) a window refunding—a series of two advance refundings, one a long-term tax-exempt issue and one a short-term taxable issue separately issued a short time apart; proceeds of the taxable (short-term) issue are invested in long-term high rate investments that produce a yield in excess of the long-term tax-exempt bond yield.

These examples are not intended to be all-inclusive; the Treasury Department is directed to write regulations to carry out the purpose of this restriction. On the other hand, the Conference Report clarifies that "low-to-high" refundings occurring to obtain relief from covenants or to restructure debt service are not *per se* prohibited.

3. *Transitional Rule.*

A transitional rule permits advance refunding of obligations that were issued before August 16, 1986 (September 1, 1986, for Joint Statement issues) and were not IDBs or consumer loan bonds when issued. These obligations must satisfy the limitation on their average maturity. In addition, these transitioned advance refundings must meet a number of the new provisions including the public approval requirement if issued after December 31, 1986, the cost of issuance limit, the arbitrage restrictions, the advance refunding rules relating to new conditions and devices, the information reporting requirement and the change in use rules. (If the refunded obligations were Joint Statement issues, the public approval requirement, the cost of issuance limit and the change in use rules do not apply.) Other than bonds for output facilities, the rule requiring volume allocation for private use in excess of $15,000,000 does not apply to transitional advance refundings. Any advance refunding bond issued to refund bonds issued as part of an issue 5 percent or more of the net proceeds of which are to be used to provide an output facility is subject to the volume limitation to the extent of the nongovernmental use of such issue.

VII. ARBITRAGE.

A. INTRODUCTION.

H.R. 3838 generally extends to all tax-exempt bonds (including refunding issues) additional arbitrage restrictions similar to those presently applicable to IDBs and single-family housing bonds. These restrictions, requiring the rebate of certain arbitrage profits and limiting investment of bond proceeds in nonpurpose obligations, are in addition to the general arbitrage restrictions applicable to all tax-exempt bonds.

B. LIMITATION ON INVESTMENT IN NONPURPOSE OBLIGATIONS.

At no time during any bond year may the amount invested in nonpurpose obligations with a yield higher than the yield on the issue exceed 150 percent of debt service on the issue for such bond year. The aggregate amount invested at a higher yield must be promptly and appropriately reduced as bonds are retired. An exception is provided for proceeds invested for an initial temporary period and for amounts held in a bona fide debt service fund. In addition, the restriction does not apply at all to governmental-use bonds (obligations that are not private activity bonds) and qualified 501(c)(3) bonds.

C. REBATE TO UNITED STATES.

An amount equal to the excess of the amount earned on all nonpurpose obligations over the amount that would have been earned if the gross proceeds of the issue were invested at a rate equal to the yield on the issue, together with earnings on such excess, must be paid to the United States in installments made at least once every five years. Rebates must be made in amounts such that at least 90 percent of the required rebate is paid in each payment period. Remaining balances must be paid within 60 days of retirement of the issue. Any gain or loss on the disposition of a nonpurpose obligation must be taken into account; however, no disposition is required if it would result in a loss which exceeds the amount which would be paid to the United States (but for such disposition) at the time of such disposition.

1. *Exceptions.*

Exceptions to the rebate requirement are provided for (i) a bona fide debt service fund with annual gross earnings of less than $100,000, and (ii) under regulations to be prescribed by the Treasury Department, an issue the gross proceeds of which (other than proceeds in a bona fide debt service fund) are expended within six months of the date of issue. Both the $100,000 exception and the six-month exception are "all or nothing" exceptions. If the gross earnings are $100,001 or $100 remains unexpended after six months, neither exception is available. [In the context of the six-month rule a limited exception exists for the minor portion amount, described below, for governmental and qualified 501(c)(3) bonds.] "Gross proceeds" of an issue include amounts received (including repayments of principal) as a result of investing the original proceeds of the issue and amounts used to pay debt service on the issue. This term has been interpreted in the IDB context to include pledged funds and sinking funds. It is unclear how it will apply to endowment funds now treated as reasonably required reserves. The Conference Report specifies that the application of the six-month expenditure requirement to pooled financings, including bond banks, is to be determined by reference to when the gross proceeds of the issue are spent for the ultimate exempt purpose of the borrowing, rather than when the loans are made.

2. RAN and TAN Safe Harbor.

In the case of revenue or tax anticipation notes, the net proceeds (including earnings thereon) shall be treated as expended for the governmental purpose of the issue on the first day the cumulative cash flow deficit to be financed by the issue exceeds 90 percent of the aggregate face amount of such issue. Thus, under this safe harbor, the six-month exception applies if within the six-month period the actual deficit exceeds the 90 percent amount.

3. Exception for Small Governmental Units.

An issue shall be treated as meeting the rebate requirement if:

    (i) the issue is issued by a governmental unit with general taxing powers,

    (ii) no bond which is part of such issue is a private activity bond,

    (iii) 95 percent or more of the net proceeds of such issue are to be used for local governmental activities of the issuer, and

    (iv) the aggregate face amount of all tax-exempt bonds (other than private activity bonds) issued by such unit or governmental units within the jurisdiction of the issuer during the calendar year in which such issue is issued is not reasonably expected to exceed $5,000,000.

D. REASONABLY REQUIRED RESERVE OR REPLACEMENT FUND.

The amount of proceeds of an issue that may be deposited into a reasonably required reserve or replacement fund to secure the payment of debt service on the bonds may not exceed 10 percent of the proceeds of the issue unless the issuer obtains a ruling. Such amount may, subject to the rebate and 150 percent rules discussed above, be invested at an unrestricted yield. Reserves in excess of 10 percent may be funded with amounts other than bond proceeds, but must be yield restricted.

The Conference Report indicates that a reserve or replacement fund in excess of 10 percent may be permitted by the Treasury Department if the master legal document authorizing issuance of the bonds (*i.e.*, the master indenture) was adopted before August 16, 1986, and the indenture:

    (i) requires a reserve or replacement fund in excess of 10 percent of proceeds, but not more than maximum annual debt service;

    (ii) is not amended after August 31, 1986, and

    (iii) provides that bonds having a parity of security may not be issued by or on behalf of the issuer for the purposes provided under the indenture without satisfying the debt service reserve fund requirements of the indenture.

The language of the Conference Report may be read to suggest that the availability of this exception to the 10 percent reserve restriction as to bond proceeds is contingent upon receiving a favorable ruling from the Internal Revenue Service.

E. Minor Portion Amount.

Bond proceeds equal to the lesser of 5 percent of the proceeds of the issue, or $100,000 may be invested at the unrestricted yield, subject to the rebate and 150 percent test discussed above.

F. Temporary Periods.

Bond proceeds may, subject to the rebate and 150 percent test discussed above be invested during an initial temporary period at an unrestricted yield until needed for the purpose of the issue. As under current law, three years is generally the extent of this exception.

In the case of pooled financings, net proceeds which have not been used to make loans within six months of the date of issue may not be invested at an unrestricted yield after such period. Once the loan is made, however, the temporary period begins again and may generally run for the balance of the three-year period. Thus, if proceeds of a pooled financing are to be used to make construction loans, the aggregate temporary period allowed to the pool and the borrowers generally may not exceed three years (a maximum of six months to the pool and a maximum of 30 additional months to the borrower). Repayment of proceeds to be used to make additional loans have a temporary period of three months. In the case of pools for tax and revenue anticipation loan financings, the aggregate temporary period to the pool and borrower may not exceed 13 months.

G. Determination of Yield.

Under current law, bond yield is defined as the discount rate at which the present value of principal and interest equals the net proceeds of an issue, taking into account the costs of issuance. H.R. 3838 provides that bond yield must be computed without regard to the recovery of costs of issuance.

H. Expansion of Investments Subject to Yield Restriction.

H.R. 3838 expands the arbitrage restrictions applicable to the acquisition of any property held for investment. Under the new rule, an arbitrage bond is any bond issued as part of an issue any portion of the proceeds of which are reasonably expected to be used directly or indirectly to (a) acquire higher-yielding investments, or (b) replace funds which were used directly or indirectly to acquire higher yielding investments.

The term "higher-yielding investments" means any investment property which produces a yield over the term of the issue which is materially higher than the yield on the issue. Investment property includes securities, obligations, annuity contracts or other investment-type property. As under current law, tax-exempt bonds are specifically exempted from treatment as higher-yielding investments and accordingly are not investment property.

I. CREDIT ENHANCEMENT FEES.

H.R. 3838 continues the current law rules under which bond insurance premiums are treated as interest expense if the bond insurance results in a reduction in the interest rate on the issue. In addition, this treatment is extended to fees for certain other credit enhancement devices (*i.e.*, letter of credit fees). The treatment of these fees as interest for yield calculation purposes is limited, however, to fees representing a reasonable charge for credit risk negotiated at arm's length. The Conference Report specifies, however, that if a fee or premium is increased to reflect indirect payment of costs of issuance, the entire fee or premium is not to be treated as an interest expense.

VIII. TRANSITIONAL RULES.

A. INTRODUCTION.

Generally, the amendments made by H.R. 3838 apply to bonds issued after August 15, 1986. The extended legislative period of H.R. 3838 together with the desire of Congress to impose certain of the new rules on transitional bond issues has produced complex transitional rules of general application, and numerous transitional rules relating to specific facilities and to certain established state programs. The transitional rules of general application and a special override rule will be discussed below.

B. TRANSITIONAL RULE FOR CONSTRUCTION OR BINDING AGREEMENTS.

1. Except as described in paragraph 2., below, the amendments made by H.R. 3838 do not apply to obligations with respect to a facility:

    (i) (a) the original use of which commences with the taxpayer, and the construction, reconstruction, or rehabilitation of which began before September 26, 1985, and was completed on or after such date,

        (b) the original use of which begins with the taxpayer, and with respect to which a binding contract to incur significant expenditures for construction, reconstruction or rehabilitation was entered into before September 26, 1985, and some of such expenditures are incurred on or after such date, or

        (c) acquired on or after September 25, 1985, pursuant to a binding contract entered into before such date, and

    (ii) described in an inducement resolution or comparable approval adopted by the issuer before September 26, 1985.

Significant expenditures are those greater than 10 percent of the reasonably anticipated cost of the construction, reconstruction, or rehabilitation of the facility involved.

2. Certain provisions of H.R. 3838 will apply to these "transitional" issues, including the 95 percent rule, bond maturity limitation, public approval requirement, arbitrage restrictions (including rebate), restriction on issuance costs, change in use restriction and information reporting requirement.

3. The volume ceiling rules are applicable unless the specified transitional exceptions described in Section IV above apply.

4. The public approval and information reporting requirements are applicable to bonds issued after December 31, 1986 rather than bonds issued after

August 15, 1986, except for bonds that are subject to these requirements prior to the enactment of H.R. 3838.

5. In connection with bonds subject to the Joint Statement, this transitional rule applies to bonds issued after August 31, 1986. In addition, the bonds are not to be treated as private activity bonds for purposes of the arbitrage and information reporting requirements, and the rules relating to public approval, restriction on issuance costs and change of use do not apply.

6. An issuer may elect out of this transitional rule.

C. CERTAIN CURRENT REFUNDING ISSUES.

1. Refundings of bonds issued before August 16, 1986 or bonds issued to refund a transitional issue described in Subsection B above are permitted if:

> (i) the issue to be refunded is retired within 90 days of issuance of the refunding bonds,
>
> (ii) certain provisions of H.R. 3838 with respect to public approval, restriction on issuance costs financed by the issue, change in use, arbitrage (including rebate), and information reporting are met,
>
> (iii) the proceeds of the refunding obligation are used exclusively to refund the refunded obligation and the amount of the refunding obligation does not exceed the amount of the refunded obligation, and
>
> (iv) the refunding obligation has a maturity date not later than the later of:
>
>> (a) the last day of the period equal to 120 percent of the weighted average reasonably expected economic life of the facilities (as of the date such facilities financed with the proceeds of the refunded obligation were placed in service), or
>>
>> (b) the date which is 17 years (or 32 years in the case of qualified mortgage bonds or qualified verterans' mortgage bonds) after the date on which the refunded obligation (*i.e.*, the original obligation) was issued.

This maturity limit is slightly more restrictive than the maturity limit contained in the refunding exception to the volume limitation, described in Section IV above, which permits the refunding bond maturity to extend to the maturity date of the refunded bond.

2. The current refunding exception applies to bonds which are part of a series of refundings of bonds eligible to be refunded under this transitional rule.

3. The provisions specified in paragraphs B. 4. and 5. above are applicable to bonds issued under the current refunding exception.

4. The $40,000,000 limitation with respect to exempt small issues does not apply to a bond issue used exclusively to currently refund a tax-exempt issue to which the $40,000,000 rule does not apply under H.R. 3838 or prior law if:

> (i) the refunding bond does not have a maturity date later than the maturity date of the refunded bond,
>
> (ii) the amount of the refunding bond does not exceed the outstanding amount of the refunded bond, and

    (iii) the interest rate on the refunding bond is lower than the rate on the refunded bond.

D. CERTAIN ADVANCE REFUNDING ISSUES.

A transitional rule is provided for advance refundings of obligations issued before August 16, 1986. See Section VI, above.

E. SPECIAL RULES OVERRIDING TRANSITIONAL RULES.

The special override rule provides that nothing in any transitional rule shall be construed as exempting any bond from the application of the following rules unless the transitional rule expressly provides otherwise:

    (i) Annuity Contracts—Annuity contracts are considered a security for purposes of the arbitrage bond rules in connection with bonds issued after September 25, 1985.

    (ii) Temporary Period for Advance Refunding—The initial temporary period for advance refunding bonds issued after December 31, 1985 is limited to 30 days.

    (iii) Determination of Yield—The yield for bonds issued after December 31, 1985 shall be determined by using the issue price of the bonds. Accordingly, costs of issuance and underwriters' discount may not be taken into account for this purpose.

    (iv) Arbitage Rebate Requirement—The arbitrage rebate rules apply to bonds issued after December 31, 1985 except for governmental bonds described in the Joint Statement. Except for certain pooled financings, the rebate rule with respect to bonds described in the Joint Statement applies to bonds issued after August 31, 1986. With respect to pooled financings described in a July 17, 1986 Joint Statement, the rebate rule applies to bonds issued after 3 p.m., E.D.T., July 17, 1986.

    (v) Information Reporting—All bonds issued after December 31, 1986 must satisfy the information reporting requirements.

    (vi) Abusive Transaction Limitation on Advance Refunding—Any advance refunding bond issued after August 31, 1986 will not be exempt from federal income taxes if a device is employed in connection with the issuance of such issue to obtain a material financial advantage based on arbitrage apart from savings attributable to lower interest rates.

IX. PROVISIONS AFFECTING MARKETABILITY OF BONDS AND TAX BENEFITS.

A. INTRODUCTION.

H.R. 3838 makes several changes to existing law that adversely affect the marketability of state and local governmental bonds. In addition, H.R. 3838 changes the depreciation system and provides for the recovery of the cost of bond-financed property on the new alternate depreciation system. These changes are briefly described below.

B. ALTERNATIVE MINIMUM TAX.

H.R. 3838 amends the alternative minimum tax imposed on individuals and corporations. The rate is 20 percent for corporations and 21 percent for individuals. Among the many amendments is a provision to treat as a preference item interest on private activity bonds issued after August 7, 1986. Exceptions are provided for qualified 501(c)(3) bonds, current refunding bonds if the refunded bond (or, in the case of a series of refundings, the original bond) was issued before August 8, 1986, and Joint Statement bonds.

In addition, another amendment provides that the alternative minimum taxable income of any corporation for any taxable year beginning in 1987, 1988 or 1989 shall be increased by 50 percent of the amount (if any) by which the adjusted net book income of the corporation exceeds the alternative minimum taxable income for the taxable year (determined without regard to this provision or the alternative tax net operating loss deduction). Adjusted net book income means the net income or loss of the taxpayer set forth on the taxpayer's applicable financial statements with certain adjustments. The Senate Report provides that a taxpayer's financial statement income includes interest on state and local government bonds. Thus there is no apparent exclusion for either governmental bonds or earlier-issued bonds. H.R. 3838 provides further that in computing the corporate alternative minimum tax after 1989, the use of financial statement income will be replaced by the use of earnings and profits in a revenue-neutral manner. Tax-exempt interest is included in the calculation of earnings and profits under current Federal law. To the extent that tax-exempt interest has been previously included pursuant to the amendment highlighted in the preceding paragraph, tax-exempt interest should be omitted under this amendment to prevent duplication of tax on the same item of income.

C. NONDEDUCTIBILITY OF INTEREST INCURRED TO CARRY TAX-EXEMPT BONDS.

Subject to the $10,000,000 exception described below, H.R. 3838 will deny banks, thrift institutions and other financial institutions a deduction for the portion of their interest expense allocated to tax-exempt obligations acquired after August 7, 1986, other than obligations acquired pursuant to a direct or indirect written commitment to purchase or repurchase such obligations entered into before September 25, 1985. The Conference Report provides that the acquisition date of an obligation is the date on which the holding period begins with respect to the obligation in the hands of the acquiring financial institution. This provision is effective for taxable years ending after December 31, 1986. The term "tax-exempt obligation" includes under this provision exempt interest dividends distributed by a regulated investment company.

H.R. 3838 provides an exception to the nondeductibility of interest with respect to certain governmental bonds [including for purposes of this provision only, qualified 501(c)(3) obligations] acquired before January 1, 1989 if the following conditions are met:

    (i) the obligation is issued in either 1986, 1987, or 1988;

    (ii) the obligation is a tax anticipation note with a term not in excess of 12 months or an obligation to provide project financing; and

    (iii) the obligation is designated by the issuer for purposes of this provision.

The issuer must reasonably anticipate that the amount of such bonds to be issued by the issuer or its subordinate entities (entities deriving their authority from the issuer or subject to substantial control by the issuer) in the calendar year will not exceed $10,000,000 (not including private activity bonds) and no more than $10,000,000 of bonds may be so designated. Refundings of outstanding bonds may qualify for this exception, and count toward the $10,000,000 limitation under the same terms as new issues. All bonds subject to this exception will remain subject to a 20 percent disallowance of deduction.

D. PROPERTY AND CASUALTY INSURANCE COMPANIES.

H.R. 3838 provides for a reduction in the deduction taken for losses incurred by property and casualty insurance companies in computing their taxable income. This reduction is equal to 15 percent of the tax-exempt interest received or accrued during the taxable year. This provision applies to interest received or accrued on state or local government obligations acquired after August 7, 1986 and is effective with respect to taxable years beginning after December 31, 1986.

E. DEPRECIATION AND INVESTMENT TAX CREDIT.

1. *Depreciation—General Changes.*

H.R. 3838 modifies the existing Accelerated Cost Recovery System ("ACRS") for depreciation by adding four additional classes into which property may be categorized and by providing for more accelerated depreciation. Thus, most personal property will be assigned a life of 3, 5, 7, 10, 15 or 20 years. The cost of real property will be recovered on a straight line basis over 27.5 years for residential rental property and 31.5 years for nonresidential property.

2. *Alternative Depreciation System.*

H.R. 3838 provides an Alternative Depreciation System ("ADS") for certain categories of property, including property financed with the proceeds of tax-exempt obligations. The cost of ADS property must be recovered on a straight line basis over its class life determined by reference to the Class Life Asset Depreciation Range midpoint life. Personal property having no class is to be recovered over 12 years. Real property, other than bond-financed multi-family housing projects, must be recovered over 40 years. Multi-family housing may be recovered over 27.5 years. The Senate version of H.R. 3838 had had a special rule for recovery of solid waste disposal facilities of eight years, but this was deleted by the Conference Committee. Thus the cost of solid waste disposal facilities must be recovered over its class life (generally 10 years for waste reduction and resource recovery projects).

3. *Allocation of Bond Proceeds.*

The Conference Report clarifies that the ADS system applies only to that portion of the cost of the property that is financed with tax-exempt bonds. H.R. 3838 provides a rule for allocation of bond proceeds under which proceeds are allocated to the cost of property in the order in which the property is placed in service.

4. *Depreciation Effective Date and Transitional Rules.*

The depreciation changes are generally effective with respect to property placed in service after December 31, 1986. In the case of bond-financed property, the effective date rule further provides that the bonds must have been issued after March 1, 1986. Two transitional rules are applicable to bond-financed property. Transition property will be recovered on the current law ACRS basis.

    a. *General Transitional Rule.*

    Property is transition property if it is described in an inducement resolution adopted before March 2, 1986, and either:

      (i) the original use commences with the taxpayer and construction began before March 2, 1986 and was completed on or after such date

      (ii) a binding contract to incur significant expenditures (10 percent of cost) for construction was entered into before March 2, 1986 and some of the expenditures were incurred after March 2, 1986, or

      (iii) the property was acquired on or after March 2, 1986 pursuant to a binding contract entered into before such date.

    If bonds are issued to refund obligations issued before March 2, 1986 and the property is placed in service after December 31, 1986, the unrecovered basis will be subject to ADS recovery, unless significant expenditures are made before January 1, 1987.

    b. *Special Solid Waste Rule.*

    Qualified solid waste disposal facilities will be transition property if before March 2, 1986 (i) there is a binding written service contract between a service recipient and a service provider, or (ii) a service recipient (or any entity related to such recipient or unit) made a financial commitment of at least $200,000 for the financing or construction of such facility, (*e.g.*, costs of feasibility studies and consultant fees).

5. *Investment Tax Credit.*

H.R. 3838 repeals the investment tax credit with respect to property placed in service after December 31, 1985. (Note that this effective date is a year earlier than the depreciation changes effective date.) An exception is provided for transition property, defined by reference to property that meets a transitional rule for depreciation. The credit amount for transition property will be reduced by 35 percent for taxable years beginning after June 30, 1987, with a phase-in for earlier taxable years. A taxpayer is required to reduce the basis of its transition property for depreciation by the full amount of the credit (after the 35 percent adjustment). No special rules apply to bond-financed property.

Index

About the Authors

ROBERT LAMB is a professor in the Graduate School of Business, New York University, and has taught at the Wharton School of Finance, University of Pennsylvania, and at Columbia University. Professor Lamb is a consultant to the U.S. Federal Reserve Board, the U.S. Department of the Treasury, major banks, and investment banks. He received a B.A. degree from the University of Chicago, an M.B.A. from Columbia University, and a Ph.D. from the London School of Economics.

STEPHEN P. RAPPAPORT is manager of the Municipal Bond Research and Financial Services Department of Prudential-Bache Securities Inc. and has taught public finance at Columbia University, where he continues to guest lecture. Mr. Rappaport is a Phi Beta Kappa graduate of Colby College, where he received his B.A. He also received an M.A. and an M.Phil. from Columbia University as a President's Fellow, and he is now a Ph.D. candidate at Columbia. In addition, he was a Wood Fellow in public finance at New York University's Graduate School of Business Administration. Mr. Rappaport has published widely on municipal bond credit analysis and public finance.